CHICKEN SOUP FOR THE DOG LOVER'S SOUL

Stories of Canine Companionship, Comedy and Courage

Jack Canfield
Mark Victor Hansen
Marty Becker, D.V.M.
Carol Kline
Amy D. Shojai

D0473980

SCHOLASTIC INC.

New York Toronto London Auckland Sydney
Mexico City New Delhi Hong Kong Buenos Aires

We would like to acknowledge the following publishers and individuals for permission to reprint the following material. (Note: The stories that were written by Jack Canfield, Mark Victor Hansen, Marty Becker, Carol Kline or Amy D. Shojai are not included in this listing.)

Patience Rewarded. Reprinted by permission of Hester Jane Mundis. ©1999 Hester Jane Mundis.

The Duck and the Doberman. Reprinted by permission of Eve Ann Porinchak. ©2004 Eve Ann Porinchak.

Now and Always. Reprinted by permission of Susan B. Huether. ©2003 Susan B. Huether.

Lucky in Love. Reprinted by permission of Jennifer Gay Summers. ©2004 Jennifer Gay Summers.

(Continued on page 394)

ISBN 0-439-86658-8

12 11 10 9 8 7 6 5 4   6 7 8 9 10 11/0

Printed in the U.S.A.   23

First Scholastic printing, March 2006

Cover photo © 2005 Best Friends/Troy Snow

Cover design by Andrea Perrine Brower

Inside typesetting by Lawna Patterson Oldfield

This book is dedicated to
dog lovers everywhere: the millions of people
around the world who have opened up their hearts
and homes to the extraordinary devotion,
unconditional love and unbridled joy of a dog,
and seen their lives richly blessed as a direct result.

We also dedicate this book to the veterinary
profession, who with unparalleled competence
and compassion, assist, protect and nurture these
life-support systems cleverly disguised as dogs.

We dedicate this book as well to the
responsible dog breeders and exhibitors who
celebrate, sustain and strive to improve the health
and well-being of their special dogs—whether
tiny or pony-size, curly-coated, otter-slick, thickly
furred or bald—preserving the unique legacy of
the canine race in all its wondrous variations.

And to the heroes, the people who give fully
of themselves in their communities to help homeless
dogs find loving homes, who aid sick, injured
or misbehaving dogs to "heal," then "heel,"
and insure that all dogs are increasingly
welcome in people's lives.

And finally, to God, who chose to
bless us richly with dogs. He knows that
through their special gifts, dogs add years
to our lives and life to our years.

Contents

2. CELEBRATING THE BOND

3. ON COURAGE

4. ONE OF THE FAMILY

8. RESCUE ME!

9. DOGGONE WONDERFUL!

10. AMAZING CANINES!

Acknowledgments

We wish to express our heartfelt gratitude to the following people who helped make this book possible:

Our families, who have been chicken soup for our souls!
Jack's family: Inga, Travis, Riley, Christopher, Oran and Kyle for all their love and support.

Mark's family: Patty, Elisabeth and Melanie Hansen, for once again sharing and lovingly supporting us in creating yet another book.

Marty's soul mate and fellow pet lover, wife Teresa, who inspires him with her inexhaustible love for, and attention to, the special love of animals. And his beloved children, Mikkel and Lex, who bring so much joy into his hectic life and remind him to relax, tease, laugh and repot himself by taking time off. Virginia Becker and the late Bob Becker, who taught farm-reared Marty to love all God's creatures from spoiled family pets to soiled dairy cows. Valdie and Rockey Burkholder, whose goodness and support have allowed Marty to thrive in the world's greatest oasis of beauty, goodness and serenity, magnificent Bonners Ferry, Idaho. And to all the pets, past, present and future who with their gifts of love, loyalty and laughter have made his life so much richer and more meaningful.

Carol's family: Lorin, McKenna and especially her dearly loved husband, Larry, who makes it possible for Carol to spend all her time writing and editing. Carol's mother, Selma, brothers Jim and Burt, and sisters Barbara and Holly, and their families, for being her favorite people in the world. Barbara's grammar and punctuation coaching was the best—thanks, Dr. P!

Amy's husband, Mahmoud, for his unflagging encouragement, love and support. And her parents, Phil and Mary Monteith, who inspired and fostered her love of pets from the beginning. Her wonderful brothers and their families, Laird, Gene, Jodi, Sherrie, Andrew, Colin, Erin and Kyle Monteith—and their assorted beloved canine family members past, present and future. And Fafnir who lives on in the hearts of his family.

Marci Shimoff, who, as always, is an inspiration, a support and, of course, the best friend ever.

Cindy Buck, whose excellent editing skills we rely on deeply, and whose friendship matters even more.

Sarajane Peterson Woolf, our literary and highly literate editor whose insights and advice were invaluable.

Christian Wolfbrandt, dog-walker and dog-sitter extraordinaire—and good friend. Your help was so appreciated!

Our publisher, Peter Vegso, who is a cherished friend, both personally and professionally, and from whom we've learned so much about writing and successfully marketing a book and remaining doggedly loyal.

Patty Aubery and Russ Kamalski, for your brilliance, insight and continued support, as well as for being there on every step of the journey, with love, laughter and endless creativity.

Barbara Lomonaco, for nourishing us with truly wonderful stories and cartoons.

D'ette Corona, for being indispensable, cheerful,

knowledgeable and as steady as the Rock of Gibraltar. We couldn't do it without you.

Patty Hansen, for her thorough and competent handling of the legal and licensing aspects of the *Chicken Soup for the Soul* books. You are magnificent at the challenge!

Laurie Hartman, for being a precious guardian of the *Chicken Soup* brand.

Veronica Romero, Teresa Esparza, Robin Yerian, Jesse Ianniello, Jamie Chicoine, Jody Emme, Debbie Lefever, Michelle Adams, Dee Dee Romanello, Shanna Vieyra, Lisa Williams, Gina Romanello, Brittany Shaw, Dena Jacobson, Tanya Jones and Mary McKay, who support Jack's and Mark's businesses with skill and love.

Lisa Drucker, for editing our final readers' manuscript. Thank you once again for being there whenever we need you.

Bret Witter, Elisabeth Rinaldi, Allison Janse and Kathy Grant, our editors at Health Communications, Inc., for their devotion to excellence.

Our great friend, Terry Burke, who takes a personal interest in all the books and who doggedly pursues sales so that, in this case, pets and people can benefit.

Lori Golden, Kelly Maragni, Tom Galvin, Sean Geary, Patricia McConnell, Ariana Daner, Kim Weiss, Paola Fernandez-Rana and Julie De La Cruz, the sales, marketing and PR departments at Health Communications, Inc., for doing such an incredible job supporting our books.

Tom Sand, Claude Choquette and Luc Jutras, who manage year after year to get our books translated into thirty-six languages around the world.

The art department at Health Communications, Inc., for their talent, creativity and unrelenting patience in producing book covers and inside designs that capture the essence of *Chicken Soup:* Larissa Hise Henoch, Lawna Patterson Oldfield, Andrea Perrine Brower, Anthony

Clausi, Kevin Stawieray and Dawn Von Strolley Grove.

Special thanks go to Frank Steele for the gift of a special friendship. Your support during the birthing of this book means so very much.

And a thousand thanks to the wonderful pet-loving writers, especially the members of Dog Writers Association of America, Cat Writers' Association, Oklahoma Writers' Federation, the "Colorado Gang" and the "Warpies" whose helping "paws" aided enormously in the success of this book. We couldn't have done it without you!

Thanks also to all the *Chicken Soup for the Soul* coauthors who make it such a joy to be part of this *Chicken Soup* family.

And our glorious panel of readers who helped us to make the final selections and made invaluable suggestions on how to improve the book:

Ellen Adams, R.V.T., Beverly Appel, Joyce Barton, Cindy Buck, Wendy Czarnecki, Roni Coleman, Jennifer Dysert, Kay Eichenhofer, Duchess Emerson, Maria Estrada, Terri Frees, Jill Gallo, Veryl Ann Grace, TracyLynn Jarvis, Erica M. Kresovich, Marcy Luikart, Kathy Moad, Erin Monteith, Phil Monteith, Mary Jane Monteith, Rebecca Morse, Mary Jane O'Brien, Tom Phillips, Kylee Reynolds, Caitlin Rivers, Barry Schochet, Betty Schubert, Patti Shanaberg, Anthony Solano, Julie Urban and Mindy Valcarcel.

Most of all, thank you to everyone who submitted their heartfelt stories, poems, quotes and cartoons for possible inclusion in this book. While we were not able to use everything you sent in, we know that each word came from a heartfelt place and was meant to celebrate dogs as the family they are.

Because of the size of this project, we may have left out the names of some people who contributed along the way. If so, we are sorry, but please know that we really do appreciate you very much.

We are truly grateful and love you all!

Introduction

Throughout the ages, our lives with dogs have been lovingly documented—from cave art to hieroglyphics and from medieval tombs of European knights to Victorian wedding portraits. In today's world, dogs are still an important and highly visible part of modern culture.

Just turn on a television or leaf through any magazine or newspaper to see a mind-boggling array of canine accoutrement for sale. Refrigerator magnets read, "Dear Lord, Please help me be the kind of person my dog thinks I am." Bumper stickers announce, "We're staying together for the sake of the dog." Two- and four-legged family members even pile on the couch together to view video-tapes of shared family vacations.

The human-animal bond, or simply "the Bond," isn't just surviving—it's thriving!

In fact, it is the strength and power of the Bond that inspired this book's creation. In response to our call for stories, we received thousands of submissions from dog lovers around the globe who shared with us the myriad ways their dogs have positively impacted their lives. *Chicken Soup for the Dog Lover's Soul* is a testament to the enduring love we humans have for the dogs who share our lives. The chapters in the book reflect the main ways that dogs benefit us: They love us, heal us, teach us, make us laugh and sometimes break our hearts with their passing. As author Roger Caras once said, "Dogs are not our whole lives, but they make our lives whole."

Dogs have been at our sides longer than any other domestic species. Perhaps this partnership arose and endured because people and dogs are so similar: We both love our families. We both enjoy snuggling in our dens. We both relish social bonds and respect loyalty.

Called the "most plastic of species," dogs exist in almost every size and shape imaginable. In addition, they occupy a wide occupational niche, from pampered lapdogs who give new meaning to the term "dog tired," to courageous canines that patrol airline terminals looking for bombs, drugs and dangerous people.

Dogs make us feel good—and are good for us. Organizations like the Delta Society describe this as "the positive effect of pets on human health and well-being." Our dogs relieve chronic pain, lift our spirits, sniff out cancer, detect impending heart attacks, seizures and migraines, lower our blood pressure and cholesterol levels, help us recover from devastating illness, and even improve our children's IQ, as well as lowering their risk for adult allergies and asthma. Just think—the unconditional love, limitless affection and to-die-for loyalty of a well-chosen, well-trained, well-cared-for dog could be just what the doctor ordered!

But perhaps our dogs help us most of all by giving us an important outlet for our love. About six out of ten U.S. households have pets, whereas only three out of ten have children. Once our children grow up—and the nest empties—dogs take on even greater importance to millions of Americans who yearn to nurture. For we humans are an extremely social species with a *need* to nurture.

Yet in today's world, many of us live alone, whether

due to divorce, choosing to remain childless, surviving a spouse or partner, or having a far-flung extended family. And sadly, too much time spent alone can leave us sick— and even shorten our lives.

Lucky for us, our canine companions provide emotional rescue for everything from a relationship breakup or bad day at work to a bad hair day—or even a *no hair* day for those of us facing cancer treatment. Dogs love us for simply being who and what we are. They don't care if we're famous, powerful, rich, important people—we're all that and more in their eyes.

At the end of the day, we may never know whether those liquid eyes shine for us or for the treat drawer, but when a tap-dancing, delighted frenzy of fur greets you at the door with a red-carpet welcome, it hardly seems to matter.

So, sit back, relax and let the love of dogs wash over you as you enjoy these charming, true tales. May they inspire you to be the person your dog thinks you are!

Share with Us

We would like to invite you to send us stories you would like to see published in future editions of *Chicken Soup for the Soul.*

We would also love to hear your reactions to the stories in this book. Please let us know what your favorite stories are and how they affected you.

Please send submissions to:

Chicken Soup for the Soul
P.O. Box 30880
Santa Barbara, CA 93130
Fax: 805-563-2945

You can also visit the *Chicken Soup for the Soul* Web site at:

www.chickensoup.com

We hope you enjoy reading this book as much as we enjoyed compiling, editing and writing it.

1

ON LOVE

*Dogs are forever in the moment.
They are always a tidal wave of feelings,
and every feeling is some variant of love.*

Cynthia Heimel

Patience Rewarded

Albert Payson Terhune, the famed dog writer of the 1920s and 1930s who authored the Lassie books, often told this story about his friend Wilson to illustrate the deep love that people and dogs share. It also shows how sometimes what seems to be in the best interest of all concerned may not apply when one of those concerned is a dog.

Wilson's dog, Jack, was an energetic, six-year-old collie that would meet him every day at the trolley station when Wilson returned from work. This was a ritual that had begun when Jack was a pup. The dog knew the route to and from the station like the back of his paw—and following that route was the highlight of his day. So when Wilson changed jobs and had to move to California, he thought it best to leave Jack on his home turf in Philadelphia with a relative. He explained all this to the dog upon leaving and told him that they both would have to adjust to new homes.

But Jack didn't want a new home. He would not stay with the family he'd been left with. He returned to Wilson's old house, even though it was boarded up, and there he passed his solitary days beside an abandoned chair beneath the portico. But every evening, tail wagging, he trotted off to the trolley station. For as long as Jack had been in the world, Wilson had always taken the same trolley home from work, and Jack had been there to greet him. But evening after evening, there was no sign of the devoted dog's master. Confused and sad, he would return alone to the deserted house.

The dog's depression grew. He refused the food left for him, and as the days passed, he became thinner and thinner, his ribs noticeable even through his thick blond coat. But every evening, ever hopeful, he'd go to the station to meet the trolley. And every evening, he'd return to the porch more despondent than before.

No one knows why Jack's new family didn't contact Wilson, but Jack's deteriorating condition did not go unnoticed. A friend who lived nearby was so upset by it that he took it upon himself to send a telegram to Wilson in California, informing him of the dog's situation.

That was all it took.

Wilson bought a return train ticket immediately; he knew what he had to do. Upon arriving in Philadelphia, he waited several hours just so that he could take the same trolley that he always did when coming home. When it arrived at the station, sure enough, there was Jack, waiting and watching as the passengers got off. Looking and hoping. And then suddenly there *he* was, his beloved owner. His master had returned at last! Jack's world was whole once more—and so was Wilson's.

Wilson later told Terhune, "Jack was sobbing almost like a child might sob. He was shivering all over as if he had a chill. And I? Well, I blew my nose and did a lot of fast winking."

Wilson took his devoted dog, Jack, back to California with him. They were never separated again.

Hester Mundis

The Duck and the Doberman

Although Jessie, our eighty-pound black Doberman, looked menacing—she snarled at strangers and attacked backyard critters—she was extremely loyal and loving to our family. We wanted a second dog, but agreed that Jessie would be better off alone; we were afraid that jealousy might compel her to hurt any dog that got between her and us.

So when our son Ricky came home from school one day with an egg, we smelled trouble. Ricky's egg came from his second-grade class project: incubating and hatching Rhone ducks. The egg had failed to hatch at school, so his teacher allowed him to bring it home. My husband and I didn't think the egg was likely to hatch outside the incubator, so we let him keep it. Ricky placed the egg in a sunny patch of grass in the yard and waited.

The next morning we awoke to a bizarre squeal coming from the backyard. There stood Jessie, nose to nose with a newly hatched peach-colored duckling.

"Jessie will swallow it whole!" I cried. "Grab her."

"Hold on," my husband, Rick, said. "I think it'll be okay. Just give it a minute."

The duckling peeped. Jessie growled and darted back to

her doghouse. The duckling followed. Jessie curled up on her bed, clearly ignoring the little creature. But the duckling had other ideas. She had already imprinted on her new "mother," so she cuddled up on Jessie's bed, snuggling under her muzzle. Jessie nudged the duckling out of the doghouse with her nose, only to have the baby squirm back to its place under her muzzle. Jessie gave a big sigh and reluctantly accepted her new role.

Ricky named the duckling Peaches and pleaded with us to keep her. Jessie didn't seem to like having a new baby, but she wasn't predatory toward Peaches either. We gave in and decided to see how things would go.

Surprisingly, over the next few weeks, Jessie really took to motherhood. When Peaches pecked at the ground, Jessie showed her how to dig. When Peaches chased tennis balls, Jessie showed her how to fetch. And when Jessie sprawled out on the leather couch to watch Animal Planet on television, Peaches snuggled right under her muzzle.

After an inseparable year of digging, sleeping and fetching together, Peaches weighed eighteen pounds. She seemed quite happy in her role as Jessie's "puppy."

Then one day something changed: Peaches' innate "duckness" kicked in. She began laying eggs once a day and became obsessed with water. During feeding times, Jessie ate while Peaches flapped and splashed in the water bowl.

One evening Jessie became frantic when Peaches disappeared. We had visions of coyotes lurking, snatching Peaches while Jessie slept. Jessie barked and howled, as would any anguished mother who had lost a child. After a thorough search of the neighborhood, we were close to giving up hope. Just then, Jessie sprinted into a neighbor's backyard. We followed her. There was Peaches, sloshing and squawking in the hot tub. Jessie hopped in to retrieve her.

As much as we wanted to keep Peaches in our family, one thing was clear: She needed to spread her wings and join the duck world. Ricky tied a red ribbon around Peaches' leg, loaded her and Jessie into the car, and we drove to a nearby pond. During the ride, Jessie curled up with Peaches and licked her head. It was as if she knew exactly what was happening and why.

As we approached the pond, Jessie and Peaches scampered toward the water. Jessie leaped in first. Peaches wobbled behind. They waded out together several yards before Peaches took off—gliding toward a flock of her own. Jessie turned around, trudged back to shore and shook off. She sat for a few minutes, watching her daughter. Then as if to say, "It's time to set my little one free," she yelped and jumped back into the car.

Back at home Ricky taped pictures of Jessie and Peaches digging, fetching and snuggling, to the inside of the doghouse. And, for a long time afterward, Jessie made weekly visits to the pond. Although we could usually see the red ribbon, we thought we could also hear Peaches' distinctive squawk, saying hello to her "birth" family.

Motherhood changed Jessie. Once unsociable and intimidating, she soon became a friend to all in the neighborhood. She snuck out at every opportunity to play with other dogs, jumped on visitors and licked their faces. Snarling was no longer part of her vocabulary.

We had feared the worst the day we saw Jessie and baby Peaches standing nose to bill. We could never have imagined that an eight-ounce ball of downy fuzz would soften our eighty-pound Doberman for life.

Donna Griswold
as told to Eve Ann Porinchak

Now and Always

A few years ago when I was looking for a small dog to add to our family, I contacted the local SPCA (Society for the Prevention of Cruelty to Animals) and got the name of a woman who was fostering some rescued Maltese dogs for them. I called the woman, and my husband and I drove to her home. As I looked around, I noticed a cute Maltese named Casper. My husband and I decided we would like to adopt him.

The foster mom asked us if there were any way we would open our hearts to Casper's companion, Kato, as well. She told us that the two boys, who had only each other for comfort, had recently been rescued from a puppy mill, where they had spent the first seven years of their lives. When the local SPCA shut down the puppy mill and seized all the dogs, Kato and Casper had been put in her foster home.

She told us that when she first picked them up, their fur was in such terrible shape they hardly looked like Maltese dogs. They were brown, the fur on their legs was matted to their stomachs, and their paws were swollen and tender from living on the wire mesh of their cage. For seven years, the only human contact these boys had was when they were thrown their food or tossed into another cage to breed with a female. What people don't realize, she said, is that the cute little puppies in the windows of many pet stores leave parents behind who live lives of neglect and suffering.

Hearing all this, I turned and looked down at the little Maltese named Kato. *But he's so ugly,* I thought. *And he isn't even friendly.* He growled and grumbled when we looked at him. Still, I felt a tug at my heart and agreed to take Kato also. As we drove home, my husband and I worried that maybe we'd taken on too much. We'd never had dogs that had been so abused for such a long time.

The first day at our home was very difficult for the two dogs. They didn't understand anything but fear of humans. They stayed close to each other and mostly hid under tables or in dark corners. In an effort to give them a fresh start, we changed their names: Casper became Thomas and Kato became Timothy.

The days turned into weeks and weeks into months. Over time Thomas became friendlier and would wag his tail when we talked to him, but Timothy still couldn't make eye contact with us. At the sound of our voices, he'd push himself against the back wall of his crate. His plastic dog kennel—the kind used to transport dogs—was the place he felt safest. Even with the crate door left open, he preferred to spend most of the day in his crate, only emerging when we gently pulled him out to take him outside. Each time I reached for Timothy, he'd flip upside down, whimpering. One day I noticed he had a gray haze over his eyes, as though there was a film on them. I asked the vet about it and he told me that it happens to dogs that live in complete fear. They retreat to another place to help themselves live through each day.

I did everything I could think of to help this dog, but

he made little progress. He would sit at the back of his crate with his head hanging down hour after hour. Nevertheless, I kept trying. When the whole house was quiet, I sat on the floor and talked to him, but he wouldn't look at me. He just stared off in another direction. One day as I sat and watched this poor soul suffering in silence, I thought about his past—the hunger, the isolation, the abuse—and started to sob. My heart aching, I began telling him how sorry I was for the pain humans had caused him. My thoughts were filled with the unhappiness and fear he had endured year after year.

As the tears streamed down my face, I felt a soft touch on my hand. Through my tears, I saw Timothy. He had come out from the back of his crate to sit near me, licking the tears that fell on my hand. Quietly, so I wouldn't scare him, I told him that I loved him. I promised that I would always love him and that no one would ever hurt him again. As I whispered over and over that he would always be warm, safe and fed, he came a step closer to me. A passage from the Bible came to my mind: Love is kind; it keeps no record of wrongs; it always protects, always trusts, always hopes, always perseveres. Love never fails. The meaning of these words was so clear as I looked at this little dog who, in spite of everything he had experienced, had opened his heart to me.

Today, I am still the only person Timothy trusts completely; we share a very special bond. When I call his name, he spins in delight and barks, his tail wagging in a frenzy of happiness. When I sit down, he climbs into my arms and licks my face. And just as I promised, I hold him, gently snuggle him and tell him I love him—now and always.

Suzy Huether

Lucky in Love

I wanted a puppy, but the timing couldn't have been worse. My three-year marriage was crumbling and the last thing I needed was a new responsibility. Trying to escape the inevitable, my husband and I decided to go on a vacation to Big Sur on the California coast. The last day of our trip, we had stopped for lunch at a restaurant. As we returned to the car, we noticed a cage by a staircase at the edge of the parking lot. I moved closer to investigate and saw a little, irresistible black ball of fluff gazing longingly out of the bars, begging me to let her out. Someone had simply left her there and put a sign on top of the cage: "Puppy for Free. Name is Lucky. Take her."

I looked at my husband, and he shook his head no, but I persisted. I needed someone to love. I took the puppy out of the cage, and happy to be free, she dove into our car. We started to drive the windy Pacific Coast Highway home. A wide, grassy meadow came into view, and we stopped so she could run. As we lay on our blanket on the grass, she trampled field daisies, sniffed for gophers and jumped in circles. Her joy at liberation was my elixir.

We renamed her Bosco, and she turned out to be a Belgian sheepdog. My loyal friend, she stayed by my side through a difficult divorce and was my guardian angel through the many years of single life that followed.

One morning, when she was nine years old, I awoke to find her panting heavily, her black curls damp and matted. With trembling fingers, I grabbed for the phone to call my veterinarian. Bosco tiredly snuggled on my lap, her labored breathing ragged on my chest, and I kissed the top of her head over and over again, waiting for the receptionist to answer.

"I'm sorry, Jennifer. The doctor's out of town." My right hand kept stroking the side of Bosco's long, smooth nose, the left hand gripping the receiver even more fiercely as I held back tears. She directed me to another veterinary clinic. How could I trust someone else with my baby? But I had no choice.

I tenderly placed my limp dog on the passenger seat of the car. With one hand I turned the key in the ignition, and with the other I gently stroked the quiet body underneath the faded green and blue stadium blanket that I used for picnics—the one I'd used the day we found Bosco.

I pulled into the clinic parking lot. I took a deep breath, said a prayer and slowly took my bundle through the doors. A matronly receptionist recognized my name and immediately summoned the doctor on call. As I waited for this unknown person to take my dog's life in his hands, I looked around the cozy, wood-paneled waiting room. A pit bull sat meekly at the feet of the woman next to me; Bosco didn't even seem to notice. A man called out my name.

Dr. Summers wore an air of urgency, his blue eyes filled with compassion and concern. As I followed him to the exam room, I noticed broad, strong shoulders and a confident stride. I laid Bosco softly on the narrow steel table and then slowly took her blanket off, clutching it in my arms. Her sweet smell still lingered on the wool. Dr.

Summers listened intently as I explained the symptoms, his gentle hands resting on Bosco's side. He thought it was gastroenteritis and wanted to keep her in the clinic for observation. But he stressed that I was welcome to come by and visit. I kissed Bosco's nose and whispered good-bye. Dr. Summers smiled. "Go home. Get some rest. I promise I'll take care of her." And somehow I knew that he would, that there was no better place to leave my best friend than in his arms.

The next day after work, I went directly to the clinic to see Bosco. The receptionist waved me into the back, and I made a beeline for the cages, trying not to run. I sat on the cold, cement floor and put my hand through the cage, stroking Bosco's fur, watching her tail give me a faint wag. When Dr. Summers discovered I was there, he came back and opened Bosco's cage. I held her tightly on my lap, happy to feel her warmth. Dr. Summers knelt on the floor near us. Talking softly so Bosco could sleep, we shared stories about our families, our careers, our dreams, our lives.

During the next few weeks, I came in every day to see Bosco and my new friend, Dr. Summers. A biopsy later confirmed bad news: lymphocytic plasmacytic enteritis (LPE). I couldn't pronounce it, let alone understand the nature of the disease. Because of the vomiting and diarrhea associated with LPE, Dr. Summers kept her in the clinic on an IV for fluids. Then, on top of LPE, Bosco developed pancreatitis, which complicated treatment.

The day came when the medicines were failing, Bosco wasn't getting any better—and I had to make a decision. Dr. Summers encouraged me to take her home, to be with her for a couple of days. He knew I needed to say good-bye. I wrapped her in her blanket and drove her home.

We snuggled on the couch, and I told her how much I had loved her, how grateful I was that a puppy named Lucky had come into my life to be my best friend. She listened, her weary brown eyes looking beyond me for peace. It was time for her to go.

Two weeks after I placed her in Dr. Summers's arms for the last time, I made a call to the clinic. I wanted to talk to someone who understood—Dr. Summers, now my friend, had been the person who had helped me close the last door. He took me to lunch and we showed each other pictures of our families. We shared memories of Bosco and he gently wiped the tears off my cheek as tears welled in his own eyes. That day opened a new door for us and we moved through it.

On April 3, two years to the day Bosco passed away, I married Dr. Summers, the man who had so tenderly cared for her—and for me. My father gave a speech during the ceremony, pausing to look up to the heavens. He smiled and said, "I know Bosco is here with us today, blessing this marriage." I smiled, too, through happy tears. Bosco had always, even in her passing, brought love into my life.

Jennifer Gay Summers

Jethro's World

My dog, Jethro—a Rottweiler/German shepherd mix—
was always low-key, gentle and well mannered. From the
moment we met at the animal shelter when he was just
nine months old, to the day he died, two things were
clear: Jethro and I had a special bond, and he had a soul of
exceptional kindness and compassion.

Jethro never chased animals. He just loved to hang out
and watch the world around him. He was a perfect field
assistant for me as I studied the various birds, including
Western evening grosbeaks and Steller's jays, living near
my house in the foothills of the Colorado Rockies.

One day while I was sitting inside, I heard Jethro come
to the front door. Instead of whining as he usually did
when he wanted to come in, he just sat there. I looked out
at him and noticed a small furry object in his mouth. My
first reaction was, *Oh, no, he killed a bird.* However when I
opened the door, Jethro proceeded to drop at my feet a
very young bunny, drenched in his saliva and very much
alive. I could not see any injuries, only a small bundle of
fur that needed warmth, food and love. I guessed that the
bunny's mother had most likely fallen prey to a coyote,

red fox or the occasional mountain lion around my house.

Jethro looked up at me, wide-eyed, as if he wanted me to praise him. I did. He seemed so proud of himself. But when I picked up the bunny, Jethro's pride turned to concern. He tried to snatch her from my hands, but failed. Whining, he followed me around as I gathered a box, a blanket, some water and food. I gently placed the baby rabbit in the box, named her Bunny and wrapped her in the blanket. I put some finely chopped carrots, celery and lettuce near her, and she tried to eat. I also made sure that she knew where the water was.

The whole time, Jethro was standing behind me, panting, dripping saliva on my shoulder, watching my every move. I thought he might go for Bunny or the food, but he simply stood there, fascinated by the little ball of fur slowly moving about in her new home.

When I turned to leave the box, I called Jethro but he didn't move. He usually came to me immediately, especially when I offered him a bone, but that day he remained steadfastly near the box. Hours passed and nothing could entice him away from his spot near Bunny.

Eventually, I had to drag Jethro out for his nightly walk. When we returned, he made a beeline for the box, where he slept through the night. I tried to get Jethro to go to his usual sleeping spot but he refused. His intention was clear: "No way. I'm staying here."

I trusted Jethro not to harm Bunny, and during the two weeks that I nursed her back to health, he didn't do anything to even scare her. Jethro had adopted Bunny; he would make sure that no one harmed her.

Finally, the day came when I introduced Bunny to the outdoors. Jethro and I walked to the east side of my house and I released her from her box. We watched her slowly make her way into a woodpile. She was cautious, her senses overwhelmed by the new stimuli—sights, sounds, odors—to which she was now exposed. Bunny remained in the woodpile for about an hour until she boldly stepped out to begin life as a full-fledged wild rabbit. Jethro remained in the same spot as he watched the scene. He never took his eyes off Bunny and never tried to approach her.

Bunny hung around for a few months. Every time I let Jethro out of the house, he immediately ran to the place where she had been released. When he arrived there, he would cock his head and move it from side to side, looking for Bunny. This lasted for about six months. If I said "Bunny" in a high-pitched voice, Jethro would whine and go look for her. He loved Bunny and was hoping to see her once again.

I am not sure what happened to Bunny. Most likely she simply lived out her life in the area around my home. Since then, other bunnies and adult rabbits have come and gone, and I've observed that Jethro never chases them. Instead, he tries to get as close as he can and looks at each of them, perhaps wondering if they are Bunny.

A few summers ago, many years after he met Bunny and treated her with such delicate compassion, Jethro came running up to me with a wet animal in his mouth. *Hmm,* I wondered, *another bunny?* I asked him to drop it. This time it was a young bird that had flown into a window. It was stunned and just needed to regain its senses.

I held it in my hands for a few minutes. Jethro, in true Jethro fashion, never took his eyes off the bird. He watched my every move. When I thought the bird was ready to fly, I placed it on the railing of my porch. Jethro approached it, sniffed it, stepped back and watched it fly away. When it was out of sight, he turned to me and seemed to give the canine equivalent of a shrug. Then together we took a long meandering stroll down the road leading away from my house. All was well in Jethro's world once more.

Marc Bekoff

The Great Dog Walk

Although I was born and raised in New York City, my parents had an exuberance for the great outdoors. Every summer Dad rented a small cottage for us on the eastern end of Long Island. The cottage was nestled in a wooded area close to the beach, so my childhood encompassed fishing, swimming, boating and the pure enjoyment of the environment. After I married and had children, we lived down the street from my parents and continued to join them on their yearly retreats to Long Island.

One year shortly before summer vacation, my parents adopted a magnificent English basset hound puppy. My two daughters were overjoyed. The dog immediately became the most important thing in their lives. They named the puppy Huckleberry Hound after the television cartoon character.

Every day after school they headed to their grandparents' house to walk and feed the dog. The trio basked in the admiring glances they received as they paraded around the neighborhood. Huckleberry was certainly a sight to behold, with his elongated body and droopy ears that nearly touched the ground. His four stubby legs were attached to extra large paws that he tripped over constantly. His narrow face held two of the most soulful eyes imaginable. Huckleberry swaggered down the street as if he knew he was special and enjoyed every moment of the attention showered upon him.

Our first summer journey to the cottage with Huckleberry was a true nightmare. He disliked the motion of the car and became violently ill. He tossed and turned on the backseat, his eyes rolling and his tongue hanging from his mouth. He drooled so much that my mother got her new shower curtain from the trunk of the car and draped it around the girls who were riding in the backseat with Huckleberry. We all arrived exhausted from the trip. Even with the shower curtain, the girls were wet with slime and smelled like the city zoo.

When Huckleberry emerged from the car, he gazed at his new surroundings, standing dumbstruck for the longest time. Then he began to bark. Where were all the tall buildings, the fire hydrants and the curbs to sniff? Where were all his loyal fans?

A flock of geese flew overhead honking loudly. Two frogs jumped directly in front of the trembling animal. A butterfly landed on his head and a stray cat hissed at him in passing. It was all too much for this poor urban creature. He fled into the house and under the nearest piece of furniture.

Huckleberry was a city hound. Give him a concrete sidewalk and he was in his element. The country offered him no benefits. He became a recluse and spent his days on the screened front porch. Huckleberry would sit and watch the girls play outside, but when it was time for his walk, he hid. We all felt sorry for him but decided to let this timid animal spend his summer as he wished, curled up on his comfortable porch chair.

One morning a pipe burst in the kitchen, and my father called the plumber, Young Charlie, who was the son of one of his fishing buddies, Old Charlie. Young Charlie was accompanied by an old black Lab named George, who announced their arrival loudly from the back of the pickup truck. The girls scooted outside to greet the dog and were thrilled to see that he wanted to play. After a rousing game of catch and a romp around the property, all were in need of a cold drink.

Huckleberry had watched them play from his window seat. When they stopped to rest, he began to howl. All efforts to silence him were to no avail. The girls hooked up his leash and pulled him outside. At that moment, the black Lab stepped up, grabbed the leash in his mouth and began to walk Huckleberry around the yard. The howling stopped. Huckleberry, head held high, a spring in his step, tail wagging, followed in whatever direction George led. Both dogs were rewarded with hugs and doggy treats at the end of their walk.

The next day, Young Charlie arrived with George and announced that his dog was very anxious to return to our house. From that day on, George, who appeared to know that he was doing a good deed, took Huckleberry on his daily walk.

The summer slipped away and school beckoned: It was time to return to the city. Both dogs nuzzled each other as we packed the car for the journey home.

The following winter was harsh. Huckleberry became ill after eating something encrusted in the snow and died within a week. The entire family was horrified. We mourned, each in our own way, and my parents decided not to get another pet. Our lives continued: Winter passed, spring blossomed and summer was at hand once more.

The trip to the country was marred by the emptiness we all felt without Huckleberry. Within a few days, Young Charlie's truck pulled into our driveway and George was lifted out of the truck. Over the winter, he had lost the sight in one of his eyes and Young Charlie felt that walking Huckleberry would enrich George's life.

Dad explained the situation to Young Charlie, who was deeply saddened by our loss. "George still gets around okay, but he's getting old. Sure makes me sad that he won't have his friend to play with this summer," he said. We all felt a lump in our throats as the pair departed.

The next morning, the girls announced that they had a plan. We drove into town and visited the town's thrift store. We purchased one extra large stuffed animal, two pairs of old roller skates and one cabinet door. I cut the board to size and my mother glued the stuffed dog onto the platform. Dad bolted the skates to the bottom of the plank and the girls made a coat from Huckleberry's chair blanket. When the coat was tied around the finished product, we called Young Charlie to bring George for a visit.

We crossed our fingers as the black Lab sniffed the creation. My daughters attached the leash to it and handed it over to George. We'll never know if he humored us or if Huckleberry's scent gave him the feeling of having his friend back. However, for the next eight weeks George took great pride in walking that stuffed animal.

The story spread around town, and many of the residents came by to take pictures of the event. Shortly after returning to the city that year, we learned that George had passed away in his sleep, the stuffed animal at his side. We cried when we got the call.

A few days later, when our summer photos had been processed and picked up, our sorrow turned to joy. The pictures of George leading his "friend" around were vivid reminders of the happy times we had spent with Huckleberry and George. We knew we had witnessed a true act of love. Now, the two dogs will live forever in the telling and retelling of one of our favorite family stories: The Great Dog Walk.

Anne Carter

OFF THE MARK, ©1999 Mark Parisi. Reprinted with permission of Mark Parisi.

Velcro Beau

Money will buy you a fine dog, but only love can make it wag its tail.

Richard Friedman

When I first saw him, he looked worried. His furrowed brow and uncertain eyes gave his regal face a haunted look. I would come to know that this was a dog who was spooked by change until he got his bearings. And that day his world had been turned upside down.

The large German shepherd had been running away on a regular basis. He always showed up at a neighbor's house where they played with him and fed him—and eventually called his family, asking them to come and get him. Sometimes when the family showed up to retrieve him, they were rough with him. The neighbors noticed that the dog never seemed too excited about getting into their truck. And lately he hadn't been looking well. His coat was rough and he was losing weight.

One day, when they called the dog's family to report his whereabouts, the family said they weren't coming to get him. They'd had enough; the dog was on his own.

Fortunately, the neighbors called a friend who was a volunteer at the shelter where I also volunteered as dog-intake coordinator and breed-rescue liaison. She took him home and then called me.

As I drove up to my friend's house, I saw her sitting on the porch with her children. The dog was sitting on the porch, too, but wasn't interacting with any of them. Instead, he was scanning the street and sidewalk with nervous eyes.

He was a stunning dog, in spite of his worried expression, rough coat and emaciated frame. I was told he was a little over a year and a half, still a pup by German shepherd standards. He was very tall and would be an imposing creature once he filled out. I had never handled a dog his size and was intimidated at first. But, aside from being agitated at the strangeness of his surroundings, he seemed perfectly friendly and readily jumped into the back of my car.

My plan was to take him to the vet for an exam and then take him to the shelter or arrange for him to go to the nearest German shepherd rescue group. But first I thought I'd stop and show him to my husband, Larry, as he'd grown up with German shepherds and loved the breed. (Over the years, I'd heard *many* stories about his favorite dog, Marc; none of our rescued mutts could compare.)

When I opened the back door of the car and the shepherd leaped out, he immediately loped over to my husband. After a cursory sniff, he lost interest and began exploring the parking lot where we stood. We watched him, and I could tell Larry was impressed. He turned to me and said, "I want him."

I was surprised. We already had three dogs—an occupational hazard of volunteering at an animal shelter—and Larry often complained that the household dog population was too high. Plus, this dog was *huge*—it would be like adding two more dogs to our menagerie! But I didn't argue; I was pleased that Larry wanted a dog for himself.

So Beau joined our family. It wasn't easy at first. He had physical problems that made it difficult for him to gain weight. He was too skinny, yet couldn't digest any fats. His digestion was, to put it mildly, finicky. All that was certainly difficult, but his behavioral problems were even more troubling.

To our dismay, we soon learned that Beau had been "reverse house-trained." He consistently messed in the house and then stood by the door, waiting to go outside. We figured out that his first family had not given him regular opportunities to visit the great outdoors. Then, when he made the inevitable mess inside, they would get mad at him and throw him out the door. He was an intelligent dog and made the obvious connection: Go to the bathroom and then you get to go outside. We had quite a time convincing him it actually worked better the other way.

But what was worse was his utter lack of interest in people. He loved the other dogs, but had no use for the two-legged members of his new family. In my experience, German shepherds were just like that. I thought of them as "big, impersonal dogs," and didn't feel hurt by Beau's coldness. Not Larry. He was deeply disappointed by Beau's aloof disinterest. It was the antithesis of his experience with Marc, whose devotion to Larry had been the stuff of family legend.

Over time, Beau got the hang of being housebroken and established his place within our canine foursome. His physical problems also gradually cleared up, and he eventually tipped the scales at 108 pounds. He was such a handsome dog that people constantly stopped us in the street to comment on his beauty.

Sometimes when I would see him lying sphinxlike in a patch of sun or running in the fields near our house, my breath would catch. He resembled a lion or some other majestic wild animal—his physical presence was simply magical. But still, his heart remained shut. He had no love to give to us. And when he looked at us, there was no spark of joy in his eyes. The lights were on, but no one was home.

What could we do? We did our best to love him and hoped we might reach him someday.

Then one day about four months after we got him, I glanced at Beau and was startled to see that he was following Larry closely with his large brown eyes. He seemed to be studying him—learning what actions signaled a chance to go for a ride or presented the possibility of a walk, treat or a scratch behind the ears. It was as if he suddenly realized that people had things to offer him—things that might not be half bad.

His interest in all things Larry began to snowball. Swiftly, it became Beau's mission to keep an eye on my husband at all times to make sure he didn't miss any opportunities for doggy fun or excitement.

Larry didn't let him down. He knew what big dogs liked to do and where they liked to be scratched. He threw balls and sticks and took Beau to interesting places. Beau soon started whining if Larry left him behind. And when Larry finally returned from those solo jaunts, Beau was beside himself with joy. The floodgates of Beau's love had opened. The dry disinterest fell away and his heart began to bloom.

Today we call him Velcro Beau, because he sticks so close to Larry's side. Every day when Beau wakes up, he stretches his long body luxuriously and then finds one of us to give him his morning rubdown. He lays his ears flat against his head and shyly pokes his large nose against an arm. This beautiful big dog, overflowing with affection, lets us know he is ready for some serious lovin'.

I am grateful that although he is clearly Larry's dog, he has included me in the circle of his love. Often, while rubbing his large chest, I lean over and touch my forehead to his. Then he lifts his paw, places it on my arm and sighs with pleasure. We stay that way for a while, just enjoying our connection.

When we finish, Beau jumps to his feet, his eyes sparkling and his large tail waving wildly. It's time to eat or play. Or go to work with Larry. Or have some other kind of wonderful fun.

To our delight, that skinny, worried dog has become an exuberant and devoted companion. Beau knows that life is good when you live with people you love.

Carol Kline

A Christmas for Toby

On Christmas morning, 1950, my parents gave my sister, Alyce, my brother, Chuck and me a black Lab puppy named Toby. I was seven and the youngest.

Toby, just two months old but large for his age, bounded out of his carrying cage, a red ribbon around his neck. Excited, he wagged his mighty tail wildly, and before we knew it, he had knocked over the Christmas tree. Ornaments went flying in every direction. Then Toby's tail got wrapped in the wiring. He dragged the tree across the floor and proudly presented it to my mother.

Mom stood stock-still, squinted her eyes and opened her mouth wide, but no sound came from her. She just stared at Toby through half-opened eyes as his tail continued a vigorous thumping against the wood floor. With every thump, more ornaments fell from the ravaged limbs of the tree, landing in shattered, colorful piles. Finally, Mom opened her eyes wide and yelled, "The tree is ruined!"

"No, Mom. We'll fix it. It'll be like new, but with fewer ornaments," I said soothingly, fearing she would banish Toby from the family. Mom stood motionless as Alyce, Chuck and I untangled Toby's tail from the wiring. I held the squirming pup while my brother and sister reassembled the tree and propped it up against the wall in the corner of the living room.

Dad tilted his head from side to side. "Doesn't look too bad," he said as he rubbed his chin. "It's really not leaning all that much. Could have been worse. Toby's just excited, Mother."

We all studied the tree, forgetting about Toby, whom I had lowered to the floor.

"What's that sound?" Mom asked as we surveyed the room.

"Toby's in the packages!" Chuck shouted. He pointed to the stack of wrapped Christmas presents. "He's tearing the ribbons."

I grabbed Toby again and took him outside to save him from himself—and the need to look for a new home.

A year passed. We all survived the loss of at least one shoe to Toby's teething. Despite his mischief making, Toby became a beloved member of our family. He grew to be the biggest black Lab anyone in our town had ever seen.

A few days before Christmas, Toby became ill and we rushed him to the animal hospital. The veterinarian thought someone had poisoned Toby during one of his unauthorized outings.

I began to cry. "Can we see Toby for just a few minutes?" I sniffled. "He'll be so lonely without us, and it's almost Christmas."

"Sure," he said. "But be careful not to excite him."

We stood around Toby's kennel. He looked much smaller than the mighty dog we so often caught gliding over the fence. His eyes were sad. His breathing was loud and unsteady.

Dad stuck his large hand through the cage's meshing so he could touch Toby. Tears filled all our eyes when Dad said, "You'll be all right, boy."

Toby lifted his head for a moment, and then dropped it back with a heavy thump against the floor. I heard that thump all the way home as we rode in silence.

The next day, when the bell rang signaling the end of class at Park Hill Elementary, my third-grade schoolmates rushed from the building into the cold December air, eager to start the Christmas holiday. I trudged in silence behind, neither feeling the joy of the season nor wanting to talk to anyone.

My walk home was filled with thoughts of happier moments when Toby would run to meet me at the end of the driveway each day after school. He'd jump up to lick my face, forcing me to the ground as he tugged at my coat sleeve. Toby only released his grip so he could carry my book bag between his powerful jaws as he marched to the door. He never asked me about my grades or if I had been chosen for the school play. And he never cared if I wore the latest clothing craze.

When I entered the house, I found everyone sitting around the kitchen table. No one was talking. Their heads were bent, their eyes directed at the center of the empty surface.

I dropped my book bag. My eyes stung. "What's the matter? Has something happened to Toby?"

Mom stood and walked to me. "No, dear." She circled her arms around me in a comforting hug. "Toby's alive. But we have another problem. It'll take a family decision. Take off your coat and come sit with us."

I did as Mom instructed, but worry didn't subside. "What's the problem, then? I mean, what could matter if Toby's okay?" A sour liquid rose into my throat.

Dad took my hand. "The vet says that Toby will need to stay in the hospital for another few days."

"That's not so bad. Why's everyone so unhappy? Will he be home for Christmas?"

"Slow down." Dad raised his hand. "Let me finish." He got up from the table to get a cup of coffee from the pot simmering on the old gas stove. He took a sip and turned to us. "The vet isn't positive Toby will recuperate. If we decide to leave Toby in the hospital, we'll have to pay a large bill. There'll be no Christmas presents." He took another sip of the hot brew before he added, "We can't afford both. You know, there really is no Santa."

It had been a long time since I believed in Santa Claus, so this news didn't come as a surprise. "I knew that. But, I still don't see what the problem is." I looked at Alyce and Chuck, who had said nothing. "You two can't want presents instead of Toby. It wouldn't be Christmas without him. We've got to try."

Alyce wrapped her leg around the chair leg. Chuck rubbed the worn spot on the tabletop and spoke first. "I was hoping for a new bike . . . but, it wouldn't be any fun riding it if Toby wasn't following, barking to make me go faster."

Alyce kept her head lowered toward the empty table. "I really can't think of anything I would want more than Toby," she said.

I jumped from the table. "It's settled then. Tell the vet we'll do whatever it takes to give Toby a chance."

The next two days crawled by. Then the day before Christmas, the vet called to tell us that Toby was going to be okay and was ready to come home.

"Hooray!" I whooped. "We get Toby—again—for Christmas."

For the first time in nearly a week, everyone laughed. Then we all piled into the family Ford. Unlike the silent trip when we left Toby at the hospital, we chattered all the way there, each sharing a favorite Toby story. A few of the more memorable tales brought a scowl to Mom's face, especially the one about last year's smashed Christmas tree.

Though the ride to the hospital seemed interminable, the minutes before Toby's arrival in the waiting room seemed even longer. Finally, the door swung open and out walked Toby, wearing a red ribbon around his neck. He was slower than he had been last Christmas, but he had the same mischievous glint in his eyes.

We all rushed to Toby, hugging and kissing him. His mighty tail thumped in happy response. Mom leaned over, and holding Toby's face between her hands, whispered, "Merry Christmas, Toby."

Tekla Dennison Miller

Blu Parts the Veil of Sadness

*A black-and-white border collie came to our
 house to stay,
Her smiles brushed life's cobwebs away.*

Only Blu knows of her life before she was tucked into a small space with wired walls labeled "Animal Shelter." We had been without a dog for a couple of months when Blu's telepathic message, "I need a loving family," reached the ears of our teenage daughter Christine.

At the time, our family of six had a home in the country. Our small acreage bordered the Plateau River outside of Casper, Wyoming. Resident pets included an assortment of aquarium fish, laying hens and a few silky chickens that resided in the chicken coop. The 4-H bunnies nestled in their hutch. A Manx cat, dressed in dolls' clothes, often accompanied our younger daughters during their imaginary adventures. And last but not least trotted Smokey, our two-year-old quarter horse.

Into our Wyoming Noah's Ark came Blu. Needless to say, she was overwhelmed. To hide from the confusion of her new surroundings, Blu sought an invisible cloak in a variety of shapes. She took cover beneath the chicken coop, under the hay manger, the water trough or the loading chute—anyplace where she was in the shadows of the activity but could observe our day-to-day routines.

Her behavior gave us clues to the abuse that she'd endured before coming to our home. It left her cowering whenever a hand was raised to pat her or voices were too loud for her sensitive soul. Yet as the weeks dissolved into months and our calendar pages went out with the trash, Blu's demeanor changed. She progressed from following us during chores to romping out front as our leader. When someone approached her with a hand for a pat, Blu no longer cringed or slunk away. Instead, she sought affection from us. If we didn't acknowledge her when she came near, Blu would nudge our hand until she received the hug and loving words she now enjoyed.

She trotted alongside Smokey when the girls rode him bareback. Blu's herding instincts were displayed when she gathered stray chickens and drove them back to the coop. After playing tag with the cat, Blu's impish smile was reflected by anyone observing her play. At the close of day, Blu rested at the bedside of one of our daughters. Like our children, she listened with rapt attention to their bedtime stories. The beauty of her canine soul touched our lives in many ways. Then one cold evening, she showed us her remarkable capacity to love.

That year, eleven-year-old Joanne and her sister Kathy were each given a calf to raise for their 4-H projects. Morning and evening, they faithfully made sure there was fresh water in the trough and food in the bunker for their calves. When the colder weather arrived in late fall, they made straw bedding inside the calving shed.

One evening the cold stiffness of winter hung icicles off the barn roof and wrapped a blanket of snow across the meadow. I had just put dinner in the oven when

Kathy yelled from the back porch.

"Mother . . . hurry . . . Joanne's calf is hurt!"

Zipping up my jacket, I ran to the barn, where I found Joanne sitting on the snow-covered ground. Blu lay close to Joanne's side while the calf lay across her lap, legs stiff. Blue wool mittens off, Joanne's one hand cradled the calf's head, the other clamped nostrils shut while she blew puffs of air into the calf's mouth. Tears streamed down her cheeks. "She's barely breathing, Mommy." She blew again into the calf's mouth. "I found her lying here . . . all by herself. I don't want her to die."

"Honey, she could have been kicked by another cow. You need to understand that she may have injuries inside beyond our help."

"I know." She wiped the tears trickling down her cheek.

"Let's get her to the house where it's warm." I carried the calf. Blu followed close to Joanne.

Only the kitchen clock marked the passage of time while we worked on the calf. Blu kept her vigil just paw steps away from Joanne.

The calf's labored breathing slowed . . . stopped.

I hugged Joanne close. "I'm sorry, honey."

"She was too little to die. Why . . . ?"

The sadness on her face was like a blow to my chest. I gulped for air. My mind whispered, *Oh honey, I wish I could protect you from death . . . but I can't.* I felt so helpless.

I said, "Injuries from an accident don't always heal; sometimes the animal or person dies. And for a little while, we cry our sadness."

Kathy took her sister's hand. "I'll share my calf with you."

"That's okay . . . I don't want another one right now."

My vision blurred while I explained to Joanne that when an animal or person died it was only the end of a tangible life, that her dad and I believed life was ongoing for the soul. Before my words were out, I realized that there would be time later for us to talk about our spiritual beliefs, to help Joanne build the personal strengths that would ease her through other losses. Just now, she was an inconsolable little girl, and I didn't know how best to help.

As I watched, Blu crawled across the floor and put her head in Joanne's lap. Blu nudged her hand until fingers moved through her black-and-white fur. Slowly Joanne bent her neck and kissed the top of Blu's head. The dog raised her head and looked into Joanne's eyes. No words were needed in those quiet moments when unconditional love touched Joanne's bruised spirit. She hugged Blu and whispered, "I love you, too."

Filled with wonder, I witnessed a black-and-white border collie—who was once afraid to love—part the veil of sadness from my young daughter's heart.

Margaret Hevel

The Haunted Bowl

It's not much to look at. Just a big old cream-colored bowl. You know, one of those old-fashioned crock bowls with a shiny glaze except on the bottom and around the rim. It's thick and heavy with short vertical sides. For almost thirty years that old bowl has occupied a place on my kitchen floor. It came from Jackson's Hay and Feed, one of those tin-roofed feed stores, the kind with a dusty wooden floor, the pungent aromas of alfalfa and bags of feed, and the sounds of cheep-cheeping fuzzy yellow chicks in an incubator. At $4.95 it represented a major invest-ment for a college student drawing $90 a month on the GI Bill.

Today, it came out of the cupboard where it was stored after Cheddar, my dear old yellow Lab, had to be put down. It had just seemed too big to feed the puppy—until now. The puppy, another yellow girl I named Chamois, is growing fast. Now, at almost eighteen weeks of age, she's ready for the bowl. She'll be the third Lab to eat from it.

Swamp was the first. For thirteen years Swamp ate her meals from the bowl. Now as I look at it sitting on my kitchen floor, I can see Swamp as clearly as if she were here. She liked to lie on the floor with the bowl between her front legs when she ate. Her last meal came from that bowl; a special food for dogs with failing kidneys. She'd been on it since September. The vet told me she had about four months left so I started looking for a puppy.

Swamp rode with me out to a farm on a windy Kansas prairie. The farmer had about ten kennel runs. On one side were Labs and on the other were pointers. He said, "I don't usually sell 'em to people who don't hunt." I confessed I was not a hunter, but Swamp worked her magic on him and soon we were driving home with a precocious yellow puppy we named Cheddar.

The bowl got Cheddar into trouble. She tried to eat from it when Swamp was holding it between her paws. A quick growl and a snap of Swamp's powerful jaws and we were racing to the vet's for a couple of stitches on her nose. I hadn't thought of that for years. Now with the bowl sitting here on the kitchen floor, it seems like yesterday. And, as if it were yesterday, I again experienced the sharp pangs of grief felt so many years ago when we drove Swamp to the same clinic and said good-bye. That night Cheddar ate her first meal from the bowl, and for the next fifteen years it was filled for her every morning.

Cheddar's technique was different from Swamp's. She'd walk up to the bowl, get a chunk or two in her mouth and walk away as she crunched the kibble. Then she'd circle back for another bite. She always ate half the food in the morning and the other half just before bedtime. It was a pattern that never varied.

That old $4.95 bowl is probably the only thing I still own that was mine thirty years ago. It has served us well, and tonight Chamois will eat her first meal from it. I wonder if she knows how valuable it is and what it means to me. I wonder if she knows it's Halloween and that her meal tonight will be served in a haunted bowl: a big old cream-colored bowl haunted by the ghosts of Swamp and

Cheddar—and a thousand poignant memories. Will she know as she eats that a black ghost will lie down and wrap her front legs around the bowl and that a yellow ghost will grab a bite and then circle back for more? Will she see the tears in my eyes before I turn away and stare into the past? Or will she just devour the food, lick her chops and wag her busy tail?

John Arrington

You Have No Messages

We were visiting our daughter when we adopted our Boston terrier, Tad. An adorable puppy, just three months old, he became the family's center of attention. Each morning, as soon as he heard my daughter Kayla moving around downstairs, he had to be taken down for playtime before she left for work. When she came home from work, we had him waiting for her at the door.

After three weeks we left for home. On the drive, we let Tad talk to Kayla on the phone each night. Once home, every time we called Kayla or she called us, we always put Tad on. He scratched the phone and listened intently and tried to look into the phone to see her.

One Saturday, Kayla called while we were out. She left a message. Tad was standing beside me when I pressed the button to listen to the message. He listened to her talking and cocked his head, grinning at me. I played it again for him.

A few days later, I was taking my shower when I heard the answering machine come on and Kayla leave a message. I thought it was strange when I heard her message repeat and the machine announce, "End of messages." A few seconds later Kayla's message began yet again.

Wondering what was going on, I climbed out of the shower, wrapped a towel around myself and headed into the living room. There stood Tad, listening to the answering machine. I stopped and watched. When the message finished, he stood up with his feet against the edge of the low table, reached over with one paw and slapped the answering machine. The message came on again. He dropped back on the floor and listened happily.

I told him "no," and distracted him from the answering machine while I erased the message. A few days later I was in the kitchen when I heard, "You have no messages." I headed for the living room. Tad had started the machine again. I watched as he cocked his head and looked at the answering machine. Then he stood with his feet on the edge of the table and tapped the button again: "You have no messages." He walked around to the other side of the table and repeated the process with the same results. This really irritated him. He returned to his first position, took both paws and began slapping and clawing the answering machine. It repeated: "You have no messages."

I said, "Tad, leave the answering machine alone." He looked at me and then turned back to the answering machine, digging at it furiously. When it repeated the same message, he ran to me and then ran back to the answering machine, waiting for me to do something. I realized he wanted to hear Kayla talking, but I had erased the message.

I called Kayla that night and asked her to call Tad and leave him a message. I explained that Tad had listened to her message, but I had erased it. When he tried to listen to it again and didn't hear her message, he had been unhappy.

Kayla called Tad and left a special message for him that he can play and listen to whenever he wants to hear Kayla's voice. We call it puppy love, twenty-first-century style!

Zardrelle Arnott

Bubba's Last Stand

A dog is a dog except when he is facing you.
Then he is Mr. Dog.

Haitian saying

During the four years I spent as an animal control officer, I learned that dogs are the first to know when spring has arrived. Dogs who never venture farther than their own backyards will somehow find themselves across town following the scent of spring. Bubba was no exception.

Each year, animal control received several phone calls complaining about Bubba—always in the spring. Bubba, an ancient, overweight and most often cranky bulldog with a profound underbite, snored in the shade of his yard all summer, and seemed content to stay behind his fence during the winter. But as soon as it began to thaw, Bubba began to terrorize the city.

Actually, Bubba was too old to terrorize anyone. His once tan and brindle coat was mixed with so much gray that he appeared at least twenty years old, and I noticed the beginning of a limp that had the definite look of arthritic hips. He never chased anyone; I don't think he could have if he tried. Still, his appearance and his perpetual nasal congestion, combined with his bad attitude, made people uncomfortable when he got loose.

Sometimes he would get it in his head to sit outside the local deli and glare. The deli owners tried throwing roast beef at him but he just sniffed at it, gobbled it up, growled and stayed right where he was. Most people just got out of his way when they saw him coming; then they called animal control.

His owner, Tim—a thin, silent man who appeared ageless in that way men do after working outdoors most of their lives—usually showed up at the pound, apologized, asked someone to tell me to drop off his ticket and took Bubba home. He wrapped his thin arms around Bubba's very large middle and heaved him into the back of his pickup truck. He never complained, never asked for a court date. He just apologized and paid his fines.

Tim didn't seem the kind of person who would be interested in having a pet, especially one as difficult as Bubba. Tim lived alone in a large dilapidated Victorian house that was in a perpetual state of renovation. He had never married, and no one really remembered if he had any family. He didn't seem comfortable showing affection to anyone, least of all a fat, grumpy bulldog. And Bubba never let anyone touch him, except for Tim, and even then he didn't look too happy about it. Yet year after year Tim spent a lot of time leaving work to come and drag his grouchy, old dog home.

One spring, it seemed as though Bubba had finally gone into retirement, only growling at passersby from the comfort of his yard. That was why I was a bit surprised when I got a call on an unusually warm June day that a very ugly, old, fat and wheezing bulldog was causing a problem up at the high school. *How did he get all the way up there?* I thought to myself as I drove to the school. The route from Bubba's home to the high school was all uphill. I had seen Bubba recently, and he surely didn't look as if he could make a trip like that.

I pulled into the high school parking lot and saw the gymnasium doors open, probably for a cross-breeze. Bubba must have entered the school through the gym. *This should be fun.* I grabbed a box of dog biscuits and the snare pole and threw a leash around my neck. No animal control officer had ever actually touched Bubba. The equipment was going to be of no real use—he would likely never let me near him. I had to figure out a way to get him to *want* to leave. I hoped the biscuits would do the job. Entering the hallway, I saw lines of teenagers standing in suspended animation along the walls. One called out to me, "Every time we even go to open our lockers, that dog growls at us. He's going to eat us!"

Sure enough, there was Bubba—holding the entire hallway hostage. I could see him standing, bowlegged, wheezing like I had never heard him before, and growling at any sudden movement. *Uh-oh,* I thought to myself. Frightening the occasional neighbor was one thing, but growling at kids on school property—Bubba was looking at some serious penalties, possibly even a dangerous-dog action complaint, which was a rare occurrence, but one with dire consequences if he was found guilty.

"Bubba," I called to him, and he managed to twist his pudgy body around to see who knew his name. He looked at me, wheezed some more and growled loudly. I reached into the box of biscuits and threw one over to him. He limped over to it slowly, sniffed it, sneezed and sat down glaring at me. So much for Plan A. I was going to have to use the snare pole on him and I wasn't looking forward to it.

Suddenly from behind me, I heard, "Hey, ugly dog. Try this." A tall teenage boy put his hand into a Baggie and threw a Froot Loop at Bubba. Bubba stared at the cereal, then up at the boy. He snuffled around it, picked it up and swallowed it. I turned to the tall boy leaning against the wall. "Can I borrow those?"

"Sure." He handed me the Baggie, and I threw a Froot Loop toward Bubba. He waddled over to suck it up off the floor. I kept dropping them as I backed toward the open doors of the gym. Bubba was in bad shape; his bowed legs seemed to have a hard time holding up his rotund body. Every step seemed to cause him pain, and the wheezing was getting worse. I wanted to pick him up, but as I started to approach, he growled and backed up. So I continued to drop one Froot Loop at a time, inching my way toward the patrol car. Finally, Bubba was at the car. He was wheezing so much I worried he would have a heart attack. I decided to just get him home and worry about the report later: Bubba was fading fast.

I threw what was left of the Froot Loops into the back-seat of the car. Bubba waddled over and stuck his two front paws on the floor to finish them up. I swallowed hard and quickly pushed Bubba's rear end into the back-seat. He grumbled and growled, but was mostly concerned with chewing the last bit of cereal. I couldn't believe it—I had touched Bubba and survived!

By the time I pulled up in front of Bubba's house, Tim's truck was parked haphazardly in front. Tim ran out of the house, letting the door slam behind him. "Is Bubba okay? I called the school, but you had already left. I'll pay the fine, whatever it is. Give me a couple of 'em. How did he get out of the house? I can't believe he made it all the way to the high school. He's so sick. How'd you get him in the car anyway?" Tim spoke more in that minute than I had ever heard him speak in the several years I had known him.

Before I could answer, Tim walked over to the patrol car and opened the door. Bubba was snoring loudly, sound asleep on his back covered in Froot Loop crumbs and looking very un-Bubba-like. Tim put his arms around the old dog and with a lot of effort pulled him out of the car, holding him as you would an infant. Bubba never even woke up, just grumbled a bit in his sleep.

"I, um, used Froot Loops. He followed a trail of them into the car," I said.

Tim lifted his eyes from the sleeping dog to look at me. "Froot Loops? I didn't know he liked Froot Loops."

The lines in Tim's pale face seemed deeper in the harsh sunlight. He looked tired; more than that, he looked worried. "I can't believe he got out. I had him locked in the house with the air conditioner on." Tim's voice dropped, "The vet says he has cancer. They told me to take him home from the animal hospital for the weekend, you know, to say good-bye."

I looked at Tim holding his old, fat, gray bulldog. Suddenly, I understood what I hadn't before. All those years that had etched the premature lines on Tim's sad face—Bubba had been there to share them. They had each other, and for them, that had been enough.

"I'm so sorry, Tim," I said and turned to get back into the car. "I'll talk to you later."

"What about my tickets? I know I'm getting a few this time, right?"

I turned around to look at Tim. "Let me see what the sergeant says first, Tim. You just worry about Bubba right now, okay?"

I started to leave again, but then remembered there was something else I wanted to ask. "Tim?" I called over to him as he was carrying his dog into the house. "Why do you think he went to the high school? I don't remember him going all the way up there before."

Tim smiled at me, another thing I had never seen him do. "Bubba really loves kids. I used to bring him to the playground when he was a pup. Maybe he remembered that."

I nodded and waved to them: the thin, tired man with the gray flannel shirt, carrying his twenty-year-old puppy into the house . . . perhaps for the last time.

Bubba died soon after that day. I never even wrote up a ticket for his caper at the high school. I figured Bubba had just been revisiting his youth, saying good-bye in his own Bubba way.

You think you know people and then you find out there is more to them than you ever could have imagined. It took Bubba's last stand to show me that loving families take many forms, all of them beautiful.

Lisa Duffy-Korpics

2

CELEBRATING THE BOND

The bond with a dog is as lasting as the ties of this Earth can ever be.

Konrad Lorenz

"He followed me home."

Some Snowballs Don't Melt

Snowball came into our lives during the winter of 1974. I was four years old. From the moment my daddy brought the plump puppy home, he and the dog formed a close bond. Though snow is scarce in Central Texas, Daddy looked at the bumbling white German shepherd puppy and dubbed him Snowball. Picking him up, my father gazed into his soulful brown eyes. "This dog is going to make something of himself," Daddy said as he stroked the pup's soft, fluffy head. Soon the two were inseparable.

While Snowball was still very young, my father began training him to prove that the dog could earn his keep. A good herding dog is essential for a working cattle ranch, so Daddy began preparing him for his role as a cow dog. Snowball's determination to please my father was amazing. To watch Daddy and Snowball herd cattle together was to watch poetry in motion. Daddy would point at a cow and Snowball would become a white blur as he zigzagged through the herd and chased the selected cow into the corral.

During the day, Daddy worked for the highway department. Every morning Snowball would mournfully watch as my father left for work in the truck. Even though it was apparent that the dog wished to go, he made no move toward the truck. Snowball knew that a pat on the head and a raised tailgate meant that he was not to go; however, a smile, a lowered tailgate and the command to "get in" were an invitation to go with my father. In that case, Snowball bounded toward the truck as if there were no limits to his joy.

At the same time every weekday afternoon, Snowball would casually stroll to the end of the driveway, lie down under a redbud tree and patiently gaze down the long gravel road, looking for my daddy's truck. Mama and I did not have to look at the clock to know that it was time for Daddy to come home: Snowball's body language clearly announced my father's imminent arrival. First, the dog would raise his head, his ears erect, and every muscle in his body would become tense. Then, slowly, Snowball would stand, his gaze never wavering from the direction of the gravel road. At that point, we could see a cloud of dust in the distance and hear the familiar whine of my daddy's diesel truck coming down the road. As my father got out of the truck, Snowball would run to him, voicing his joyful delight. Despite the dog's great bulk, he danced around my father with the grace of a ballerina.

One Saturday morning when Snowball was six, Daddy took him and Tiger—our other cow dog, an Australian shepherd—to work cattle at my granddaddy's house, while my mother and I went to visit my mother's mother, Nana, who also lived nearby. While we were there, the phone rang. From my perch on a stool near the phone, I could hear the panic-stricken voice of my father's mother on the other end of the line. The blood drained from Nana's face as she motioned to Mama to take the phone receiver. Granny told Mama that, while Daddy was working Granddaddy's cattle, a Hereford bull had trampled him.

Although the extent of his injuries was unknown, it was obvious that Daddy needed medical attention. It was decided that I was to remain at Nana's house while Mama took Daddy to the emergency room. Tearfully, I sat huddled in a corner of an ancient sofa while Nana tried, unsuccessfully, to console me.

A short time later Granddaddy called Nana's house and asked her to bring me over to see if I could do something with that "darn dog." As Nana and I drove to Granddaddy's, I sat on the edge of the seat and pushed against the dashboard, willing the car to go faster. As Nana drove her wheezing Nova up the sand driveway, I could see my daddy's battered blue truck parked underneath a lone pine tree close to my grandparents' house. When I got out of the car, I heard a mournful wail. It pierced the stillness of the afternoon, causing the hair on the back of my neck to stand on end. In the back of the truck stood Snowball, howling his heartbreak and misery to the world. Granddaddy had hoped that the sight of me would calm Snowball, but Snowball and I had never been that close. I did everything I could to comfort him, but nothing worked.

As I tried in vain to soothe the dog, Granddaddy pointed a gnarled finger at Snowball and said, "That dog is a wonder. He probably saved your daddy's life."

Granddaddy told us that all the cattle, except a Hereford bull, were herded into the corral. The stubborn beast refused to go in, despite Snowball and the rest of the dogs doing their best to herd him. Granddaddy guessed that the extreme heat of the day had enraged the bull. His patience tested to the limit, the bull turned and charged at my father, who was standing nearby. Catching Daddy off guard, the bull knocked him to the ground and ran over him. As the bull pawed the ground in preparation to charge again, a blur of white streaked between the bull and my father. Snarling at the enraged bull, Snowball stood firmly planted in front of my father. Then, with a heart-stopping growl, Snowball hurled himself at the bull, and began to drive the Hereford away. According to Granddaddy, Snowball's action gave my father enough time to crawl under a nearby truck. Trotting to the truck that my daddy lay underneath, Snowball took a wolflike stance and bravely turned away each one of the determined bull's attacks. Working as a team, Snowball, Tiger and my uncle's dog Bear, kept the bull away from the truck until my granddaddy and uncle could reach Daddy.

Later that afternoon Mama returned home with my father, and everyone in the family was greatly relieved to learn that Daddy had no life-threatening injuries. Snowball, on the other hand, remained inconsolable until Mama let him into the house to see my father. On silent feet, Snowball padded into the bedroom and quietly placed his head on my parents' bed. Daddy petted him and thanked Snowball for saving his life. Satisfied, the shepherd padded outside, a "doggy grin" on his face.

Unfortunately, Snowball wasn't able to save my father six years later when Daddy was killed on the job. On that terrible day, the faithful dog went to his place at the end of the driveway to wait for his master. There was confusion on his old face as he watched car after car turn into our driveway. I could read his thoughts: *So many cars, so many people, but where is my master?* Undeterred, Snowball kept his vigil far into the night, his gaze never leaving the road. Something happened to Snowball after Daddy died—he grew old. It appeared that it was his love and devotion for my father that had kept him young and had given him the will to live. Day after day, for two years following my father's death, the dog staggered to his spot at the end of the driveway to wait for a master who would never return. No amount of coaxing or pleading could convince Snowball to quit his vigil, even when the weather turned rough.

It soon became very obvious to Mama and me that it was getting harder for Snowball to get around. The weight that he gained over the years was hard on his hip joints. Just the effort of lying down or getting up was a chore, and his once-powerful strides were now limited to a halting limp. Still, every day he returned to his spot at the end of the driveway. The day finally came when Snowball was unable to stand by himself. He whined his frustration and pain as Mama and I helped him to stand. After getting his balance, the old dog, his gaze never wavering from his destination, made his way out to his daily lookout post.

After two months of helping Snowball to stand, my mother and I tearfully agreed that it was time to do the humane thing for the fourteen-year-old cow dog. Our neighbor's son was a vet, and we arranged for him to come to the house and give Snowball the injection. Snowball lay down on the ground and placed his head in my mother's lap, his eyes filled with love and understanding. We all felt he knew what was about to happen.

After the vet gave him the injection, Snowball smiled his "doggy grin" for the first time since my father died, then slipped away quietly in my mother's arms.

Our throats choked with tears, we wrapped the body of the gallant dog in an old blanket and buried him beneath the spot at the end of the drive that he had occupied for so many years. The group huddled around the dog's grave all agreed that Snowball had "smiled" because he knew that, once again, he would be with the person he loved the most. If there is a heaven for animals, which I hope and believe there is, I can picture Daddy and his beloved dog together there, once again sharing the joy of each other's company—this time for eternity.

Debbie Roppolo

Greta and Pearl: Two Seniors

When the phone rang and the gentleman on the other end said he wanted to place his dog, an eleven-year-old German shepherd named Greta, I winced. He had sold his house, was moving to a temporary apartment and would soon be leaving the country. As the director of Southwest German Shepherd Rescue, I agreed to see and evaluate the dog with a note of realistic caution to the owner: he'd better start thinking about a contingency plan.

Greta sure was a nice old gal. We put her information on our Web site right away and did receive a couple of inquiries, but no one wanted to deal with the little annoyances that sometimes come with an aging dog.

Rescue organizations function within a large cooperative network. One day I received an e-mail from a woman named Suzanne who ran another rescue group. She said that she had an elderly woman, Pearl, looking for an older, large German shepherd. I suggested that Suzanne visit our Web site, where she could view the two senior-citizen canines currently in our rescue program. About a week later Suzanne e-mailed me Pearl's phone number and advised that, although the woman was eighty-six years old, she felt that it would be worthwhile to pursue the adoption.

I immediately phoned Pearl and told her all about Greta. I explained that she was on medication, and Pearl laughed and said they could take their pills together. I made it clear that the average life span of a German shepherd is between ten and twelve years, but many reach thirteen to fifteen years of age. I also asked about her mobility and ability to care for such a dog. Pearl was undaunted and informed me that, in her younger days, she'd run a Great Dane rescue program. She told me that she would make arrangements for Greta to live with her granddaughter, on her forty-acre ranch, should anything happen to her (Pearl). Further, Pearl said that she was still driving her car, and if need be, was able to make trips to the vet.

I explained our policies and advised that I would be paying her a home visit.

We don't usually place German shepherds in apartments for a number of reasons, however in this case, it seemed appropriate. Greta didn't need a lot of exercise— what she needed was a lot of TLC, a sense of security and a devoted companion who was around all the time. And Pearl's needs were exactly the same.

After meeting Pearl and her husband, Bert, and checking out what would be Greta's new home, I agreed to introduce them. We arranged to meet at a nearby park. The meeting went so well that Greta went home with them on the spot.

Every time I made a follow-up call, I held my breath. And each time, Pearl told me everything was going great. I asked that she periodically contact me with updates. Whenever I heard Pearl's voice on the other end of the phone, I found myself waiting for the other shoe to drop.

During one call, Pearl told me that Greta had a bath and had gone to the vet for a checkup. She had her tested for every disease known to man or beast, and apart from a sluggish thyroid, Greta was in fine shape. In subsequent conversations, Pearl related that Greta shadowed her everywhere. She spoke about how Greta would place her body across Pearl's if she sensed any unsteadiness. The next call was to tell me: "If I were to have molded a dog from clay and given it life, it would have been Greta. I cannot imagine life without her." I assured Pearl that I was certain Greta felt the same.

We were into week five of Pearl and Greta's union when I received a phone call from a very distraught Pearl. The management of her apartment complex had informed her that, despite the fact that she was permitted to have pets weighing up to a hundred pounds (which we had verified), certain specific breeds were excluded: Rottweilers, German shepherds, Dobermans, chows and pit bulls. There was no mention of this restriction in her lease, nor had Pearl ever been made aware of this policy. Nonetheless, Greta would have to go.

I assured Pearl that we would fight all the way to court if necessary. She informed me that she would rather live in her car than part with her new companion, yet I could sense the panic associated with the possibility of being uprooted at nearly eighty-seven years of age—with an ailing husband, to boot. I advised Pearl that I would need a few days to do some research. I had to read the Landlord/ Tenant Act and familiarize myself with that aspect of the law.

In the meantime, I suggested that Pearl obtain a letter from her doctor stating that she needed Greta for her psychological and physical well-being, that Greta assisted both her and her husband with balance issues and provided them with a sense of security. Pearl's husband, Bert, was going blind as a result of his diabetes and spent a good deal of time sleeping, leaving Pearl lonely and depressed. That is, until Greta came along. Both she and Greta had become reignited. This was truly a mutually beneficial relationship.

I put in a call to the cofounder of REACH (Restoring and Extending Ability with Canine Helpers). I asked if she thought getting an eleven-year-old German shepherd certified as a service dog was feasible. In essence, she said that as long as the dog could fulfill Pearl's needs as outlined by her doctor, and provided Greta could pass the Level One Assistance dog test, "Yes, assuming you feel that Greta's temperament is sound enough." I asked her to start the process and told her I'd get back to her.

I checked with Pearl to verify she had her doctor's letter and to let her know that a small army would be marching into her home in a few days. She had no other information and no preparation.

One week after that distraught call from Pearl, the certified REACH evaluator (with clipboard and score sheet in hand), an additional temperament tester, two strangers to the dog and family, two children and one female German shepherd unknown to both Greta and Pearl arrived at their home. It was a cool day but I was sweating. I had no idea how the obedience aspect of the evaluation would go. I did not know how much control Pearl would need or have over Greta as Greta faced strange dogs inside her home territory, unfamiliar kids bumping into her, food temptations while being called and so on. I was confident that Greta would be fine with everything else.

Forty-five minutes later the score sheets were given to the REACH evaluator: Greta had passed with flying colors! At the tender age of eleven, Greta became a Certified Level One Assistance Dog, and Pearl became the proudest lady in Arizona. As they were presented with their official certificate and Greta's badge, Pearl held out her arms to the entire room, proclaiming, "I love you!"

As the "team" was pulling out of the parking lot, we saw Pearl, with the letter and certificate in hand, and Greta, with her badge hanging from her collar, heading in the direction of the manager's office. I phoned her that evening to ask her how it went. Upon seeing their credentials, the manager had said, "Well, I guess she can go just about anywhere now," to which Pearl had crowed triumphantly, "You got *that* right!"

Stefany Smith

Bullet's Dog

Dogs love company. They place it first on their short list of needs.

J. R. Ackerley

One morning in early June, I went outside to feed our horse Bullet. Usually, Bullet waits patiently at the fence for his breakfast, but this morning he was lingering near the two tall oak trees in the center of the pasture where he liked to spend the hottest hours of the day.

Curious why he wasn't eager for his breakfast, I peered across the pasture at him, hoping he wasn't sick. Then as he began to slowly walk toward me, I noticed a blotch of red fur hunkering down in the tall grass beneath one of the trees. So this was what held Bullet's attention this morning: another stray dog had found its way onto our property. Most of them shied away from our large retired racehorse, but this dog seemed to feel safe in the shelter of the tall grass in spite of Bullet. I placed a bucket of alfalfa cubes inside the fence. After Bullet ate them, I would give him a few of the oatmeal cookies he loved more than anything.

It was a glorious morning, so I sat down on my back steps, reluctant to go back inside and start my day. As Bullet ate his alfalfa cubes, the dog rose cautiously to its feet. The dog stared at Bullet for a long moment and then slowly made its way toward the horse. It paused every few steps and looked at me intently to make sure I wasn't a threat. As the dog drew closer to Bullet, I held my breath. I didn't know how Bullet would react to an animal that approached while he was eating. Knowing that a kick from a horse can be fatal to a dog, I was about to shout at the dog to scare it away. Just then Bullet swung his head and looked at the dog for a moment. Unperturbed by the approaching animal, he turned back to his food and began to eat again.

The dog drew close enough to snag a cube that Bullet had dropped. My heart broke as I watched the dog—a female—chewing on the alfalfa. I knew she had to be extremely hungry to attempt to eat horse feed.

I went inside the house to find something that the dog could eat. I had some leftover meat loaf in the refrigerator that I had planned on serving for dinner. I put the meat loaf in an old aluminum pie tin and walked toward the fence with it. The dog ran to the safety of the tall grass near the oak trees as soon as I took one step in her direction. I put the food down on the ground and tried to coax her toward me. After several minutes, I gave up and went back inside the house. She would probably come for the food as soon as I was out of sight.

A little while later, while folding laundry, I realized that I had not yet given Bullet his cookies. I grabbed a handful out of the box we kept under the sink and went back outside. To my surprise, Bullet was kneeling in the grass with the dog next to him. I smiled at the warm picture they made. Knowing that I carried his treat, Bullet got up quickly and galloped to the fence to meet me. The dog watched as I tossed the cookies over the fence. I noticed that she had not yet gotten the courage to venture outside the fence to get the meat loaf I had left for her.

Again I sat down on the back steps, trying to think of how to get the dog to overcome her fear and come for the meat loaf. For some reason, she seemed to feel safe within the confines of the pasture. Noticing that Bullet was eating, the dog began to move forward slowly, watching me all the while. *He might share his alfalfa with you, but he'll never let you at his oatmeal cookies,* I said to myself. But to my surprise, Bullet watched with only mild interest as the dog leaped forward and grabbed a cookie. She swallowed the cookie in one famished gulp, then darted forward to snatch another one. There were no more cookies left, but the dog stood beneath Bullet and scurried for the crumbs that fell from the horse's mouth, licking the ground furiously to get at every last morsel.

When Bullet walked back toward the shade of the oak trees, the dog trotted along beside him. All day long, whenever I looked out the window toward the pasture, the dog was always close to Bullet, either running along at his side or lying in the grass near him. The dog appeared to be devoted to the horse, who had willingly shared his food with her.

It was three days before I coaxed the dog out of the pasture. She got down on her belly and crawled toward me, her large brown eyes begging me not to hurt her. Whimpering, partly in fear and partly with joy, she allowed me to gently pet her. I noticed that she was young and quite beautiful, in spite of being malnourished. I found myself calling her Lucy, and knew that this stray was here to stay.

Though Lucy eventually warmed to my husband, Joe, and me, she always preferred Bullet's company the most. She spent most of the day inside the pasture with him.

They would run together with great exuberance and joy until they got tired and then drop in the grass beside each other to rest. Bullet always shared his cookies with Lucy. Often Bullet would lower his head and nuzzle Lucy, and she would reach up and lick his face. It was obvious that they loved each other. At night Lucy slept in the stall next to Bullet.

When visitors commented on our new dog, we always laughed and said, "Lucy isn't our dog. She's Bullet's."

Lucy brought joy into the life of an aging racehorse, and much amazement and wonder into ours.

Elizabeth Atwater

Daisy Love

In our early days of working together at the grooming shop, my husband, David, and I had a field day studying humanity as it passed through our door on the other end of a dog leash. Things were less hectic then. We had plenty of time to dissect our customers' personalities and discuss our observations.

George was one of these character studies. Despite his gruff personality, he was a sentimental man, an uncommon trait in cool, reserved New England where we strive to keep a stiff upper lip. George wore his heart on his sleeve, notably for Evie, his wife of forty-five years whose death after a lingering illness had been a traumatic blow to the craggy old gentleman.

Each April on the anniversary of Evie's passing, George would grace the editorial page of the local newspaper with a poem written in her memory.

"Every year about this time, we know we can count on two things," David remarked as he leafed through the paper. "Income taxes and a poem from George."

"I happen to think it's touching," I argued. "And I'll tell you something else: If George doesn't get his dog to the vet soon, he'll have somebody else to grieve for."

For almost a year, I had been upset whenever George brought his terrier mix, Daisy, in for grooming. I had noticed small lumps growing on her body, but each time I suggested he take the little Benji look-alike to the vet, he changed the subject. I agonized over the situation with David, who also worked as a psychiatric nurse. "People like George will not act until they are ready," he told me. "In the mental-health field, we refer to this as denial."

I empathized with George's dread. In his mind, if he didn't name the demon, it didn't exist. And Daisy was much more than a pet to the lonely widower. A heavy smoker and drinker in his younger years, George's retirement had been hastened by poor health, but now he worked at keeping fit. His daily walks with Daisy were a big part of his regimen.

His life revolved around the little dog. There was the morning ride to the doughnut shop where Ruthie the waitress always saved him a plain, and Daisy a coconut, cruller. "I know it's not health food, but it's my only vice," he told me. Once home, they'd relax in his recliner to watch *The Price Is Right,* then take a walk before lunch. After a nap, they arose in time to greet the school kids getting off the bus in front of their house. No matter what the chore—leaf raking, fence painting, bulb planting or lawn mowing—Daisy happily tagged along at her master's heels as he addressed her with a steady stream of chatter.

His pride in the little mongrel showed every time he picked her up after grooming. "Well, well, don't you look pretty," he'd enthuse as Daisy wagged her whole body with delight. "Show us how you dance!"

The little dog dutifully twirled on her hind legs, then yipped for a cookie. "Show Kathy how you go for a walk," he'd tell her, as she picked up the leash in her mouth and trotted to the door.

"Now let's go visit your mother and show her those pretty bows." Off they would go to tend the flowers on Evie's grave.

Another winter came and went before George got to the vet with Daisy. By this time, the lumps were harder and larger. I felt a sense of grim foreboding when he said the vet had decided not to operate. "He said she would be more comfortable if you gave her medicated baths." Somehow I did not believe those were the vet's only instructions.

As the months passed, Daisy grew less energetic. She found it increasingly hard to stand, so I took to trimming her while she was lying down. She still performed her little tricks at the end of each visit. "Show Kathy how you act shy," he told her as she ducked her head and covered her eyes with a paw.

When I returned from my summer vacation, my new assistant, Trudy, conveyed the news I had been dreading: Daisy had passed away. "George was very upset that you weren't here," she told me. "He even called the vet a quack. It got worse when he started crying."

Unable to reach him by phone, I sent George a letter expressing our condolences. Months later, when he dropped by to see us, he looked as though he had aged several years. We reminisced about Daisy, her funny tricks and endearing ways. "My son keeps telling me to pull myself together. If he tells me once more, 'Dad, it was only a dog. . . .'" All I could offer was a hug.

"The worst part is, it was all my fault," he said tearfully. "I blamed the vet, but if I had taken her to see him when you folks told me to, I'd still have her now."

David gently placed his arm around the old man's shoulder. "We've all learned some lessons the hard way, George," he told him.

A few weeks later, fate intervened when a young

woman came into the shop, dragging a dirt-caked terrier mix that was matted from head to tail. The raggedy creature's pungent odor told me it had recently gotten up close and personal with a skunk.

"This here is Fanny. She belongs to my aunt and uncle, but they wanna get rid of her."

As I reached down to examine the dog, she jerked its chain. "I gotta warn ya, she's a bad dog. She barks all day, and she don't like kids."

"She barks in the house?" I inquired.

"No, she don't come in the house. They keep her tied out in the yard."

Poor Fanny was frightened and jumpy. Grooming her was not easy or pleasant. When she emerged, de-fleaed and de-skunked, her bones jutted out from her bare skin. Yet somehow she looked eerily familiar.

"Who does she remind you of?" I asked David.

"Sinead O'Connor?" he guessed.

"No! Doesn't she look like Daisy, George's old dog?"

It would take some convincing. George had sworn he would never have another pet.

"I just can't go through it again," he told me. "I don't deserve it after what happened to Daisy."

"But, George, you know you've been lonely," I prodded, as determined as a used-car salesman.

"Everybody's lonely," he grumped. "What else is new?"

"The poor thing spends her life tied to a rusty chain in a muddy backyard. She's totally unsocialized." I warmed to my subject. "Maybe you shouldn't take her after all. She's going to need an awful lot of training, patience and love. You might not be up to it."

"I guess I could take her on a trial basis," he mumbled.

"Well, if it doesn't work out, you can always give her back," I offered brightly.

The first thing George did was to rename the dog

Daisy II. Her coat grew out, soft and fluffy, and she learned to walk on a leash and come when called. She still got anxious when he left her for grooming, then exploded in a yapping fury when he came to pick her up.

"Watch this," he said one December day, placing his car keys on the chair beside my counter. "Daisy, want to go get doughnuts?"

In a furry flash, she raced to the chair, jumping up and then landing squarely at his feet, head cocked to one side and keys gripped tightly in her mouth. George beamed proudly.

David and I stood in the doorway, watching the happy pair walk across the snow-dusted parking lot as the church bells chimed a Christmas carol. "Merry Christmas, George!" I called after him. "And don't forget—if it doesn't work out, you can always give her back!"

Kathy Salzberg

Devotion

To your dog, you are the greatest, the smartest, the nicest human being who was ever born.

Louis Sabin

The truck chugged into the parking space beside me in front of the supermarket and shuddered to a stop. Its rusty hinges protested as the man leaned his shoulder against the door to force it open. The truck was old, its red paint so faded and oxidized, six coats of wax could not have coaxed a shine from its ancient hide. The man, too, was old, stooped and faded like his truck. His washed-out red and black checkered flannel shirt and colorless trousers were a perfect match for the aura of age surrounding him and his truck. *A farmer,* I thought, judging by the leathery, tanned skin of his heavily lined face and gnarled, dirt-encrusted hands. The creases radiating from the corners of his eyes bore witness to years of squinting against the sun. As he stepped out of the truck, he turned to address the only youthful thing in the whole picture, a lively young springer spaniel attempting to follow him.

"No, Lady," he said. "You stay here and guard our truck.

I won't be long." He didn't roll up the window, apparently secure the dog would hold her post.

As he entered the grocery store, the dog moved over to assume a position behind the steering wheel, her eyes following the man's progress. As the door closed behind him, she settled back on her haunches, staring almost unblinking at the closed door.

The minutes passed. The dog did not move, and I began to feel her anxiety.

"Don't worry, girl," I said. "He'll be back soon."

I knew she heard me by the way her long brown ears perked up and by the sound of her tail as it thumped a tattoo on the seat beside her. Her nose twitched and the brown freckled fur covering her muzzle shivered in response, but her eyes never wavered from their scrutiny of the door through which the old man had disappeared.

No Buckingham Palace guard could have maintained a more steadfast devotion to duty. Each time the market door opened, the dog stiffened in anticipation, settling back when the emerging figure was not the one for whom she waited.

At last he appeared, carrying a laden plastic bag. The sedate little lady on guard duty erupted into a brown and white flurry of pure joy. She yipped a series of sounds that could only have been interpreted as laughter. She chased her tail in a tight circle, sending up a cloud of dust from the dirt-encrusted seats. When he finally wrested the protesting door open, she launched herself at him, standing with her front paws on his shoulders, licking his face with great swipes of her pink tongue. The spray of white lines at the corners of the man's eyes disappeared as his face crinkled in response to her pleasure. His broad smile revealed strong, slightly stained teeth, probably the result of years of smoking the scarred old pipe peeking out of his shirt pocket.

"Move over, Lady, I'll drive now," he said as he gently pushed the dog to the other side and slipped behind the wheel. That did not end her display of affection. She jumped on him again, her tongue washing his face and ears, knocking off the old misshapen hat protecting his head. From her throat rolled a garbled stream of sound, a language only he understood. Taking her face in his hands, he ruffled the hair at the base of her ears and looking into her eyes said, "I know, I know. I took longer than I expected. But guess what I brought you."

Her hips stopped their frantic swinging as she sat back, alert, watching his every move as he pretended to search his pockets and then the plastic bag, finally producing a package of beef jerky. The dog licked her lips as he slowly tore open the package, removing at last a strip of the hard, dried beef. Gripping it in his strong teeth, he let it protrude from the corner of his mouth as if it were a cigar. Her eyes never left the promised treat. She sat beside him, quivering with anticipation until he nodded. Then she stretched her neck and using only her front teeth, pulled the blackened meat from his mouth. She didn't eat it immediately. Instead, she sat back, watching and waiting, drooling, as the jerky protruded from her mouth in the same way as it had from his.

A smile twitched the corners of the man's lips as he took another piece, placing it into his mouth as he had before. They looked like two old cronies settling back to enjoy a quiet cigar. I felt a smile spread over my own face. He nodded again and the dog flopped down to begin enjoying her treat. He glanced over, seeing me for the first time.

We both grinned sheepishly. I, for having been caught eavesdropping on a private display of a man's affection for his dog. He, for having been caught in the foolish little game he played with her. He snatched the beef strip from his mouth.

As he coaxed his old truck into protesting life, I remarked, "That's a fine dog you have there."

He bobbed his head and replied, "She's a real champion, all right."

Giving me a parting smile, he backed out of the parking space, the old truck resenting every demand being made of it. I watched them as they drove away and noticed the jerky was back in the man's mouth. The dog, having wolfed down her prize, was sitting erect again, eyeing his share, too. I was willing to bet she'd get the last bite of it before they reached their destination.

Marjie Lyvers

Dixie's Kitten

Dixie was a pretty dog, an English setter dressed in a white coat adorned with black and brown markings. In her younger days she had spent many happy hours in the fields, running and hunting quail. But now Dixie was so old that she spent most of her time lying in the sun, basking in the soothing warmth of its rays. She especially loved to lie in the yard. There was a full water bucket and brimming food dish within easy reach, and her outdoor shelter was lined with clean, fragrant hay. There were times when her old bones ached and pained her, and she would groan as she stood up to move to another patch of sunlight. But sometimes there were wonderful days when somebody brought by a young bird-dog pup, and a spark would leap in her tired eyes. She adored puppies and would forget her age for a little while as she romped with the younger dogs.

"It's been a long time since you were a puppy, old girl," I told her one day, stopping to comb my fingers through her silky hair. She wagged her tail and looked toward the pup being admired in the front yard. Then with a soft whine, she eased her aching body into a more comfortable position and dropped her chin to her paws. Her eyes were fastened on the younger dog and she seemed lost in thought. Probably dreaming about the days when she was running through the fields teaching the younger dogs to sniff out quail, I decided. I gave her one last pat on the head, and went into the house.

Lately Dixie had seemed lonely. I remembered the family of ducks that used to cross the road in front of our house every evening to share her dish of dog food. Not once had Dixie growled or snapped at the ducks, and sometimes she would even move aside so they could have better access to her food. Visiting cats were always welcome to join in the meals, and it wasn't unusual at all to find her with her nose in the same bowl with several ducks, cats and whatever stray dog may have wandered up. Dixie was a gentle, social soul and nowadays there just didn't seem to be as many guests dropping by to chat over dinner.

One day there was a knock at my door. I opened it to find my next-door neighbor standing there with a concerned look on his face. "Have you seen my kitten?" he asked. "He slipped out and is missing."

It was a cute, fluffy little thing, not much bigger than a minute, and I knew my neighbor was right to be concerned. A tiny lost kitty would be no match for the coyotes and wild cats that roamed our rural area.

I told him I hadn't but that if I spotted it, I would give him a call. He thanked me, sadness etched on his face. "He's so little," he said as he headed for the next house. "I'm afraid if I don't find him soon, something bad will happen to him."

Later that afternoon I carried dog food out to Dixie. She was in her house and I could hear her tail thumping a greeting as I poured the food into her bowl. I fetched the water hose and filled her bucket, then called her out to eat. Slowly she emerged and painfully, carefully, stretched. As

I reached down to pat her head, a tiny gray kitten stepped out of the dark doghouse and twined itself around Dixie's legs.

"What have you got there, girl?" I exclaimed. Dixie glanced down at the kitten, then looked back up at me with a gleam in her eye. Her tail wagged harder. "Come here, kitty," I said and reached for it. Dixie gently pushed my hand aside with her nose and nudged the kitten back inside the doghouse. Sitting down in front of the door, she blocked the kitten's exit and I could hear it meowing inside. This had to be my neighbor's lost kitten. It must have wandered through the thicket of bushes between our places and straight into Dixie's doghouse.

"Crazy dog," I muttered. Dixie wagged her agreement, but didn't budge from in front of the door. She waited until I was a safe distance away before she stood up to begin nibbling at the pile of food. I went into the house and telephoned my neighbor.

"I think I've found your kitten," I told him. I could hear the relief in his voice, then the laughter as I told him that Dixie had been hiding it. Promising to come over to collect the runaway cat, he hung up after thanking me again.

He showed up, eager to look at the kitten. "Yep, that's my cat!" he said as the little gray fur ball stepped out of the doghouse. Dixie backed away from us and nosed the kitten toward the door. Gratefully, the man reached for the cat. In the same instant, Dixie snarled at him.

I was shocked. She'd never growled at anybody before! I scolded her, and my neighbor reached for the kitten again. This time Dixie bared her teeth.

"Let me try," I said. I reached for the kitten but Dixie shoved it inside the doghouse, then followed it in and flopped down, blocking the tiny cat from us with her body. Nobody was going to take her kitten!

We could hear the kitten purring loudly inside the

house. Then it stepped up, bold as brass, and rubbed itself against Dixie's face. She licked its fur and glared out at us. It was plain that she had adopted the little cat and planned to keep it. "Huh," I said. At the moment, it seemed the only thing to say.

"Well, it looks like the kitten's happy," my poor neighbor said after a few minutes. The little gray cat had curled up between Dixie's front paws and was grooming itself intently. Every once in a while it stopped to lick Dixie's face. Kitten and dog seemed perfectly content. "I guess she can keep the kitten, if she wants it that bad."

So Dixie was allowed to help raise the kitten that she had claimed as her own. Thanks to the kindness and understanding of my neighbor, the tiny cat and the old dog spent many happy hours together. The kitten benefited from the arrangement and grew into a fine, healthy cat. And Dixie was happy to live out her days basking in the sun, dreaming of kittens and puppies and romping in the fields.

Anne Culbreath Watkins

Bashur, the Iraqi Dog

My son, Mike—Major Mike Fenzel of the 173rd Airborne Brigade—parachuted into northern Iraq on March 27, 2003. After two weeks on the ground, Mike and the three thousand others in his unit began their mission to capture the city of Kirkuk.

During the first hours of the mission, they made a brief stop to refuel by the side of the road. The unit's intelligence officer noticed something moving in the grass. Looking closer, she saw it was a tiny puppy, no bigger than a dollar bill. The puppy was alone and in bad shape; the officer knew it would die if she left it there. So she scooped the pup into her arms and took it with her into Kirkuk.

When they finally reached Kirkuk, the puppy was brought to headquarters, washed off and fed. There was a vet on hand whose primary responsibility was to check food for the troops, and he gave the puppy a distemper shot. After that, they released the tiny dog on the airfield to roam with the hundreds of other wild dogs who lived on the base. Over the next few weeks, the little puppy made an impression on the soldiers living on the base, including Mike. The men in the unit made sure the little female pup—whom Mike had named Bashur after the airfield they had parachuted into—had enough food, giving her leftovers from the mess hall and from their MREs (Meals Ready to Eat).

Bashur survived being hit by a Humvee in her first weeks on the airfield. After recovering from a badly bruised hip, Bashur grew strong and healthy. Although she had the run of the base, she mainly stuck around the headquarters building where she received food as well as lots of attention from the men going in and out on their round-the-clock missions.

Bashur stood out from the other dogs on the airfield. Not only was her coloring distinct and beautiful—she had a caramel-colored head with a well-defined white blaze and the soulful amber eyes of a hound—but she was determined to be with the soldiers. She bounded up happily to everyone who passed, tail wagging, eyes sparkling, ready for a game or a cuddle, a comforting sight after the stress of the soldiers' missions. She was a one-dog welcoming committee and the soldiers loved her for it.

But an army camp is a busy and sometimes dangerous place, and one day a pickup truck speeding across the camp ran over Bashur's paw, crushing it. By then, Mike had become very fond of Bashur, and when he heard she had been hit, he ran to find her.

After carrying her to his room, he brought in his medics to give her attention. Mike decided to keep Bashur with him while her paw healed and then possibly until they left Iraq, to prevent her from becoming another casualty. Soon Bashur recovered fully, and Mike began taking her to the battalion headquarters where he worked each day. There he tied her up outside so that she couldn't run free and be hurt again. The men provided her with a special red collar with an "Airborne" patch on it to identify her as their mascot.

Over the next six months, though Bashur remained the unit's mascot, Mike and Bashur developed a special bond. Mike told me that caring for Bashur kept his mind in a positive place. Every morning they jogged together and every evening they relaxed together. Mike marveled at the power of her companionship to lift his spirits.

Living with Bashur had other benefits as well. Once when I was on the phone with Mike, Bashur began to bark wildly. Mike said, "Must be incoming, Dad. Gotta go." It turned out that Bashur could detect mortars and artillery rockets long before human ears could register the sound. When she would look up, startled, Mike knew another enemy artillery strike was on the way.

In February 2004, Mike realized he would be leaving Iraq soon. He knew he couldn't leave Bashur behind, so when he called home he asked me if we would take Bashur if he could manage to get her to us. My wife and I knew what Bashur had come to mean to him and I told him we would.

At first, Mike thought he would be able to ship her through the country of Jordan with the help of an official at the Baghdad zoo. But nothing is certain in a country at war. First, Jordan stopped allowing dogs to transit through their country and then his contact at the zoo left, taking with her Bashur's best chance of leaving Iraq.

Time was running out, but Mike kept trying. Finally, he found an international veterinary hospital in Kuwait that would be able to ship Bashur to the states. The next hurdle was getting her to Kuwait. As it happened, Mike was the executive officer of a battalion that was preparing to redeploy to Vicenza, Italy—through a port in Kuwait City. He would take Bashur with him when they left.

On the day that his battalion left Kirkuk for Kuwait with their 140 vehicles, Mike loaded Bashur in his Humvee, and they made the 600 mile journey to Kuwait

City together. Bashur already had her required shots but had to spend a week in quarantine at the International Veterinary Hospital. Luckily, the hospital was located right next door to the port site, so Mike was able to visit her every day.

The last obstacle Mike faced was finding a crate large enough to ship Bashur home in—she had grown a lot since the day she had been found on the side of the road. There were none available in Kuwait City, so the veterinary hospital built an immense wooden box to meet airline requirements. The refrigerator-sized container had a steel grate in front so that Bashur could breathe and see out.

At last, Bashur, snug in her specially made crate, was loaded on to a KLM plane headed to Amsterdam. From Amsterdam, she would make the final leg of her journey to O'Hare Airport in Chicago.

At the appointed time, I drove to O'Hare to meet Bashur. The KLM freight employees needed a forklift to get the big wooden container onto the terminal floor. When the door was opened, there were probably nine men—including me—clustered around Bashur's crate.

Bashur was cautious, not sure what to expect. She stuck her head out and looked both ways. When I said, "Bashur, how's our baby?" she looked up quickly, recognizing her name.

I had heard she was a big dog, but I really wasn't prepared for her size. When she started to walk out of the crate, one man in the group exclaimed, "My God, when is she going to stop coming out of that crate?" Bashur just kept coming until all forty inches of her emerged.

I dropped to one knee and took her collar. I immediately recognized the "Airborne" patch. Putting the side of my face to hers, I gave her a big hug and then attached her new leash.

We walked outside into the early March sunshine and crossed the parking lot to my waiting van. I had spread a thick blanket behind the front seat, and Bashur stretched out on it like the Queen of Sheba—but not for long! As soon as we began to move, she jumped into the passenger seat, plopped her rear end on the seat, front paws on the floor and chin on the dash, to take in the passing scenery. I shouldn't have been surprised she was good in the car, as she'd had lots of experience in army vehicles for most of her life.

When we got to the house, Bashur jumped out and made a beeline for my wife, Muriel, who took one look at the big dog and immediately melted. Bashur can do that to you. She has a huge tail that is always wagging and eyes so full of love that no one can resist her.

Bashur was officially home.

Now each morning Bashur and I leave the house at six and head to my office—a car dealership northwest of Chicago. Everyone at work loves her. The floor of my office is strewn with her toys and chew bones. Being raised by a battalion of soldiers, she prefers men, and her favorite type of play is wrestling and roughhousing.

When the newspaper printed a story about her, she received countless baskets of goodies from well-wishers— so many that we began to donate them to the local animal shelter—and two women came to take pictures of Bashur to send to their sons overseas. Their sons, soldiers who had known Bashur in Iraq, wanted to make sure that she was okay.

At noon Bashur and I take our daily walk in the fields around the office. It is a special time for both of us. I love watching her bound joyfully along, gazing with fascination at birds or becoming enthralled by a smell her large hound nose has unearthed. She seems amazed by all the wonderful things in her new life.

Bashur has certainly found her way into my heart as she has done with so many others. Sometimes when she sleeps, she rolls over and sighs, content, and I am happy. We *owe* this dog, and we want her to have the best life we can give her. There is really no way to repay her for the comfort she brought our son and so many others like him. But we can try. . . .

John Fenzel, Jr.

My Furry Muse

Newlyweds always face challenges as they learn what to expect from each other. My Iranian husband, Mahmoud, came from a country, culture and especially a family very different from the close-knit, pet-loving household I'd experienced. But we had faith our love was enough to build a life together.

In November 1979, our world blew up. We struggled to understand the taking of hostages half a world away, and we worried about Mahmoud's relatives caught in the insanity of that awful nightmare.

The crisis threatened our relationship as well—we were so very different. The stress became unbearable. Sometimes we hurt each other expecting too much. We'd misunderstand a word, a glance, a gesture that had different meanings for each of us. Would our love survive?

So when Mahmoud suggested a puppy for my birthday, the gift meant everything. In his homeland, dogs were considered dirty, dangerous creatures suitable only for outdoor guard duty—inviting a dog into our home meant he understood me. That he wanted me to be happy. And that he knew what would help me most during the most frightening and challenging time of our lives.

The German shepherd puppy kept me company when Mahmoud worked nights. Fafnir listened when I worried out loud, clowned to make me laugh and licked away my tears—and there were many tears. I felt out of place in the small eastern Kentucky town where we lived and missed my distant Indiana family. I struggled to be a "perfect" wife, and of course failed miserably.

But Fafnir made me feel important. He didn't care if meals never tasted like Mom used to make, he never called me a Yankee and we seemed to have a common language that needed no words. He thought I was wonderful—and I knew he was special, too.

Then Mahmoud was laid off, so we moved to Louisville where he attended graduate school. Less than a week after the move, I found a position as a veterinary assistant near our apartment. As a special bonus, I could take Fafnir with me to work. Our neighbor's small cockapoo, Fidget, became best buddies with Fafnir. Things were looking up!

Then Fafnir developed a limp. He favored first one paw, and then another. Medicine temporarily relieved his limping, but his paws turned red, itchy and swollen. He scratched constantly and only seemed happy when playing tag with Fidget.

I tried everything. Antibiotics made him sick. A special diet didn't help, and his weight dropped to fifty-nine pounds. Despite my discount, the treatment costs added up—and up. Nothing seemed to help. Fafnir was allergic to the air he breathed—the molds, pollens and other allergens of the Ohio Valley region. His condition grew worse day by day. Fafnir no longer looked like a German shepherd. When I stroked his black coat, his fur pulled out in clumps with flaking skin still attached. His once-expressive ears were naked on the outside, the tender inside lined with pustules and slow-to-heal scabs. Constant licking and chewing stained his tummy black except where the red, oozing sores broke the skin. Swollen feet prompted a halting, limping gait more appropriate to an aged, arthritic canine.

When he visited the clinic with me, pet owners now shrank away and pulled their dogs out of sniffing range. They didn't want Fafnir to give his "horrible disease" to their beloved pets. Although he wasn't contagious, I couldn't blame people for their concern. Fidget still invited games, but Fafnir could no longer play. He hurt too much. And he smelled.

He was only fourteen months old.

Had love blinded my eyes and my logic? If this poor creature belonged to somebody else, would I also shrink from touching the affectionate dog? How could I justify continued treatment? Was there a better, more compassionate option? *No! Not my Fafnir!* I veered away from the thought before it fully formed, but a calmer, more reasonable voice insisted that I face the facts and realities of the dog's condition. Was I being selfish? Would death be the kindest treatment of all?

I couldn't bother Mahmoud with the question—he had enough to worry about. For two days and nights I argued with myself, one moment sure that any life was better than an early separation from my beloved dog; the next trying to find strength within myself to stop his suffering.

The third morning, driving the short distance to work, it was hard to see the street through my tear-clouded eyes. Fafnir licked my neck, excited as always to visit the clinic and see his friends. Maybe he'd get to sniff a cat (oh, doggy joy!).

The busy morning moved quickly from case to case, while Fafnir rested in his usual kennel. Each time I dug into my pocket for suture scissors or pen and touched the crumpled paper, my eyes filled again. It was the euthanasia authorization form I'd decided to complete during lunch break after playing with Fafnir one last time.

Then an emergency case arrived. A young woman, nearly hysterical with fear, carried a Pomeranian puppy into the clinic. "It's Foxy, please help! He chewed through an electric cord." The woman's two small children watched with wide, tearful eyes.

The veterinarian began immediate treatment. "A transfusion would help since the pup's in shock. Lucky we have Fafnir here as a donor."

I froze. For an endless moment I couldn't breathe. Then without a word, I brought my boy out of the kennel. His eyes lit up at the chance to sniff Foxy's small, shivering body. Fafnir's scaly bald tail wagged, and he grinned. I had to coax him away to draw twelve cubic centimeters of precious blood from his foreleg, to be given to his tiny new friend.

By lunchtime, Foxy's gums transformed from white to a healthy pink, and he breathed normally. The red puppy even managed a feeble wag and sniffed back when Fafnir nosed him through the kennel bars.

For the first time in three days, I could smile through what had become happy tears. Without looking at it, I pulled the euthanasia paperwork from my pocket, crumpling it and tossing it into the trash. What if I'd made that decision even an hour earlier? If Fafnir hadn't been there for Foxy, the puppy would have died.

Fafnir grinned up at me, and I realized he didn't care how he looked. Fafnir patiently put up with the unknowns in his world—with uncomfortable baths, bitter pills and scary needle sticks he couldn't control—simply because he loved me and trusted that I would keep him safe. Fafnir willingly came to Foxy's rescue, just as he'd rescued me during the first troubled months of my marriage. That's what we do for our friends, for the ones we love. We pass it on to strangers, too, simply because it brings such joy.

Six months later, Mahmoud attained his master's degree, found a great job, and we moved from Louisville to Tennessee. Away from the allergens that had plagued him, Fafnir quickly recovered and no longer needed medication. My heart swelled with quiet thanks during each afternoon walk when neighbors admired Fafnir's proud stride and glowing coat and begged to pet him.

In Tennessee, I began to write about my experiences working at the vet's office. My first published article told Fafnir's story and launched my pet-writing career. Fafnir has been my furry muse ever since. More than that, his infectious grin, his quiet trust, and his delight at meeting new critters (looky, a cat!), fill the pages of my heart with a joy beyond words.

Amy D. Shojai

After Dooley

On my wife's fiftieth birthday we were awakened in the middle of the night by the violent shaking of our bed. Dooley, our eighteen-year-old miniature dachshund, lay between us, jerking in convulsions. He was so fevered that I could feel the heat without actually touching him. We rushed him to an all-night animal hospital and waited for the inevitable heartbreak. He did not die that night, but his old and tired body had taken more than it was meant to tolerate. A few days later, with a powerful tranquilizer running through his veins, our dog fell asleep for the last time as I held him in my arms.

Dooley was a puppy when my wife, Patricia, and her two sons received him as a gift. Five years would pass before I came into their lives. Growing up, I always had pets, but Patricia had never considered herself a "dog person." In fact, Dooley had been her first. Other dogs made her very nervous. So, after Dooley passed, when I suggested that we consider bringing another canine into our home, she said she would go along with the idea *only* if I accepted certain conditions.

First, we wouldn't rush into anything. Our loss was still very fresh in our minds, even after several weeks of mourning, and we were both concerned that replacing Dooley too soon might somehow disrespect his memory. Second, we would consider only a puppy since an older dog might be more aggressive, and, therefore, more difficult for my wife to handle. Finally, our new dog could not weigh more than ten to fifteen pounds when fully grown.

We decided to start our search in late March, around the time of our wedding anniversary. That way, if we found a dog we liked, we could purchase him or her as a mutual gift. Still, I knew that Patricia was doing this more for me than for herself.

On our first visit to the local animal shelter, I saw him immediately. As soon as the door to the back room opened, we were greeted by a chorus of thirty to forty barkers wildly competing for our attention. The cages stood side by side and facing each other, forming a U around the cool, semidark room. He was there in the first cage to the right, a full-grown Lab mix calmly taking in the cacophony around him. Black as night, he nearly blended in to the dimly lit recess beyond narrow steel bars. I caught his eye and quickly looked away without a word to my wife. Too old and too big, he did not match our predetermined profile.

After a short tour and a cursory examination of the younger residents, my wife and I left the shelter empty-handed but promising to come back soon.

More than a week had passed when we arrived home from work to find a vaguely familiar voice recorded on our answering machine. "Where have you been?" were the first few words we heard. The message was from Vicky, the animal shelter manager, urging us to come and check out some recent arrivals.

The next evening we went back for another visit, but again, our search for the perfect puppy came up empty. As we were about to leave, I noticed the dog I had admired the previous week, still watching us hopefully and with quiet dignity from that first cage on the right.

I stopped and turned to my wife. I was certain of the reaction I was about to receive, but like a child who cannot help asking for the one thing he knows he can never have, I took my shot: "How about this guy?" I said.

A few minutes later, Patricia and I were alone in a quiet room across the hall. I could hardly believe it when she had agreed to take a closer look at a dog four times the size of Dooley. Now I could sense her apprehension as we sat there on a pair of folding chairs waiting to meet the orphaned animal I was certain would never be coming home with us.

The door opened and in popped a furry black head. He hesitated in the doorway, clearly assessing the situation. He looked at me, then at my wife. As if he knew which of us he had to win over, he walked straight up to Patricia and gently placed that beautiful head in her lap. Amazed, I watched my wife instantly fall in love. I will never forget the look of compassion on her face or the conviction in her voice when she turned to me and said, "I want this dog."

Exley has now been a part of our family for just over four years. I'm still dumbfounded at the thought that this gentle, loyal and loving animal was once abandoned to the streets. Likewise, I'm surprised that someone else didn't come along to adopt him in the days between our first and second trips to the shelter. Maybe we just got lucky. Or maybe there was something else behind our good fortune.

My wife is certain that we had some help. She believes Dooley's spirit was with us that night, nudging the bigger dog in her direction and somehow finding a way to let us know that he was the ideal new companion for us.

"Yeah, right," I tell her, not bothering to hide my skepticism. "Believe whatever you like if it makes you feel better."

But sometimes, when I find myself on the couch enjoying a few peaceful moments with Exley—listening to his
soft breathing and feeling his warm body pressed as close
as he can get against my leg—I remember our visits to the
shelter and how I nearly passed by this wonderful dog
without speaking out. In those moments of contented
companionship, so like the times I spent with Dooley, it
doesn't seem at all far-fetched that the spirit of an old
friend might find a way to help his surviving family pick
out the perfect new friend.

Gary Ingraham

When Harry Met Kaatje

No matter how little money and how few possessions you own, having a dog makes you rich.

Louis Sabin

December 1994. In Holland on a business trip, I had completed my assignment and was heading home. It was early morning on a cold and rainy Saturday, and I was on my way from the hotel to Amsterdam Central Station to catch the train to the airport.

Just outside the train station, I came across a homeless man. I'd seen this particular man a number of times in the past, as I'd traveled through Amsterdam quite often, and usually gave him some change. Many homeless people call Amsterdam Central Station their home, but this man really stuck in my mind because he was always so good-natured.

That day, because of the holidays, I was feeling particularly upbeat, so I handed the man fifty guilders (about twenty-five dollars) and wished him a Merry Christmas. With tears welling up in his eyes, he thanked me profusely for my generosity and asked my name. I told him mine was Dave, and he said his was Harry. We chatted briefly and went our separate ways.

As I walked up to the ticket vending machine inside the train station, I reached into my wallet, but found nothing. I realized that I had just given Harry the last of my money, and the bank was not yet open for currency exchange. I had no Dutch money left to buy my ticket to the airport. As I stood, pondering my predicament, along came Harry. He saw me standing there bewildered and asked if I needed help with the ticket vending machine, as it was entirely in Dutch.

I explained that this was not the difficulty. My actual problem was that I had no money. Without the slightest hesitation, Harry punched out the code for a ticket to the airport, and deposited the change required. Out came a ticket. He handed it to me and said, "Thank you."

I asked why he was thanking me when it was I who was indebted to him.

He said, "Because I have been on the street for many years. I don't have a lot of friends, and you are the first person in a long time that I have been able to help. This is why I thank you."

Over the next eight years, I continued seeing Harry at the train station when I passed through Amsterdam, which was almost every month. He usually saw me first and came over for some conversation. A number of times we had dinner together. Dinner with Harry isn't what most people think of as a normal meal. We would purchase pizza or fries from the outdoor vendors and sit on the curb to eat, since Harry wasn't welcome in restaurants. I didn't care; I considered Harry a good friend.

Then, starting in June 2002, I stopped seeing Harry at the train station. I thought the worst—that Harry, even though he was fairly young and healthy, had probably frozen to death or been killed.

In early 2003, I was in Amsterdam for my monthly visit. It was 5:30 on Saturday morning, and I was on my way to the train station. Suddenly, I heard a voice yell, "Hey, Dave."

I turned to see a clean-shaven, casually dressed gentleman walking a medium-sized brown and white collie-type dog. They were coming my way. I had no idea who this person was. He walked up to me, shook my hand and said, "It's me. Harry."

I was in complete shock! I couldn't believe it. I had never seen the man without ragged clothes and layers of dirt all over himself, and now he looked completely respectable. He began to tell me the story of where he had been for the last several months.

It all began with the dog he was now walking. Kaatje, his new companion, had just shown up one day and started hanging out with him at the train station. He and the dog lived on the street for a few months until one day Kaatje was run over by a car. Harry rushed the dog to a vet, who informed him that the cost of surgery to repair the dog's hip was going to be very expensive. Harry, of course, had no money. The vet made Harry an offer: if he performed the operation, Harry would take up residence on a cot in the back of the vet's office and work for him by watching the dogs during the night shift until the surgery was paid off. Harry readily accepted the offer.

Kaatje came through the hip surgery with flying colors. Harry kept his end of the bargain. Because he was so kind to the animals and was such a good worker, when the bill was paid off, the vet offered Harry a permanent position. With a steady salary, Harry was able to get an apartment for himself and Kaatje. Harry was no longer homeless. His love for Kaatje had rescued him from the streets. He stood before me now, looking like any pleasant young man out for a walk with his dog on a Saturday morning.

It was time to catch my train. Harry and I shook hands, and Kaatje gave me a nice good-bye face wash.

"Let's get together the next time I'm in Amsterdam," I said.

"I'd like that," Harry said with a warm smile.

We made plans to meet for dinner near the train station on my next trip and parted ways.

Just before going into the train station, I turned so I could watch man and dog walking happily back to a place people sometimes take for granted—a place called home.

Dave Wiley

Gremlin, Dog First Class

In the spring of 1943, a detachment of seven planes from the VPB-128 U.S. Navy Bombing Squadron was sent to Guantanamo Bay, Cuba, where a German submarine had been sighted. The weather was hot and humid. Most of the pilots and crew were young men, away from home for the first time. Many were homesick; all were afraid. Just a few months earlier, they all had been civilians in different walks of life. Now they were sailors, struggling to survive war.

One day around lunchtime, one of the aircraft crews was seeking shade underneath the wing of their plane when they spotted what appeared to be a half-starved rat trotting in their direction. As the animal neared them, they saw that it was a small dog. The dog was so undernourished that his ribs were clearly visible through his thin brown and white fur.

"Come here, boy," one of the sailors called.

The dog stopped in his tracks and stared.

Eyeing the protruding ribs, the young sailor was filled with compassion and offered the dog his sandwich. At first the dog seemed reluctant, his brown eyes fearful, but he was so hungry he couldn't resist. With his head down and tail between his legs, the little dog inched forward, then gobbled down the sandwich. It took several days and a lot of sandwiches before the dog trusted the men enough to follow them into the mess hall where he indulged in military chow: fresh oranges, boiled eggs and Spam.

The dog learned to love the enlisted personnel who gave him their undivided attention. And although he tolerated the officers, the sailors noticed that he had *no love* for civilians. The dog would study civilians from a distance, but closely monitor them if they approached him. If they got too close, he would bare his teeth and growl. It was assumed that the dog had been so abused by civilians that he could never forget it, and after investigating to make sure he was a stray, the men decided to keep him.

When the detachment was ordered back to the squadron, the sailors couldn't stand leaving the dog behind, so they smuggled him aboard an aircraft.

Shortly after takeoff the dog barked as the men began playing with him. The pilot asked, "What is that noise?"

The radioman replied, "It must be a gremlin, sir."

According to the dictionary, *gremlin* means "a mischievous, invisible imp said to ride in airplanes and cause mechanical trouble."

The dog barked again, and the men had to come clean. They took him into the cockpit where he was enthusiastically welcomed by the rest of the crew.

"This must be our gremlin, sir," the radioman said, and the name stuck.

Gremlin was indoctrinated into the U.S. Navy when the squadron returned to New York. Induction papers were signed with a paw print, and he was issued an ID card and dog tag. A crew member donated a dress-blue uniform jacket from which a cape was cut and attached to a harness. The uniform bore the insignia "Dog First Class," and Gremlin seemed very proud to wear his uniform. He was also issued Air Combat Crew wings and eventually earned several campaign ribbons, all attached to the uniform. Gremlin seemed to sense that his uniform was special and would stand at attention during the squadron's infrequent personnel inspections and would move only when the unit was dismissed.

He usually slept with the enlisted personnel and was completely house- and plane-broken, never relieving himself while in quarters or in flight. However, immediately upon landing, like all crew members, he searched for a place of privacy.

Gremlin soon became the most popular member of the VPB-128 and often flew on noncontact missions with his human counterparts. Gremlin's navy career took him to five of the world's seven continents: North America, Europe, Africa, South America and Asia, in that order.

Gremlin had several primary caretakers, some of whom lost their lives during the course of the war. When that happened, another sailor was always ready to take over tending the dog.

While many dogs are enthusiastic automobile riders, Gremlin loved airplanes. At the first turn of the prop of the PV-1 bomber, he would spin in circles, bark loudly, wag his tail furiously and strain against the wind of the prop, his ears and cape flapping in the wind, reminding the men that he wanted to go, too.

Once, Gremlin disappeared during a short stay on the Midway Islands. Rumor had it that one of the submarine crew members had picked up the dog and taken him to their base on a neighboring island. The skipper realized this would be a great loss and morale would no doubt suffer. He sent three squadron aircraft crews over to find him, but the submarine had left—probably with Gremlin aboard. The men kept searching and calling for their beloved friend. Hope dwindled with each passing moment.

Then one man saw a small mass huddled under a park bench. It was Gremlin—but he was shaking and wouldn't come when called. The sailor quickly gathered the dog up and yelled to the rest of the searchers, "I found him!"

The men came running. It seemed too good to be true, but there he was. They stroked the frightened dog and spoke softly to him, and finally Gremlin began wagging his tail. He was back where he belonged—with the VPB-128.

When the squadron was sent to Samar, a hot spot in the war zone, the men had to spend most of their time concentrating on the enemy. Gremlin didn't seem to mind. It was almost as if he understood their purpose for being there, and he was content so long as he was with the sailors.

It was in Samar that an enlisted man by the name of McKirdy assumed primary care of Gremlin. McKirdy, with his crew, was ordered on a follow-up attack of a Japanese submarine tied up to the dock at Cebu City. McKirdy's plane was shot down and fell, flaming, into the water. At that time, bombers carried so much gasoline that even a slight crash or hit would cause the plane to burst into flames. Several planes went down that day and many members of the VPB-128 lost their lives.

There was a lot of confusion in the days that followed the loss of McKirdy's plane, but someone finally noticed that Gremlin hadn't been seen for a while. They finally realized that Gremlin had been on that plane—the brave and loyal dog had gone out on his last mission.

Gremlin, Dog First Class, rescued from a life of hunger and abuse in the slums of Cuba and brought into a world filled with love, unending attention and adventure, died for his country and the men he loved on March 21, 1944. He accomplished his mission with the highest degree of loyalty, compassion and love.

JaLeen Bultman-Deardurff

My Blue-Eyed Boy

I think we are drawn to dogs because they are the uninhibited creatures we might be if we weren't certain we knew better.

George Bird Evans

My dog, Harry, and I are very close. Harry, an eighty-pound Dalmatian, listens to me when I am upset, comforts me when I am blue and goes everywhere with me. He cares for no other person like he does for me, his beloved mama. Having raised him since he was an eight-week-old pup, I feel the same way about him—he is my blue-eyed boy.

One beautiful Sunday morning, Harry and I went to Central Park. Harry was running off leash on Dog Hill, along with all the other city dogs, while their owners enjoyed a spring day in the park.

I was feeling down because I had been recently laid off from the job I'd held for ten years. Being in the park with Harry was one of the ways I forgot for a while that I was out of work—and that my prospects were not looking good in a tough economy.

I was standing at the bottom of Dog Hill talking to another dog owner, when all of a sudden, we heard someone shout, "He peed on my leg!" I turned to look, and, lo and behold, at the top of the hill I saw a lady gesticulating at my beloved boy, who apparently was the culprit. Horrified, I rushed up the hill. Harry had never done anything remotely like this before.

When I got to where the woman was standing, I reached down quickly and grabbed hold of Harry's collar in case he decided to do anything else untoward. The woman was bent over, trying to clean up her leg. She was pulling off her shoe because the pee had dribbled down her leg all the way into her shoe.

We straightened up at the same moment, and for a shocked instant, we looked at each other.

"Alexandra!" she said.

"Valerie!" It was my former boss—the one who laid me off three months before.

I apologized to Valerie for Harry's behavior, but all the way home, I laughed and laughed, and gave Harry lots of kisses and hugs. Harry, of course, was thrilled that he clearly had pulled off a winning stunt—though, fortunately, he has never repeated his performance. To this day, when I think about all of Harry's wonderful qualities, his "revenge for mama" still makes me laugh the hardest.

Alexandra Mandis

The Subway Dog

I was twenty years old and living away from home for the first time. For companionship, I had a dog named Beaufort, who, although gentle, weighed more than I did and had a mouthful of sharp teeth. I felt safe going anywhere with Beaufort at my side.

In order to be free during the day to enjoy walks in the park and other things I liked to do, I took a job working the four-to-midnight shift in downtown Boston. The only downside of this arrangement was that I had to ride the "T"—the Boston subway—home from work late at night. As time passed, I discovered that keeping to oneself was an important survival mechanism. I avoided making eye contact and carried a book under my arm to read while I rode.

One night, I had finished work and was heading home. Every night, I rode the Red Line from Park Street Station to Andrew where I would get off and walk the six blocks home, knowing Beaufort was waiting patiently.

That night was different.

Park Street Station has a steep flight of stairs leading down to the underground platforms. I was tired as I fumbled for a token to put in the turnstile. I knew I had one—I always did. I rummaged around from pocket to pocket, but found nothing.

"Oh, man," I groaned.

The station was quiet at that time of night with only two or three more trains scheduled before the "T" closed at one in the morning. I walked over to the collector's booth and pulled out a dollar.

"One token, please."

People who ride the "T" often regard the token collectors inside the booths as only one step removed from ticket machines, so it was understandable that I wasn't paying attention to the man behind the booth's thick glass and the metal bars. But he was paying attention to me.

He slid the token and my change under the window. Then he spoke, "Hey, would you like a dog?"

Startled, I looked at him, not sure I had heard him correctly. "Excuse me?"

"Would you like a dog?" he repeated.

He looked down, motioning with his chin. I leaned over and it was only then that I saw the subject of his inquiry.

Inside the booth was a dog—a very small type of terrier with lots of wild, wiry hair. The dog appeared to be trembling but looked at me as if to say, *Yeah, and what's your problem?*

I was surprised, and as an animal lover, a little troubled. "Where'd he come from?" I asked.

"He's a stray; he showed up about eight o'clock. He's been here ever since." The big man picked up the dog and set him on the narrow counter, gently rubbing him behind the ears. "He has a collar but no tags. No one has come looking for him and my shift is almost over."

My rational side knew that rescuing this little wanderer was noble but totally impossible: I mean, what about Beaufort?

The token collector sensed a soft spot in me. "I've asked every person who has come through here if they wanted him. No one would take him."

"What about you?" I inquired.

He smiled and laughed softly, "Me? No honey, my wife would kill me."

I couldn't take my eyes off the dog. How in the world did he get here and why was no one looking for the poor little guy?

The collector made his final pitch: "You know, if you don't take him, I'll have to let him go when I leave."

I couldn't believe it! "What do you mean you'll let him go? We're downtown. He'll get killed. He'll starve! He's so . . . little."

He explained that there were only a couple more trains scheduled to come before he closed. He couldn't leave the dog in the booth, and he couldn't bring him home. No one else had taken him. I, in other words, was the dog's last hope.

I was wavering, and both man and dog sensed it. Oh, Lord, what was I going to do?

We stared at each other for what seemed a very long time.

"Is it a male or a female?" I sighed finally.

He grinned. "A female. I called her a 'him' just 'cause it's easier," he explained hastily.

I shook my head and added halfheartedly, "But I don't have a leash."

"That's okay, I've got it all worked out. Here's a piece of twine; it's stronger than it looks. What stop are you getting off at?"

"Andrew."

"Oh, great! That's only four stops. You'll be fine—the twine will last you until you get home."

His face flushed with excitement, the collector unlocked

the heavy door, stepped out of the booth and without fanfare handed me my new pet. "Thank you so much," the guy said with relief, "I really didn't want to let him loose upstairs."

The dog and I looked at one another.

"Hey, you guys look good together!" the man crowed. With that he opened the gate and allowed me to pass without paying, a satisfied grin on his face.

The dog and I walked to the next set of stairs that would take us down one more level to the subway tracks. I spoke to my new friend in soothing tones. "It's okay, everything's going to be okay," I promised.

The minute the collector told me that the dog was female I had decided on a name: Phyllis, after Phyllis Diller, the comedienne with the wild, unkempt hair. It came to me immediately and was as right as rain. "Oh, Phyllis," I sighed, "Wait till Beaufort gets a look at you."

We descended the stairs, my new friend and I, stepping onto the dirty platform together. Park Street Station is one of the biggest and busiest train stations in Boston. It is so big that it has three platforms instead of the usual two. One side leaves Boston heading toward Dorchester and the other side goes farther into town and on to Cambridge and quirky Harvard Square. In the middle is an extra platform to accommodate the many riders who frequent the station.

As if on cue, my fellow travelers all turned to look at Phyllis and me. Even the young man who played guitar, collecting coins in his open guitar case, stopped.

All at once the whole crowd broke into applause. Looking around, I didn't recognize the place. Most nights, people kept to themselves—like me, burying their noses in books or newspapers and ignoring everyone around them—but not tonight. Tonight everyone was smiling and clapping, giving me a thumbs-up and a right-on! Phyllis began to bark, all bluster.

A young couple two tracks over on the far side to Cambridge pointed and waved. "Look!" the girl gushed, "She took the dog. She took the dog."

Joined by the length of twine the collector had given me, Phyllis and I stood together, basking in the attention of the cheering crowd. It didn't matter that we were big-city strangers in the middle of the night—for a brief moment we were all joined in the euphoria and camaraderie that only happy endings can bring.

Elizabeth Lombard

"Dog" and Mr. Evans

"She's famous, you know," the elderly man said humbly, half looking at the floor, while I examined his dog's swollen ear. But I could hear the pride in his voice.

A few moments earlier, just before entering the exam room, I had glanced over the chart for the patient in Room One. When I saw the patient's name, I thought, *How original. A dog named Dog. Probably another backyard lawn ornament that's barely noticed and doesn't even get enough attention for someone to come up with an actual name for her.* But then I also noticed she had been brought in for yearly exams and had received all our recommended vaccinations and preventative care. Perhaps this wasn't a neglected dog after all.

Inside the exam room, I met Mr. James Evans, eighty-four, and Dog, his eleven-year-old Weimaraner mix. I guess you could say they were pretty close to the same age. Mr. Evans had noticed the swelling and "dirty ears," and brought Dog right in to have her checked out.

As I continued the exam, he told me how he stumbled upon Dog's high intelligence when he started teaching her simple tasks. He taught her these mainly in case of an emergency since he had heart and other health problems. He noticed how quickly she caught on and began teaching her more tricks. Her most famous were counting and solving math problems. They started "showing off" for family and friends, then Mr. Evans began taking her to nursing homes, schools and other small groups to perform.

"The people seem to enjoy it," he said. "Everyone's always asking how she does it. I tell them I don't know, she hasn't told me yet," he laughed. "Maybe she can read my mind. I don't know . . . but she gets the answers wrong when I'm not concentrating."

When he first started telling me all this, I thought, *Yeah, yeah, everybody thinks their dog is a genius.* But I could now tell by the way his eyes lit up, and how Dog never took hers off him, that he wasn't boasting, but doing what he always did: sharing this special animal and her stories with others. He sensed that I was genuinely interested and told me he would bring a video of her next time. He readily agreed to my recommended preanesthetic blood testing and treatment of the ears.

Mr. Evans brought me the videotape the next time he brought Dog in, which was for her annual visit. Later that day, a few members of the staff and I watched it. Although it wasn't the best-quality tape, two things were evident: how much the small audiences enjoyed the performance and how Dog never took her eyes off her partner. *Was* she reading his mind? Or was she so adept at reading his body language that she was picking up on some subconscious cue he was giving her, something he didn't even know he was doing—and isn't that almost the same thing? However they did it, it was a result of both of them being completely in tune with and trusting each other.

Several months later, they were back in my exam room, both a little feebler. Mr. Evans wanted me to check those ears again. He thought she might be losing her hearing. She was also having some trouble getting around. "But so am I," he chuckled as I carefully checked her over. Her ears were fine—just some wax, no infection—but her hips were arthritic.

The next time I saw them, Dog had to be carried into the exam room. Two years had passed since our first meeting. She was now thirteen and he was eighty-six. I dreaded this exam.

Before I even started, Mr. Evans looked straight at me with moist eyes and said, "Now, she's been too good to me for me to let her suffer. I would never let her down like that."

With that, I went on quietly with my exam. She was so weak. Laboring to breathe, her heartbeat was muffled and her eyes were dim. He agreed to leave her overnight so we could do more tests. He wanted to take the time to find out everything, but didn't want to allow her to be uncomfortable any longer if nothing could be done. I said I understood.

X-rays, EKG and blood work confirmed congestive heart failure, which had also caused liver disease. After treating her with heart medication, she was breathing a little easier and able to eat and drink. Something told me, though, that she was just holding on—holding on for him . . . for now. I prayed that she wouldn't die, not that night, not without him beside her.

I held my breath that morning as I entered the treatment room, trying to read my staff members' faces for the answer to the questions I didn't want to ask: How was Dog? Had she made it through the night? She was alive, but very weak. I had to call Mr. Evans. He seemed to already know what I had to report.

Mr. Evans patted her head as I injected the bright-pink liquid, tears streaming down my face, my hands shaking. I glanced at my assistant, hoping to find a steady face. No luck. Her eyes were pools of water. Dog's leg, my hands, the syringe were now nothing but a blur. She took one last, deep, long breath.

Mr. Evans's son John carried out the large box. For the first time, James Evans looked old to me. I wondered how he would be without her.

Later that afternoon, John Evans called to let us know that his father had passed away—he had suffered a heart attack while Dog's grave was being dug. I couldn't believe the pain that hit my own heart. I don't know how long I stood, stunned, before taking another breath.

I felt responsible. I had ended Dog's life, and because of that, Mr. Evans's life had ended, too. But then I realized they wouldn't have wanted it any other way. The family knew this, too. They had Dog's body exhumed and cremated. And they placed her ashes with her best friend.

I am grateful to Dog and Mr. Evans. They did more for me as a vet than I did for them. For at those times when I feel discouraged, dealing with the aftermath of a person's neglect of a pet, I remember Dog and Mr. Evans, and my confidence in the bond is restored.

Andrea B. Redd, D.V.M.

3

ON COURAGE

Even the tiniest poodle or Chihuahua is still a wolf at heart.

Dorothy Hinshaw Patent

Calvin: A Dog with a Big Heart

Blinded in a Nazi concentration camp at the age of twenty-one, I arrived in America with my wife in 1951. We worked and raised two sons; now, at eighty-two, I have five grandchildren. For most of those years, I depended on a white cane as my mobility aid. I envied my blind friends who had guide dogs—they had so much more freedom of mobility than I did. My problem, although I was reluctant to admit it, was that I had a fear of getting too close to dogs.

In spite of my fear, the day I retired I decided to apply for a guide dog at the Guiding Eyes for the Blind Guide Dog School. I so wanted the freedom a dog could give me, I had to make the attempt.

When I arrived, Charlie, the training supervisor, had a few cheerful welcoming words for the twelve of us beginning the May 1990 class. After the welcoming ceremonies, I took Charlie aside and said, "I would like to have a guide dog, but because of my negative experiences with dogs, I am not sure I could ever bond with one." Charlie, curious, asked me if I minded telling him about my negative experiences.

"I am a Holocaust survivor. In one of the Nazi concentration camps I was in," I explained, "the commandant had a big, vicious German shepherd. Sometimes when he entertained guests and wanted to show how cruel he could be, or how vicious his dog was—or both—he told a guard to bring a group of prisoners into his courtyard. Once, before I was blinded, I was in that group. I watched as he chose one of us to stand apart. Then he gave the dog the command, 'Fass!' meaning, 'Fetch!' With one leap, the dog grabbed the victim by the throat. In a few minutes, that man was dead. The dog returned to his master for his praise and reward, and the audience applauded the dog for a job well done. More than four decades later, nightmares about this still torment me," I confided to Charlie.

After a moment of reflection, Charlie said, "No human being is born evil; some become evil. No dog is born vicious; some are trained to be vicious. Give us a chance to prove to you that the dogs we train and the one you get will guide you safely, love you and protect you."

His words strengthened my resolve. I was determined, I told Charlie, to give myself a chance. Should I fail, it wouldn't be for lack of trying. Charlie called a meeting of his staff to reexamine my file and decided Calvin would be the right match for me. Calvin was a two-year-old, eighty-pound chocolate Lab. Following our four-week training period, I went home with Calvin and found myself struggling to forge a bond with him. I was in the process of learning to love him, and although I understood the helpful role Calvin was to play in my life, I was still cautious around him, never fully relaxing and accepting him. This struggle affected Calvin as well. During this period, Calvin ate, but lost weight, and the vet told me it was because the dog could sense my emotional distance. I often recalled Charlie's words: "No human being is born evil, and no dog is born vicious. . . ." My instructor called me several times, offering advice and giving me encouragement.

Slowly but surely, Calvin and I began to break down the invisible barrier between us. Finally, after about six months—twice as long as the average human/guide dog team—I began to trust Calvin more fully. I went with him anywhere I needed to go and did so with confidence.

Any lingering doubts I had about Calvin were dispelled one day as we stood at a busy intersection, waiting to cross the street. As we had been trained, when I heard parallel traffic start to move, I waited three seconds, then gave the command, "Calvin, forward." When we stepped off the curb, a motorist suddenly and unexpectedly made a sharp right turn, directly in front of us. Calvin stopped on a dime, slamming on the brakes! He had reacted exactly as he had been trained to react in such a situation. Realizing that he had saved us both from serious injury, I stepped back onto the sidewalk, crouched down, gave Calvin a hug around the neck and praised him for a job well done.

It was the turning point in our life together. After that, the love between us flowed freely and Calvin blossomed.

Out of harness, Calvin became as playful and mischievous as any other dog. When my granddaughter Hannah, a one-year-old just starting to get steady on her feet, came to visit, Calvin let her painstakingly position herself to grab his silky ear. Then he moved deftly to the side, his tail wagging a mile a minute, as Hannah reached in vain for him. Calvin's game made Hannah squeal with delight.

Calvin also formed a loving relationship with my wife, Barbara. She was coping with several chronic physical conditions and was homebound, and they became inseparable pals and playmates. At her periodic visit to the doctor, he noticed that her blood pressure was lower than it had been for a long time. Barbara asked the doctor if Calvin's companionship could have anything to do with her lowered blood pressure. "Most unlikely," he replied. "I'll change your prescription, though, since your blood pressure is better. Come back in two months." The blood pressure stayed down. The doctor, although un-convinced, grudgingly accepted that Calvin's compan-ionship might have had a favorable effect. Barbara and I had no doubt. The facts spoke for themselves.

Time and time again, Calvin proved he had a big heart, big enough for Barbara and me: He not only gave me the extra measure of independent and safe travel I had craved for many years, he also became a beloved member of the family.

Yes, Charlie, you were right. "Give us a chance," you said. "Your dog will love you, guide you, protect you." Calvin did all that and then some.

Max Edelman

Fate, Courage and a Dog Named Tess

*What counts is not necessarily the size of the
dog in the fight; it's the size of the fight in the dog.*
                                    Dwight D. Eisenhower

I had just picked up my young niece Hannah from
school when I first saw the confused dog darting in and
out of traffic at a busy intersection. She was a lanky
German shepherd, and I cringed as I watched several cars
swerve or stop to avoid hitting her. She appeared to be
lost, and Hannah immediately began begging me to inter-
vene. I resisted. I was in a hurry to get home to cook dinner for Hannah and her parents and brother. I had a
schedule to maintain, and right then, helping a stray dog
was the last thing I wanted to do.

However, as soon as I was able to, I turned around. As
we approached the intersection from the opposite direction, we saw her again. She had moved out of the street
and was now making friendly advances to everyone
walking by, only to be ignored or shooed away by people
in a hurry to get home at the end of their workday. With
a hopeless sigh, I pulled over and parked my car.

"Okay, Hannah," I said. "This is what we'll do. I'll open the car door and give her one chance to get in, but if she doesn't, we're going home. I won't try to force her."

I got out, opened the door and made a halfhearted call to a pup more than fifty feet away. At the sound of my voice, she pricked her ears, looked directly at me and came running in our direction. In an instant she was in the car, wagging her tail and showering us with doggy kisses as if she'd known us forever. I couldn't help but laugh. What a sweet dog! And miracle of miracles, she was wearing a chain collar that I hadn't noticed before. Even though she didn't have a name tag, surely someone was missing her. A phone call or two, and with any luck, I'd be able to return her to her family. This might not be so bad after all. I took her home firmly believing she would soon be out of my life.

A week later, after running ads in the paper and making repeated phone calls to the local Humane Society and rabies control, I finally resigned myself to the hard reality that whoever had placed the collar around her neck didn't want her back. I lived in a small house and already had two dogs, so keeping her wasn't an option. I decided I would find her a home where she would be cared for and appreciated by a loving family. My first step was to make an appointment with my vet, who pronounced her in perfect health, although obviously underweight. I named her Tess and began to teach her about in-house living, knowing she needed some better manners to increase her appeal.

With lots of food and grooming, she filled out and her scruffy coat began to glisten. She thrived under all the attention. Within six weeks she was completely housebroken and beautiful. I wrote a story about her and convinced the editor of our local paper to run it in the weekend edition. The story was typed and ready to be dropped off at the newspaper office the next day, and I felt certain we were spending one of our last evenings together.

Just as I was getting ready for bed, the doorbell rang, and because it was late, I answered wearing pajamas, thinking it was probably a neighbor wanting to borrow something. Instead, much to my dismay, an unkempt man stood before me, asking to use my phone. No way I wanted this guy in my house, but I offered to make a call for him if he would supply the number. Without another word, he opened the storm door and pushed his way into my living room. My mind raced. Why in God's name hadn't I checked to see who it was before opening the door? My two dogs—an English springer spaniel and a shih tzu—and Tess, all stopped their effusive greetings, sensing, as I did, that this guy was trouble. The three of them looked at him, then looked to me for some sign that things were okay.

But things were definitely not okay. I was too terrified to speak or move. I stood frozen, waiting, trapped in a dangerous situation from which I feared there was no escape.

Suddenly, the German shepherd I had taken in to save from a life on the streets stepped between me and this stranger who threateningly stood before us. Tess was only eight or nine months old, big, but still very much a pup, and yet, there she was, head down, hackles raised, emitting a low-pitched, menacing growl as she glared at the intruder. For maybe five long seconds we all stood there, motionless. Then, very slowly, the man took one backward step. He raised his hand slightly as he implored me to hold my dog, and he carefully backed out of my house and down the walk.

At last, finally able to move, I shut the door, locked it and turned to hug my friend, the stray dog I had rescued—and who, now, had rescued me. Magically, with the danger gone, she transformed herself back into the wiggling, tail-wagging, pain-in-the-neck pup I had come to know. The next morning I called and canceled the appointment I had to drop off the story about her. Tess didn't need a home; she already had one. Two dogs had become three, but the lack of space didn't seem nearly as important as it had before.

Since that night Tess has never once growled or shown the least bit of hostility to any other human being, and, although her muzzle is now graying, she still often acts like the pup who, without hesitation, bounded into my car—and my life—eleven years ago. I have learned a lot from Tess, especially on that memorable night when she taught me about fate and courage. But most important, she showed me how a random act of kindness can bring blessings to your life.

Susanne Fogle

In Her Golden Eyes

An animal's eyes have the power to speak a great language.

Martin Buber

My six-year-old daughter, Mariah, held on to my hand as we walked through the animal shelter. We wanted to pick just the right puppy for her sister Vanessa's twelfth birthday. I scanned each cage, noticing all the pairs of needy brown eyes staring back at us. It was neediness for love and a happy home—things the girls and I also hungered for since their father and I had divorced.

"Here are our newest arrivals," the volunteer said. He led us to a cage where three puppies were sleeping. They were the size of small bear cubs with beautiful fur.

"What kind are they?" I asked, stooping down to take a closer look.

"They're chow mixes," the boy said. "I've never seen such awesome-looking dogs."

My heart quickened as the pup in the middle suddenly yawned and looked up at us. She was breathtaking, with oversized paws and silvery-black wolf markings on her face. Most of all, it was her eyes that struck me. They were so gentle and sweet. As golden as her fur. Something told me that she was the one.

As long as I live, I'll never forget Vanessa's face when we surprised her with her new companion. It almost made the pain of the last several months disappear.

"I'm going to name her Cheyenne," Vanessa beamed.

In the coming days, Cheyenne accomplished exactly what I was hoping for. Instead of the children feeling homesick for the life we'd lost, they spent time playing with their new puppy. Instead of feeling depressed over missing their daddy, they romped and laughed for hours. It gave me hope that they would make this very difficult transition a bit better—if only something would help me do the same.

It was on a late April afternoon that things took a horrible turn. The girls were in the backyard playing with Cheyenne while I went to the store. When I got back home and pulled into the driveway, a pickup truck came speeding down our street. I got out of my car, keys in hand, and saw that Cheyenne had gotten loose. She ran past me in a blur.

"Cheyenne!" I called out. "No! Get back here!" But it was too late. She chased after the truck, caught up to the front tires, and was flipped in the air before landing with a thud on the side of the road.

Luckily, the vet was still open and they took her right in. I kept watching Cheyenne's side, willing her to keep breathing as the vet put her on the examining table.

"The front leg appears to be the worst of her injuries," he said, pinching between her toes with a silver clamp. "The nerves have been damaged and she doesn't have any feeling. I'm afraid we'll have to amputate."

The day of Cheyenne's surgery was the longest day of my life. Nothing prepared us for what we would see once we went to pick her up. In the bottom cage, Cheyenne lay panting and blinking sleepy eyes, the entire right side of her body shaved clean from her stomach to her neck. A huge white bandage was wrapped around the shoulder area where her leg used to be. A plastic tube was also taped to the area to help the surgical site drain. She looked totally miserable. Tears slid from my eyes as I saw Cheyenne's tail give a faint wag.

That night we all camped on the floor to sleep next to Cheyenne. As she moaned in agony and lay on her side unable to move, I kept trying to picture her as she used to be: running, playing, jumping up on the bed to snuggle down next to me. I felt frightened and uncertain, wondering how she would ever be that same carefree pup again. In a way, I understood the kind of trauma she was going through. One day you were happy, then life just shattered, inexplicably, leaving you in a world of pain.

Vanessa and I took shifts for the first few nights. We'd keep watch, try to comfort her, give her pain pills and feed her vanilla ice cream from a spoon. She'd doze, but usually she was too uncomfortable to sleep. Every few hours, we'd carry her outside and help her stand so she could go to the bathroom. We were exhausted, but nothing was more important than Cheyenne coming back to us—even if she would never be the same again.

On Monday I had to take care of her myself when Vanessa went to school. Mariah kept busy with her coloring books while I constantly hovered over Cheyenne. I changed her bandages and made sure she wasn't trying to bite at them. I stroked her head and kept telling her how strong she was. Seeing her so miserable and watching the blood ooze from her drainage tube broke my heart over and over again. I missed her sweet eyes looking at me with love instead of so much suffering.

"You're a survivor," I whispered in her ear. "We need you,

so you have to get better. Those children are depending on you, so please . . . don't give up. Fight and get through this."

As I said these things to her, something struck me deep inside. The same words applied to me. It had been a nightmare since the divorce, the pain so deep that I wanted to curl up and die; I didn't see myself able to stand on my own. But weren't the children depending on me, too? Didn't I have to fight and get through this? Tears ran down my cheeks as I lay my face against Cheyenne's muzzle. It was so soft and her breath fanned my skin. Breath that reminded me how precious life was.

"I'll make a deal with you, girl," I said. "If you fight and get through this, I'll fight my way back, too. We'll learn how to walk on our own together."

From that day on, things steadily improved. Cheyenne looked more alert and comfortable, daring to take her first steps, while I started crying less and smiling more. A healing was beginning to take place and it felt so very good. One day at a time, one step at a time, Cheyenne and I were making it together.

"Look, Mom! She's doing it! Cheyenne's walking on her own!" Vanessa pointed as Cheyenne wandered about the yard one week later. She managed just fine with the front leg missing. In fact, it seemed as if she didn't miss it much at all.

Mariah clapped happily. "Just like her old self!"

I thought about that a moment and had to disagree. "Actually, sweetheart, I think Cheyenne's going to be better than she used to be. She'll be stronger because she's a survivor now. Just like us . . . better than ever."

In that instant, Cheyenne stopped and looked at me. The gleam was back in those golden eyes. We both had a new life to look forward to, one precious step at a time.

Diane Nichols

Ballerina Dog

One April afternoon a few days after my twenty-first birthday, my parents announced that they were ready to give me—their live-at-home, frazzled, college-student daughter—a belated birthday present.

Wheelchair-bound since birth, I propelled myself from my bedroom into the living room where my parents anxiously waited.

"Bring it on! Good things come to those who wait," I joked, as I closed my eyes and extended my hands waiting to feel the weight of a beautifully wrapped gift.

"Why are you holding out your hands?" my dad laughed. "Your gift isn't coming in a box this year."

"Huh?" I opened my eyes to study the glee stamped on both of their usually calm faces. "I know! It must be that handicapped-accessible van I've been praying for!"

"No, it's not a van, but it's almost as good," my mom chuckled. Then she said more seriously, "Jackie, we know you were devastated when Buck passed last year. We all were. He was a great dog. But we think our house has been void of doggy joy long enough. It's time to hear puppy noises again."

"So today, right now, in fact," my dad broke in, "we're

going to a place where you'll be able to select the puppy of your choice."

"But," I stammered, but there was no time for protest as he scooped me out of my chair and into our car. My parents chatted to each other while I sat in the back, desperately trying to quell overwhelming waves of sadness.

Sadness because not so long ago, this trip would have seemed incomprehensible—a betrayal. After all, it had been only seven months since Buck lay on my cold bathroom floor drawing his last breaths. Seven months since I slid from my chair onto the floor, gently caressing his gray-streaked black-and-white fur, as his spirit passed from this world to the next. Sobbing, I vowed to him and to myself that I would never get another dog . . . but now here I was, about to break that promise.

Finally, my father turned to me and asked, "It'll be nice to hear the pitter-patter of paws again, won't it?"

"Yeah," I said flatly, trying to conjure up the excitement he'd expected. But I couldn't. Tears began to roll down my cheeks. I wiped them away quickly as my father, unaware of my tenuous emotional state, continued.

"When we get there, should we make a beeline to the shih tzu puppies? I know they're your favorites."

My favorite was Buck, I thought, *not his breed. Buck, my constant companion, who climbed up on my lap and, like a salve, soothed my spastic, palsied muscles in a way that no drug ever could.*

"Buck is irreplaceable!" I wanted to scream, but I held back, opting for something kinder. "Breeds don't really matter. It's their heart that counts. I'll look at them all." I paused, then continued as we pulled into the parking lot, "Who knows? I may not find any and walk out empty-handed." I wanted to prepare my parents for this possibility.

"I doubt that," Dad smiled at me, as he plopped me in my chair and headed toward the building, "but we'll see."

A chorus of barks and howls heralded our arrival, as a friendly employee offered to show us the available puppies. My parents accepted, but I lagged behind, gazing at the other dogs, shimmying and shaking, pleading to be released from their four-walled prisons. I smiled, but held myself in check, determined to keep my vow. Until . . .

Until I saw my father's face shining like the noonday sun. "Over here," he called to me.

Intrigued, my heart began to race, as I pushed toward the pen where my parents stood. Struggling to get a better look, I hoisted myself up, my legs tightening with the effort. There, nestled in the pen, were two angelic shih tzus. The male, a fluffy caramel and white pup, was gregarious and charged right at me. His smaller sister, a beautiful midnight-black-and-white puppy, was more demure, waiting for me to lean in a bit, before licking my nose. *Aww, she looks like Buck,* I said silently, my heart beginning to soften. Then suddenly, before I knew what was happening, my resolve toppled. I was hooked.

"Well, it looks like we won't be going home empty-handed," my mother said, as if voicing my thoughts.

"Wonderful." My father was pleased. "Which one?"

I was leaning toward the male; he was obviously the alpha and far more playful. Yet the girl was so tiny, her ebony eyes captivating and sweet.

I held them both, the male against the center of my chest, while the female lay curled in the warmth of my lap. It was nearly closing time as the male nibbled the ends of my hair, and the female slept serenely against my atrophied legs. Still, I was hopelessly undecided.

The employee, observing my deadlock, lowered his voice to a whisper and said, "Look, if I were you, I'd take the boy because the female's disabled. Her legs are deformed; she stands like a ballerina in first position."

Stunned at his insensitivity, my eyes widened. *Hadn't*

he seen my legs or the wheelchair I sat in? I wondered.

Noticing my expression, the employee continued, "I don't mean to upset you, but she'll need constant care. And the last thing you probably need is another pile of doctor bills."

Wanting to prove him wrong, I placed her on her feet. Instantly, her two bowed legs scissored, as she strained to keep her balance. Yet, despite her valiant effort, her tiny disabled legs faltered and she tumbled onto her side.

"See her legs cross?" he said quietly. "She's our little ballerina dog."

My eyes glistened as I listened to her tiny panting. I knew her struggle far too well. I recalled those times when I had used all my strength to stand upright—and that glorious second when I stood tall—only to come crashing down. I wanted to take her, but the employee was right: could I really afford her care?

"Okay . . . I'll take him," I said sadly.

As we were saying our good-byes to the little female, she struggled back up. Her eyes bursting with determination, she pushed her brother out of the way and then carefully placed one foot in front of the other, as she began her slow, steady ascent across my lap and up my shirt. She wobbled and stumbled but didn't stop until she rested against my heart.

Laughing and crying at the same time, I whispered, "I hear you, ballerina dog. You're coming home with me." Contented, she closed her eyes, knowing her mission was complete. We would manage whatever care she needed; it would all work out.

"Excuse me, sir," I announced loudly, "there's been a change of plans. I'm taking Ballerina Dog."

Jackie Tortoriello

The Dog Who Loved to Fly

Copper's yearning to fly was apparent from puppy-hood. You wouldn't expect a dachshund to want to spend his life airborne, but from the day he cleared the rail of the playpen that was supposed to keep him out of trouble while I was at work, to his last valiant effort at leaving the Earth, there was no stopping him.

It was Copper's soaring spirit that made me choose him as my first dog. The rest of the litter was cute in the traditional puppy way. Copper, however, would have nothing to do with touching noses or cuddling up next to me. He managed to drag himself up on top of the sofa, and before anyone could stop him, off he jumped. He landed with a "poof!" as the air escaped from his tiny belly. Seven-week-old dog legs aren't meant to support skydiving. I knew that, but he didn't.

I'm not big on following rules either, so Copper was the obvious choice for me. I whispered in his little ear, "I like you, flying dog. Do you want to come home with me?" He stared at me intently as if to say, *Okay, but don't expect me to obey Newton's Law of Gravity!*

Copper's pilot training began the moment we arrived home. He surveyed the landscape, identified the highest elevations and spent his days scampering up and flying down from everything he could. For months, every floor in the house was covered with pillows, blankets, towels and anything soft I could find to cushion his landings.

One day when he was about five months old, I came home to find Copper standing in the middle of the dining-room table with that look on his face that said, *Fasten your seat belts and hang on for the ride!* I ran as fast as I could toward him to catch him, but he hit the ground before I could yell, "No flying in the dining room!"

From that day on, I put the dining-room chairs upside down on the table every morning before I went to work. When friends and neighbors asked why, I'd just shrug and say it was an old German custom.

I wished Copper could be happy doing regular dachshund stuff—sniffing the carpet, rolling in strange smells, barking at squirrels and learning to be disobedient in two languages, but it just wasn't in him. "What am I going to do with you, flying dog?" I'd ask him every night when I got home from work. I got him a dog tag shaped like an airplane and prayed that he was strong enough not to get hurt in his airborne escapades.

One day when he was five, Copper jumped up on the back of the couch and flew off. When he landed, he hurt his back. I rushed him to the vet, who said he'd blown a disc and would need surgery. My heart was broken. *If I had been a good dog-parent,* I thought, *I'd have found a way to stop him from flying.*

Copper pulled through the surgery with a wagging tail and that same rebellious spark in his eyes. And now that he had a reverse Mohawk from the surgery, he looked even more independent. The last words I heard at the vet were, "Don't let him jump off things!"

I tried, really I did. For three weeks, whenever I wasn't with him, I kept Copper in a crate. He gave me a look that said, *How can you take away my freedom, my spirit, my reason for living?* And he was right; I had grounded not only his body, but his spirit as well. So as he got stronger, I started letting him out of the crate. I gave him a stern warning to behave himself, but he and I both knew he wouldn't.

As the years went by, Copper found it harder to get around. When he got too old to easily clamber onto the sofa with me, I built him a ramp. Of course, the first thing he did was to use it as a springboard to fly from. And he was just as proud of himself as he ever was.

Then at age thirteen, Copper's entire back end became paralyzed; he couldn't jump at all. I don't know who was sadder that Copper's flying days were over, him or me.

The vet couldn't find anything wrong, so I got Copper a K-9 cart, a little wheelchair for dogs. "Now, Copper," I said, "I looked for a little cart with wings, but they just didn't have one. So I guess you'll just have to stay on the floor like a real dog from now on."

A few minutes later, while I was in the kitchen cooking dinner, I heard a noise in the living room. I ran in and saw Copper at the top of the ramp, with that look in his eye. Before anyone could stop him, he turned and wheeled down the ramp at full speed, his ears flying behind him.

Copper could still fly. I should have known better than to doubt his soaring spirit. And once he landed his new "aircraft," he wheeled back up the ramp and took off again, as elated by his accomplishment as the Wright Brothers must have been.

Copper flew up and down that ramp with his wheels spinning behind him for almost three more years before he escaped the bonds of Earth once and for all.

Leigh Anne Jasheway-Bryant

Locked In

April afternoons are warm in suburban Philadelphia, and the temperature inside a parked car rises quickly. Ila, my two-year-old daughter, was strapped into her car seat, pink-cheeked and sweaty. D'Argo, my ten-month-old chocolate Lab, was bounding from the front seat to the back, barking and panting. Helpless, I could only stand and wait.

They had been locked in the rented truck for fifteen minutes when the police car finally pulled into my driveway.

"No spare key, ma'am?" the young officer asked. The only key I had was attached to the remote door lock control, which was lying on the driver's seat, along with my purse, the after-school snack for the older kids, my book, the mail and the dirty dry cleaning. I had tossed everything onto the seat, buckled Ila into her car seat and shooed D'Argo into the passenger side, closing doors as I went. Just as I reached the driver's side door, I heard the clunk of the door locks. D'Argo was standing on the driver's seat, tail wagging and his oversized puppy paws on the remote.

"It's a rental," I explained. "The agency doesn't keep spares, but the agent is trying to get a new key cut. He said he'd send it right over."

One hand on the nightstick in his tool belt, the officer circled the truck, trying all the doors, tugging at the lift gate. D'Argo trailed him from window to window inside. They came face-to-face at the front passenger window. D'Argo, his nose pressed against the window, wagged his tail and drooled, leaving large globs of spit and nose prints on the glass.

Two more officers arrived. After a quick briefing, the older, heavier officer took a long metal tool with a flat hooked end from the trunk of his squad car. He wedged it into the gap between the driver's side window and door and slid it slowly in and out, trying, unsuccessfully, to jimmy the lock. Then he attacked the keyhole with a screwdriver, succeeded only in making a few gouges in the metal and gave up. "These new cars, like Fort Knox," he muttered. "Sorry, ma'am."

I called the car-rental company again. They were "still working on it," my friendly rental agent said. I pressed my face against the window, shading my eyes to see through the tinted glass. D'Argo had flopped down next to Ila's car seat, his long body stretched out across the seat and his big brown head resting in her lap. Ila's face was flushed and shiny. Drops of sweat rolled down her cheeks and her blond curls were dark and matted against her forehead. Ila looked up into my face.

"Mommy! Uppie!" she said, holding up her arms. Her wide blue eyes leaked tears.

"Mommy will get you out as soon as she can," I said, straining to sound calm and cheerful. Her face crumpled.

"Mommy! Mommy! I wan' you!" she wailed. She twisted and strained against the car seat, crying harder, legs pumping, arms reaching. D'Argo jumped into the front seat and joined in, baying with a low, guttural moan.

Fidgeting with his nightstick, one of the officers turned to me.

"We could break a window," he said, giving the front driver's window an experimental tap. D'Argo flinched, hair rising across his back, but didn't back away.

"The baby'll be okay in the backseat, but I'm afraid I'll hurt your dog, ma'am."

"We can't wait for the key anymore," I said, "we need to get them out." The men looked at each other.

"Like I said, ma'am, we might hurt your dog."

"I don't want you to hurt him either, but they've been in there too long."

The younger officer pulled his nightstick out of his tool belt and walked around to the passenger door. D'Argo met him at the window, barking and howling.

"Can you call him? Get him away?" he called.

"D'Argo! D'Argo! Come!" I yelled, banging frantically on the driver's side window. D'Argo stopped barking and looked back, but stayed where he was. The policeman raised the baton, then hesitated, looking through the window at D'Argo and then at me.

"Do it!" I yelled.

He swung down hard, smacking the glass with the nightstick. D'Argo leaped back. The nightstick thudded against the window again. D'Argo vaulted into the backseat.

"D'Argo, off! Getta offa me, D'Argo!" Ila screamed, but her voice was muffled in D'Argo's chest. The dog was standing over her car seat, covering her with his body. She beat her fists against his side and kicked her feet at his legs, but he would not move.

Suddenly, there was a loud crack as the nightstick splintered. The three officers stood together, staring at the pieces of the broken baton, then looked up at me as I came around the truck. I ran for the toolbox in the basement and grabbed the sledgehammer, the heaviest tool I could find. I handed it to the younger officer, who started pounding on the window. The sound was deafening. Ila was still screaming, punching and kicking frantically at D'Argo, who stood squarely over her, his back to the action at the window. His large body covered her small one almost completely.

The glass fractured suddenly with a crackling sound. One more blow from the sledgehammer and the window shattered. The officer reached in and unlocked the doors. I wrenched open Ila's door and D'Argo flew past me. There were shards of glass everywhere on the backseat and floor, but none in the car seat. I fumbled with the buckle, unlatched it and pulled Ila out. She was flushed, warm and sweaty, her T-shirt soaked through and her hair plastered to her head in ringlets, but she was not hurt. I squeezed her tight and sank onto the ground, both of us sobbing. I sat there for a minute, hugging her. Then I looked for D'Argo. He was twisting and lunging, trying to get away from the older officer, who was holding him by the collar.

"He's not hurt," he said, struggling to hold on, "but I'm afraid he'll run away."

But I knew he wouldn't.

"It's all right," I said, "you can let him go." D'Argo flew straight for us, wormed his big head between Ila and me and licked both our faces until we were laughing instead of crying.

M. L. Charendoff

The Telltale Woof

Every dog is a lion at home.

H. G. Bohn

The veterinarian's words came as no surprise. "I'll do what I can, but I'm not optimistic. Call me tomorrow morning."

I smoothed the black fur on Yaqui's head and ran my fingers across the small brown patches above his closed eyes. His normally powerful body was limp, and I could barely detect any rise and fall in his rib cage. Turning away, I reached for Frank's hand, leaving our shepherd-cross companion stretched out on the polished steel surface of the examining room table.

I barely remember the drive home. Lost in worry, I didn't realize we had reached the turnoff to our ranch until I heard the frantic barking of the dog we laughingly called "Yaqui's Great Enemy." From behind his front-yard fence, Yaqui's Great Enemy, who guarded the house at the crossroads, dashed back and forth, waiting for Yaqui's reciprocal challenge. When greeted with silence, he bounced to a standstill, stared at the car, then trotted off toward his den under the porch.

After Frank left for work I wandered about the house, picking aimlessly at chores. Yaqui's pal, Simba, a hefty mastiff, padded quietly after me, stopping every so often to gaze up at me with questioning eyes.

Dinner that night was subdued as we reassured ourselves that Yaqui would pull through. Both Frank and I privately chastised ourselves for what had happened.

Six months earlier, we had moved onto a ranch in the foothills of the Pine Nut Mountains in western Nevada. Our dogs, who had been used to the confines of backyard suburban living, thrived in their new freedom, spending their days sniffing around the barns and corrals. Often, though, we found them standing by the fence that surrounded the ranch buildings, looking out across the pastures. Yielding to their entreating eyes, we would take them for walks, letting them prowl through the sagebrush, following tantalizing scents and animal trails. In time, we all became familiar with the sparse desert landscape.

Although we made a conscientious effort to keep the gates shut, occasionally we found one open and the dogs nowhere in sight. But even when they were gone for hours, we rarely worried. There was almost no traffic, and because they were big dogs, we believed them safe from coyotes and mountain lions.

One evening in early December, Simba returned alone. We called into the darkness, listening for Yaqui's answering bark, but all we heard were the echoes of our own voices. A dozen times during the night we rose to check the circle of light on the porch, but the dawn arrived as empty as our spirits.

For three days we searched. At first we drove for miles along the ranch roads with Simba beside us in our old Suburban, hoping she might give some sign that Yaqui was nearby. Then, as gray clouds moved in from the west and temperatures dropped into the low teens, Frank and

I saddled up our horses. We crisscrossed the brush-covered slopes and picked our way through boulder-clogged draws, looking for recent tracks or signs of blood.

On the second afternoon, while we scoured the upper limits of the foothills close to where Red Canyon sliced into the mountain front, we thought we heard his voice, but when the wind settled, the countryside was still. Only the rhythmic sound of Simba's panting broke the silence.

By the morning of the fourth day, snow was falling steadily. Frank stared out the window as he dressed for work. Neither one of us wanted to verbalize what we were thinking. Then as he picked up his jacket, he called out, "Come on, let's check the road to Red Canyon one more time."

Straining to see, we eased the Suburban along the barely discernible dirt track to the top of the slope. There, in the eerie silence of the swirling snow, we sat for a moment. Both of us sensed the search was at an end.

Just as Frank slipped the car into gear, Simba whined. I turned around as she leaped up and pressed her nose against the rear window. She pawed at the glass, her tail waving. It batted against the backs of the seats and stirred the air above our heads. Staring at us, the huge dog tipped her head back and emitted a long, low howl.

No more than twenty feet away was a black shadow, struggling out of the gloom. Clamped firmly on his right front paw was a large, steel jaw-trap. Behind the trap, attached by a knotted strand of barbed wire, trailed a thick, four-foot-long tree limb. The wood was gouged with teeth marks and the wire crimped where desperate jaws had torn at the rusty surface, exposing slashes of fresh steel.

All three of us piled out of the Suburban. Simba licked her friend's face. Joyfully, she romped away from him, then returning, she bowed her greeting, challenging him to play. But Yaqui only stood and shivered. Cautiously, she approached him again and sniffed at the paw that was swollen beyond recognition, engulfing the metal teeth.

Frank grabbed the trap and stepped on the release mechanism. The rusty hinges refused to budge. He stamped harder on the lever and the jaws scraped opened. Yaqui sank to the ground, whimpering softly as we pried his foot loose.

Scooping up Yaqui's emaciated body, Frank laid him gently in my arms for the trip to the veterinary hospital. When we approached the main crossroads, Frank slowed, and there as always, barking behind his fence, was Yaqui's Great Enemy. Too feeble to sit up, Yaqui lifted his head and gave one weak *woof*. Right then I should have known he would be all right.

The following day the doctor called to say he thought Yaqui would survive but definitely would lose his leg. The day after that, he said Yaqui would keep his leg but would surely lose his foot. The third day, the foot seemed out of danger but a few toes would have to go.

Yaqui survived with all his digits intact, but for the next ten years he wore a prominent scar across the top of his foot. On cooler days he walked with a faint limp, but his spirit was never scarred.

We identified the wood attached to the trap as belonging to a species of tree that grows only in the upper reaches of the canyons, many hundreds of feet above where we found Yaqui. Dragging the trap and its anchor, he had struggled beyond the limits of credible endurance to return to us, trusting that we would be there for him. Thankfully, we were.

Eleanor Whitney Nelson

4

ONE OF
THE FAMILY

*Acquiring a dog may be the only opportunity
a human ever has to choose a relative.*

Mordecai Siegal

"I think he's spending too much time with the kids."

Moving Day

He was a street dog of indeterminable pedigree. Not too big, but scrappy.

He found my husband on St. Patrick's Day, 1988. A New York City police officer, Steve was patrolling the Park Slope section of Brooklyn. The skinny blond dog with the white stripe on his face and stand-up ears he never did grow into, fairly leaped into the patrol car through the open window.

I got the call that afternoon. "Can we keep him?" My big strong husband sounded like a kid.

We kept him. Steve named him Patrick, in honor of the day he'd found him. We didn't know how he'd ended up a homeless pup. But it didn't matter. He was safe now. The vet estimated that he was about six months old and that he'd been on the streets only a few days. He was healthy, but awfully hungry.

I fed him boiled chicken and rice, easy on his stomach, and determined to start putting some meat on the ribs that were a bit too prominent. After that meal—and after every single meal I fed him for the rest of his life—he thanked me with several sloppy kisses on my hands.

Things were hectic that March. The kids were growing

and we were in the process of moving into a larger apartment.

Patrick watched with an odd expression; but it was an odd move. We didn't really pack. We simply rolled everything into the hall, loaded it in the elevator, went two floors down and rolled the stuff off and into the new place.

The new apartment gave our kids their own rooms. Patrick's space was an alcove at the end of the hall leading to the master bedroom. I cut a piece of carpet to fit his "room" and piled his toys in one of the corners. I bought "Dawn Lane" and "Michael Lane" signs for the kids, so of course I bought a "Patrick Lane" sign for him. I think he liked it. When I put it on the wall he licked the sign, then me.

March 17 became his birthday. On the first anniversary of the day he found us, I threw a "Patty Party," inviting all the grandparents. I'd done it tongue-in-cheek, but it became an annual event. We got Patrick a kelly-green birthday hat and a big matching bow tie. Another dog might have been embarrassed; Patrick wore them with pride.

To repay us for rescuing him, Patrick protected us with zeal and an unerring ability to tell good guy from bad. He could pick the "perp" out of a lineup a block long. He knew guns, too. When Steve cleaned his service revolver, Patrick would eye him strangely, from a safe distance, as if to say, "What's a nice guy like you doing with a thing like that?"

In 1992 Steve retired. We bought a house in Jersey near my folks, but couldn't close until October. The kids stayed with my parents so they could start the year in their new school. We brought them home on alternate weekends. Michael's room now became the "Box Room."

Every day I knelt in that room, placing breakables on the pile of papers, wrapping them up and tucking them into boxes. And every day Patrick watched from the room's other doorway. I told him all about "our" new house and described the fun "we" would have.

Our last night in Brooklyn approached. We'd lived in that apartment four and a half years, and in the building for fifteen. Though excited about moving into our own home, we were a bit sad to leave the city we'd lived in all our lives. Patrick understood. He patrolled the apartment restlessly, sniffing every nook and cranny as if to commit to memory the security of the only loving home he'd ever known.

We closed on the house on Friday, then drove back to Brooklyn with the kids. The "Box Room" was nearly full, but the packing paper still lay on the few square feet of remaining floor, ready to protect our last-minute treasures. I gave the kids their "Dawn" and "Michael" boxes, instructing them to finish packing their toys. We had something quick for dinner. I don't remember what. I only remember what happened after.

I walked into the kitchen and happened to glance into the "Box Room." I was stunned.

"Hey, guys," I called. "You won't believe what Patrick did." They followed me through the kitchen. Patrick poked his nose in from the living-room doorway, a very worried expression on his face.

There, nestled in the canyon of cartons, lying right on top of the newspaper used for wrapping breakables, was Patrick's favorite toy.

I said, "Patty, are you afraid we're going to move away and leave you? Is that what those other people did to you?" He didn't need words. His eyes told me.

"Well," I told him. "You don't have to worry. We're not going to leave you. You're coming with us."

Then I rolled up his toy in the paper. I'd planned to put his things in the "Patrick" box. Instead, it went in with our dishes. It seemed the thing to do.

His bushy blond and white tail wagged like mad, and if asked under oath I'd have to swear he laughed. We all wound up in a heap on that stack of papers, getting licked to death by one very happy—and grateful—dog.

I'm sorry to say I'd never considered Patrick's feelings through that whole tumultuous process; never thought he was worried as he sat day after day, intently watching me wrap up and pack away our things; never realized he didn't know he was part of the "we" I kept mentioning. After all, he'd been with us four and a half years and we'd moved with him before. But I guess the vast amount of packing required for this move dredged up old memories and threatened his sense of security. Elephants never forget; dogs don't either.

When I think about Patty now, all I can say is: I'm thrilled he picked Steve. He brought joy to our lives that we would have sorely missed otherwise. He left us in November 1997 and we still miss him. He's with us, though, in a pretty wooden urn—and he smiles at us every day from his picture, dressed so smartly in his kelly-green birthday hat and matching bow tie.

Micki Ruiz

Refrigerator Commando

Ever consider what they must think of us? I mean, here we come back from a grocery store with the most amazing haul—chicken, pork, half cow. They must think we're the greatest hunters on earth!

Anne Tyler

A golden barrel on legs—that was our first impression of Max when my wife and I saw him at the Animal Welfare League. His unique ability to inhale a full cup of dog food in less than seven seconds had enabled Max to enlarge his beagle-mix body into the shape of an overstuffed sausage. Even after Heather and I adopted him and helped him lose weight, we were continually amazed at his voraciousness. His escapades became the stuff of family legend: his seek-and-destroy mission involving several pounds of gourmet Christmas cashews, his insistence on chasing birds away from the feeder so *he* could eat the seeds, his discovery (far too gross to discuss here) of the yeasty joys of Amish Friendship Bread batter. And of course the refrigerator story . . .

One day during her lunch break, Heather called me at work. "Did you shut the refrigerator door tight this morning?"

"Think so. Why?"

She paused just enough to let the suspense build. "Max raided the fridge."

We got off lucky: we were overdue to go to the grocery store, so there hadn't been much in there. He'd gotten the last couple of pieces of peppered turkey and maybe a third of a bag of baby carrots—no surprise there, Max loves carrots (then again, Max loves potting soil). Still, no real damage done. We wrote it off to a sloppily closed door (probably my doing), and the next morning I made sure everything was shut good and tight before I left. After all, we had just loaded up with groceries the night before, and we wouldn't want my carelessness to help Max get himself into trouble, right?

Turns out Max didn't need my help at all.

Again a phone call to me during Heather's lunch hour, this time straight to the point: "I think he knows how to open the refrigerator," she said.

"What?!"

Max had made himself a sandwich. A *big* sandwich: a pound of turkey, a pound of Swiss cheese, a head of lettuce, half a tomato and an entire loaf of bread. He'd also ripped open another bag of carrots and polished off the remnants of a bag of shredded coconut (for dessert, I assume). Heather found him lying amid the flurry of destroyed plastic bags, tail desperately thumping at her displeasure, as if to say, *Please don't be mad, it was just* SOOOO *good . . .*

Still, we didn't really believe it. He couldn't reach the handle, and the door seal was tight. How was he doing it? I caught him that night, after putting away our second load of groceries in two days. I just happened to be passing by the darkened kitchen when I saw his stout little body wiggling, pushing his narrow muzzle into the fridge seal like a wedge. Then, with a quick flick of his head, he popped the door open.

Apparently, Max, while not understanding the gastrointestinal distress that results from eating sixteen slices of cheese, had a full understanding of the concept of the lever. Where was this dog when I'd been in science class?

This was serious. He now had the skill, the determination and, most important, the appetite to literally eat us out of house and home. The next morning, as a temporary fix, we blocked the refrigerator with a heavy toolbox. Surely he couldn't move a barrier loaded with close to twenty-five pounds of metal, could he?

Another lunchtime phone call. I think I answered it: "You've got to be kidding!"

The moving of the toolbox still remains a bit of a mystery. I'm guessing he used that lever principle again, wedging his muzzle between the box and the door and then just pushing for all he was worth. And once that barrier was gone, he got *serious*.

More bread, more meat, more cheese. The rest of the carrots. Apples—many, many apples. A packet of cilantro, smeared like green confetti across the kitchen floor. He'd also popped open a Tupperware bowl of angel hair pasta and had been working at its sister container of tomato sauce when Heather found him. The only items left on the bottom two shelves were beer and pop, and the only thing that saved those was his lack of opposable thumbs.

That night we decided to hit the grocery store for a *third* time and invest in a childproof lock for the fridge. Before we left the house to buy it, we hovered anxiously around the refrigerator for a while. There wasn't *much* left in there, but still, what if he tried to climb to the top shelves? What if he conquered the freezer?

But what could stop him? The toolbox had been no

match. Finally, I half lifted, half dragged the seventy-five-pound safe from my office closet, dragged it to the kitchen and thudded it onto the floor, flush against the door.

Max sat behind us, watching. Calculating.

Heather leaned into me, almost whispering. "Do you think it will work?"

I said, "Well, I think we'll find one of three things when we get back. One, everything will be fine. Two, the safe will be budged a couple inches, and we'll have a beagle with a very red and throbbing nose. Or three, we may come home and find he's rigged up some elaborate pulley system that's lifted the safe out of his way. If that's the case, I say from now on, we just stock the bottom two shelves with whatever he wants."

We dashed to the store and back in record time. We practically ran into the kitchen and found him lying there, thinking deeply. No sore nose, no pulley system. We sighed big sighs of relief and got the plastic and vinyl childproof strap installed. So far it's done its job. So far . . .

Sam Minier

"Well, at least he's not begging
at the dinner table anymore . . ."

The Offer

We were both pups when my parents got her—I about eighteen months old, she somewhat younger but older by far in wisdom and experience. She had already had a brief career in the movies, having played one of Daisy's puppies in the Dagwood and Blondie films. But now, too old for the part, she had been given to my father in lieu of payment for a script he had turned in. He was a comedy writer for radio, and occasionally, movies, and excelled in writing jokes and scripts but not in collecting the fees owed him.

Her name was Chickie, and she was a wonderful mix of Welsh corgi and bearded collie. A white star blazed on her chest, and she had four white feet and a white-tipped tail to complement her long black fur. Even though she was scarcely over a year old, she was already motherly and sat by my crib for hours on end, making sure that no harm would come to me. If I cried, she would be off to my mother, insisting that she come immediately. If I wanted to play, she would bring toys, hers as well as mine.

My dad caught on that this was a special dog with high intelligence plus something else. He taught her many tricks, learned from the dog trainers at the movie studio. Lassie's trainers gave him pointers on how to get Chickie to respond to hand signals, as well as to climb ladders, bark on cue, walk on beach balls, dance on two legs and jump rope with a willing human. This she did readily and well, but there was more to her still—perhaps one could call it a deep sense of ethics. She seemed virtue incarnate, a Saint Francis of Assisi of dogs, who took on responsibilities of saintly cast. I thought of her as my sister and, what with all our travels, my constant companion and closest friend.

Thus it was a shock when one day one of the actors in a picture my father was working on came home with him, saw Chickie and immediately wanted to buy her.

"Jack," said the actor, "that is the greatest dog I ever saw in my life. I'll give you fifty bucks for that dog."

"Can't do it, pal," said my father. "It's the kid's dog."

The actor persisted. "I'll give you a hundred bucks for the dog. I know you need the money."

Indeed, we did, and driven by the panic of imminent poverty—the one thing he dreaded more than anything else—my father acted in an uncharacteristic manner. Excusing himself, he went into the kitchen to discuss this with my mother.

"Certainly not!" she adamantly declared. "It's Jeanie's dog."

"You're right, Mary," my father sheepishly agreed. "It's just that I think I'm going to lose my job at the studio and am damned scared of not being able to bring home the bacon."

"Well, you certainly cannot bring home the bacon by selling the child's dog," my mother fumed. "Anyway, if we go broke again, I'll just do what I always do—start an acting school for children."

A few days later the actor came back, saying, "Jack, I've got to have that dog on my ranch. I want that dog. I'll give you 250 bucks for the dog."

During this ordeal Chickie and I were sitting on the floor behind the couch, listening in horror. I was already making my running-away plans with her.

"Well, I sure do need the money," said my father. "Just a minute; I've got to talk to my wife."

"Mary, he's offering 250 bucks for the dog! We can always get Jeanie a new dog at the pound!"

"No way!" said my mother.

The next day the actor returned. He had rarely known failure and was not about to start now. "Jack, I'll give you 250 bucks and my secondhand car. I know you need a car to get around."

"Wait a minute," said my father. "I'm sure this time I can convince my wife."

Upon hearing the latest offer, my mother, bless her heart, stormed out of the kitchen, stormed up to the actor and chewed him out.

"Ronald Reagan," she railed, "how dare you try to take away my child's dog!"

At least he knew a good dog when he saw one.

Jean Houston

Sammy's Big Smile

What dogs? These are my children, little people with fur who make my heart open a little wider.

Oprah Winfrey

When I was a child my Aunt Julie had a dog named Sammy, a little black Chihuahua mix with a tongue as long as her body. Sammy could run up one side of your body, lick your face clean and run down the other side before you knew what happened. This adorable black dog always greeted you with a "doggy smile." Sammy owned my Aunt Julie, and everyone in our family knew it.

One afternoon I was visiting my aunt. We were all dressed up and going out. I don't remember the occasion, but I do remember that we were in an awful rush. My family comes from a long line of people who feel that if you're not fifteen minutes early for an event, you are late! As usual, time was of the essence. Sammy, however, wasn't in any rush. The only thing Sammy was interested in was getting some attention.

"No, Sammy, we cannot play," my aunt scolded, "We have *to go! Now!"*

The problem was that we couldn't "go," because Aunt Julie had misplaced her false teeth. The longer we searched for her teeth, the later we got for the event and the angrier Aunt Julie became—and the more attention Sammy seemed to demand. We ignored Sammy's barking, as we looked frantically for the missing dentures.

Finally, Aunt Julie reached her breaking point and gave up. She plunked herself down at the bottom of the stairs and cried. I sat next to her, counseling her with that special brand of wisdom eight-year-olds possess. "It's okay, Aunt Julie, don't cry. We can still go, just don't smile," I said, which made her cry even harder.

At that moment, Sammy gave a few shrill barks, this time from the top of the stairs, and then was quiet. As we turned around to see what she wanted, we both exploded into laughter. There stood a "smiling" Sammy—with Aunt Julie's false teeth in her mouth—her tail wagging a hundred miles an hour. The message in her sparkling eyes was obvious: *I've been trying to tell you for a half hour—I know where your teeth are!* A vision that, thirty years later, still makes me laugh out loud.

Gayle Delhagen

Phoebe's Family

In rural Oklahoma, where I was raised, dogs were big and lived outside. They protected the cattle and barked when someone walked down the dirt road. If the temperature dipped below freezing, they might come inside, but they sat right inside the front door, looking ill at ease until we let them out again in the morning.

Then I met Phoebe.

Around the time that my future husband, Joseph, and I became "more than friends," his family bought a Boston terrier puppy. Phoebe had the bug-eyes and big ears of her breed, and the sharp claws and swift tongue of her age. She was smaller than any dog I'd ever known, but she was pure energy, throwing herself at my legs, clawing her way up my body to nuzzle my face with a cold nose and slobbering tongue. She had her own bed, her own chair and an entire family waiting on her hand and foot, speaking to and about her as if she were not the dog but a newly adopted member of the family. And she was *allergic to grass*. She had to get shots for this condition.

I found all this faintly ridiculous and was uncertain how to treat a dog like Phoebe. Phoebe sensed this. When I came in the door, she bowled me over completely, launching her body through the air to crash into my legs. To defend myself from her claws, I quickly learned to wear jeans when visiting the house. I stood outside the door, steeling myself for her advances, trying to set a cheerful, dog-confident expression on my face in the hopes it would trick her into thinking I knew what I was doing. It never worked. Every time, Phoebe would barrel past everyone to hurl herself at me, and every time, she would be reprimanded by my future in-laws. The only thing worse than being unable to fend off Phoebe's exuberant advances was feeling that her family thought I disapproved of her—and therefore disapproved of them. Every time it happened, they would apologize and hold Phoebe back, saying, "Be still, Phoebe. Stacy doesn't want to pet you."

But the odd thing is that I *did* want to pet her. She was sleek and beautiful, the first Boston terrier I'd seen except in photographs and paintings. She knew how to do all kinds of tricks our farm dogs wouldn't have considered. Her eager eyes and excited, wiggling body made me laugh. She was fun and boisterous, like Joseph's family— just the opposite of my close-knit but quiet Native American family. In the same way that I wasn't sure how to fit in with a family so different from mine, I wasn't quite sure how to make friends with Phoebe, who was so different from every dog I'd ever known.

Joseph was in the army and I was attending college, so we carried on our relationship mostly through letters and phone calls, only getting to see each other in person when he was home on leave. Phoebe grew bigger and smarter, but not less energetic. Because I was an infrequent visitor, she treated me to the grand, excited welcome of a brand-new person every time I came to the house. With other new guests, she would eventually settle down and play fetch or sit on her chair, looking cute. Not with me. No matter how I tried to distract her with toys, her main goal was to stand on my chest, claw at my shirt, lick my nose and bite my long hair. I was trying to impress my future in-laws with my good manners and poise. As you can imagine, it was difficult to be either graceful or witty with an excited dog attempting to clean my eyeglasses with her tongue. Still, I gamely kept trying to find a way to relate to Phoebe that would satisfy us both.

In December 2002 Joseph asked me to marry him, and three months later, he parachuted into Iraq with the 173rd Airborne. I moved nine hours away from our families to attend graduate school in Mississippi—and wait for him. I kept in touch with his family and visited whenever I was home from school. I never did become entirely comfortable with Phoebe, but I grew to value her even more when I saw what a comfort her cheerful, loyal presence was to Joseph's parents during this stressful time.

Joseph was wounded in October 2003 and sent home for two weeks' leave. We were married in a quiet ceremony before he returned to Iraq. Now officially part of the family, I continued to keep in touch with my in-laws as we waited and hoped for Joseph's safe return. Every time I visited them, it was as if Phoebe and I were meeting for the first time. Our relationship became a kind of running joke: "You're a cat person in a dog family!" my niece said. I loved my in-laws, but I worried that I would always be the "cat person." In a dog family, this could be serious.

When Joseph called to say he was coming home, his parents drove to Mississippi to help me move, leaving Phoebe with his grandparents for the two-day trip. On our way back to Oklahoma, Joseph's grandparents called to say that Phoebe, who had been fine when my in-laws left, would not play or eat. We expressed sympathy for her, but we weren't truly worried. We all joked about how spoiled Phoebe was, and I envisioned my father's reaction to the news that *now* Phoebe was visiting a dog psychologist.

When we arrived at their house late that night, we expected a jubilant welcome. Instead, a quiet little Phoebe walked up to us wagging her stub-tail, then lay down under the end table. Everyone petted her and tried to get her to eat, with no success. We decided to take her to the vet first thing in the morning. I was sorry that Phoebe wasn't feeling well—and felt guilty too. I was finally comfortable with this new sick Phoebe, who sat on the floor with her head on my knee, as I petted her gently. It was a drastic change from the tug-of-war using my shirtsleeve and the slobbery game of fetch that had become our routine.

The next morning, Joseph's mother loaded Phoebe into the truck and left. She was back much sooner than we expected, and when she walked in the door, Phoebe was not with her. "She died on the way to the vet," she announced, her usually animated face completely still with grief.

Shock and disbelief pounded through my body. I didn't know what to say. Joseph's father went to his wife and put his arms around her. They cried together, and I was filled with a bittersweet gratitude, knowing that their relationship had served as an example for my husband. He had grown up with the kind of marriage where two people were willing to share this much love for each other, for their children and even for a demanding little dog, no matter how much it might hurt at times.

In my family, we very seldom cry in front of people. Our emotions are shown through our actions, so I put on my shoes and prepared to help bury Phoebe, despite my in-laws' protests that it was too cold. It was a miserable, sleeting day. The ground was a little frozen, and we took turns pounding the shovels into it. Phoebe was wrapped in a quilt with one of her toys. When the little grave under the lilac bush was covered, we patted it down one more time and came inside. As I washed the mud from my hands in the privacy of the bathroom, I cried for Phoebe.

For although I'd never quite learned to handle her, I *had* loved her. From the beginning, she'd pulled me headfirst into the process of becoming comfortable with my new family. And though I was awkward and stiff around her, she never gave up trying to connect with me.

Today, when my in-laws' new Boston terriers, Petey and Lucy, run up to play with me, I know what to do. I roll around on the floor with them—and don't even care if I look silly. I can finally be myself with Joseph's family, who I see now have always welcomed me with open arms. I think Phoebe would be pleased.

Stacy Pratt

A Canine Nanny

The dog was created especially for children.

Henry Ward Beecher

I was physically and emotionally exhausted. At night, I was awake more than I slept, caring for our three-week-old daughter, Abigail. By day, I chased our older daughter, Bridget, an active two-year-old. My already taut nerves began to fray when Abigail developed a mild case of colic. Bridget demanded attention each time her sister fussed. Our dog, a purebred Brittany named Two, was constantly underfoot, and stumbling over her repeatedly did not help my state of mind.

I also felt isolated. We were new to the area, and I didn't know anyone in town. My parents, our nearest relatives, lived 150 miles away. Phoning my mother on the spur of the moment to ask if she'd drop by and watch the kids for an hour while I got some much-needed sleep wasn't realistic. My husband helped as much as he could but needed to focus on his job.

One day Abigail woke from a nap. As babies sometimes

do, she had soiled her clothing and crib bedding. I tried to clean her up as fast as possible, but her cries developed into ear-shattering wails before I was through. I wanted to comfort her, but I was at a loss. I had to wash my hands, I couldn't put her back into the crib and the floor hadn't been vacuumed for days. Strapping her on the changing table, I wedged a receiving blanket between her and the railing. I promised I'd be right back. As her screams followed me into the bathroom, I neared complete meltdown. Women had handled this for generations—why couldn't I cope?

I had just lathered up with soap when Two trotted purposefully past the bathroom door. A moment later the crying ceased. Hurriedly, I dried my hands and entered the nursery to find the Brittany standing on her hind legs, tenderly licking Abigail's ear. The baby's eyes were opened wide in wonder. Two dropped down and wagged her stubby tail in apology. With a canine grin and her ears pushed back as far as they could go, she seemed to say, "I know babies are off limits, but I couldn't help myself."

At that moment, I realized why I had been tripping over Two all the time: she wanted to help! When Bridget was born, Two had enthusiastically welcomed the newest member of her family. But because she had difficulty curbing her energy, we had watched her closely. Now, at six years of age, with a more sedate disposition, Two understood she had to be gentle.

That day marked a turning point for me. During Abigail's fussy moments, I laid her blanket on the floor and placed her next to Two. Often Abigail quieted as she buried her hands and feet in the dog's warm soft fur. Although Two relished her role as babysitter, objecting only when Abigail grabbed a fistful of sensitive flank hair, I still kept a vigilant eye on them, or Abigail would likely have suffered a constant barrage of doggy kisses.

When Abigail turned four, we enrolled her in preschool. Her teacher as well as several of the other parents commented on how she was always the child who reached out to those who were alone. Extending an invitation to join in play, Abigail often stayed by someone's side if she didn't get an answer, talking quietly and reassuringly. I like to think that Two's willingness to remain lying next to a screaming infant somehow contributed to our daughter's sensitivity.

I admit I've spoiled Two since that first day when she comforted Abigail. If I leave the table and a half-eaten meal disappears, I know who the culprit is. But I don't have the heart to punish her for being an opportunist. I'm indebted to her, and losing out on several bites of cold food is a small price to pay.

Two is still part of our family, and although we all dote on her, there is an unmistakable connection between her and Abigail. Now nearly twelve years old, Two has more than her share of aches and pains. During winter, she often rests in front of the heat register. When Abigail wakes in the morning, she covers *her* dog with her old baby blanket and fusses over her. And when Abigail wanders away, Two trails after her, the tattered blanket dragging along on the floor. Two still considers Abigail her special charge, and I'm happy to have her help. I hope they have many more days together, looking after each other with such loving care.

Christine Henderson

Two Old Girls

Wobbles was a fragile, shaken fistful of fur that slipped and slid across the green marble floors of my grandmother's house, her eyes tightly shut to keep out the terrifying sight of our concerned family crowding around her. My grandmother was unimpressed and remained unaffected at the sight of this forlorn, abandoned pup bought from a village lad for the ransom of one rupee (one-fortieth of a dollar). We knew her thoughts on the matter: a dog's place is downstairs, preferably outside the house. Human space could not, by her stringent standards, be shared by an animal, however dear!

"But she's not a dog yet; she's just a puppy," my brother and I cried.

Gran was unmoved by our wails and pleas, as were my two bachelor uncles, who were sticklers for cleanliness and order. A dog of any size, pedigree or shape was still a dog. And our Wobbles was definitely of an undistinguished family tree.

Still Wobbles came to stay—outside only!—growing from a scruffy puppy with unsteady footwork into a medium-sized white mongrel. We grew, too. Time lowers guards, increases acceptance levels and brings patience. A dog in our lives eventually rearranged our inner mental complexities into simpler expressions of affection and emotion.

This was especially evident in Gran. Every afternoon at 1:30, before she ate her own lunch, she'd call for the cook and ask in a vitriolic and imperious tone: "Has any one thought of *her* lunch or are we only interested in our own food?" "Her" referred to Wobbles, the name being quite unpronounceable in the Indian tongue. Gran's English was rudimentary, and she hadn't gotten as far as *W*. My brother and I would smile secretly at each other over our own half-eaten lunches.

When the cook—a moody but brilliant concoctionist— disappeared for a week, we watched in amazement as Gran covered her nose with one hand and carefully took out Wobbles's lunch every day. This was remarkable since Wobbles's lunch consisted of a meat mush or stew. Normally, our rigidly conditioned vegetarian Gran wouldn't consider going close enough to inhale its offensive odor, but she not only smelled the lunch, she also warmed it, then laboriously panted down the twenty-two steps and gave the "lunchtime" signal: banging Wobbles's dish twice on the shed's cement floor, at which sound Wobbles, wriggling joyously, would appear from nowhere.

"You move away from me, you stupid dog. Don't touch me or I'll have to bathe in this afternoon heat. Do you want to kill me with two baths in one day?" Gran asked shrilly, waving her fragile arms as Wobbles whined and wagged her ridiculously curly tail.

But as I looked down from the balcony, I thought I saw— or was it the sun in my eyes?—Gran petting Wobbles with her slippered foot before slowly going up the stairs to the safety of her cool, incense-scented living room.

Several summers later the monsoons came down with a fury. For weeks streets were waterlogged, traffic held up, and pedestrians found themselves in a quandary. One day our family jalopy, trying to make its way through the crowded city in one such rainstorm, became stranded. Two glum-looking uncles, three squirming, sweaty nephews and nieces and our worn-out mother in an after-work state of exhaustion, sat waiting for the already harassed, out-of-control traffic cop to regain his breath and create some semblance of order. Gran was the only family member at home. This meant that, except for the half-blind watchman who was as old as the foundation stone, there was no one to look out for Gran. The grown-ups worried about her as the lightning and thunder crashed and the children giggled and squirmed.

At home, the downpour steadily increased, its volume crashing down on the parapets and balconies, as the old watchman struggled to close the windows against the elements. Once he had accomplished this, the old man sat patiently within range of Gran's call, nodding off as my grandmother counted off prayers on her prayer beads.

The old watchman was Gran's unacknowledged favorite. Tall, snowy-haired, soft-spoken, he had stories by the trainload to tell in his nasal twang—and oh, he loved Wobbles to a fault! The first hot leavened bread rising on his mud-baked oven was always Wobbles's breakfast. This religious old man seemed to see some divinity in this pet of ours. Though Wobbles snarled at the arrogant, swearing cook and snapped at me for tweaking her tail, her behavior was always angelic with the watchman.

The storm continued to rage. The water kept rising, flooding the driveway and then entering the ground floor landing. Gran and the watchman heard a sound: pattering paws and a very wet whine. Suddenly a dripping nose with drooping wet whiskers peered into the room. My grandmother let out a small scream of surprise. The entire three years Wobbles had lived with us, this was only the second time she had trespassed and entered Gran's spotless living room. The old watchman got busy with his head cloth wiping Wobbles, while my horrified Gran watched the puddle from Wobbles's dripping coat grow ever larger on her precious marble floor. What could she do? None of her kitchen rags could be used for the purpose of swabbing dog water off the floor!

All of a sudden, there was a large crack outside the window as lightning brought down a sizable portion of the blackberry tree in our yard. Ears flattened, Wobbles howled piteously and crawled from under our watchman's caressing hands to lie shivering near Gran's feet. The terrified dog refused to budge. Gran, solidly ignoring the errant gate-crasher, continued counting her beads. This was the scene that greeted us when our tired, fidgety lot finally returned home.

After that day, although no one ever spoke of it, whenever there were thunderstorms, the dog came to lie at Gran's feet. Wobbles had won Gran's crabby old heart!

Seven years later, Wobbles passed away quietly—lying on the driveway, just like that—on a scorching May afternoon. The watchman, blinder and older, came to tell my grandmother that the gardener and cook were taking Wobbles away. I was sitting beside Gran doing homework. At the news, Gran lay motionless with eyes closed.

All she said was, "Give her some water to drink." (Hindu last rites include wetting the lips of the dying with holy water.)

The old watchman nodded and shuffled off. The room was silent. From her tightly shut eyes, protected by her horn-rimmed spectacles, a solitary tear coursed down Gran's wrinkled cheek—and then another and another.

I knew it was up to me. I stood up and prepared to go out and say good-bye to Wobbles. From me—and from Gran.

Atreyee Day

A Dog's Love

After two months of my puppy playing tug-of-war with me, one day he just stopped. No matter how much I dangled the rope in front of Rusty, he would not pull on it. The most he would do was take it and chew on it, but the second my hand touched the rope, he would drop it.

Several days later he began to lay his head on my stomach when I sat on the couch. This was cute until he began to growl at my husband or daughter when they approached me. It was irritating, but didn't seem too serious until he actually nipped my daughter for jumping on me. After that, my husband and I decided that we needed to find Rusty a new home, probably one without any children. We thought it was very odd because he had been so very friendly and good with our daughter up until that incident.

Weeks later when we had finally settled on a new home for our puppy, I discovered I was pregnant. My husband and I felt that Rusty had somehow sensed that I was pregnant before we did and, with his odd behavior, was only trying to protect the baby growing inside me. I was the happiest I had been in weeks. We called the people we had found to give Rusty a new home and told them we had changed our minds.

Later that day I called our veterinarian's office and told them what had been happening. Apparently, this is normal for dogs who have developed a strong attachment to females. They suggested that my husband and daughter approach me at a slower pace and try to be gentler when they touched me.

We tried this, and after a week or so, Rusty began to ease up and let them sit by me. He continued to rest his head on my stomach and acted protectively when he felt I was threatened. As time went by he began to bark at me if I lifted anything heavier than clothes or if I started to clean the house. By the time I was three months pregnant, he even pulled on my pant leg if I was on my feet for too long. As soon as I sat down, Rusty would let go and lie at my feet or next to me with his head on my stomach. He often fell asleep this way and would wake up if I moved. Until that time I had no idea that dogs could be so protective or so sensitive to their humans' needs.

When I reached the four-month point in my pregnancy, Rusty's behavior toward me changed abruptly. One night, I was sitting on the couch watching TV when he got up on the couch and laid his head on my stomach. Nothing unusual about that—until he jumped back up and started barking, looking directly at my stomach. My husband and I were baffled.

After that Rusty would not go anywhere near my stomach. He let me pet him for a few minutes but no more. He no longer seemed comfortable around me for any length of time. I grew increasingly nervous as the days passed. I just knew that Rusty was trying to tell me something. My husband insisted I was being silly because I was not having any problems with my pregnancy and there were no signs to indicate that anything was wrong.

A week later I went to an appointment with my doctor—and discovered that the baby's heart had stopped beating.

It was what Rusty had been trying to tell me.

I was crushed, left to wait out the miscarriage I would soon have. After returning home from the doctor's, I could tell that Rusty sensed how upset I was, but he still kept his distance. It was the same wary distance he had kept for the last week.

My husband was still at work and my daughter at school. Miserable, I sat down on the couch and began to cry. Rusty slowly inched closer and closer to me. Finally, he jumped on the couch. I could tell that he was tense. He sat stiffly, making sure to stay away from my stomach. As I continued to weep, he sat beside me, watching me, his eyes full of concern. Then slowly, he leaned over and I felt his tongue on my face, licking away the tears that rolled down my cheek. This released a fresh flood of tears. I wrapped my arms around him, hugging him tightly. He stayed close, licking me and letting me cry my heart out into his warm, furry neck. His body slowly relaxed and soon I felt better, soothed by his loving presence.

It took me two weeks to miscarry. The whole time Rusty would not leave my side. He followed me wherever I went. If I sat on the couch, he was right there next to me, doing all he could to comfort me. Whatever deep natural instinct had kept him away from me had been overridden by his care and concern for me. I was so grateful. Rusty's love was the bright spot in that dark time in my life.

Kelly Munjoy

Lady Abigail

"Why don't you get a better job?"

"Why don't you get up and clean the house?"

My boyfriend hurled these insults at me during yet another of our frequent fights. I had heard it all before:

"You know, if you'd just lose ten pounds, you'd be really pretty."

"I don't care what you do tonight; I'm going out with the guys. . . . No, I don't know when I'll be back, why don't you go out with your friends? Oh, yeah, I forgot: you don't have any. Look, do whatever you want, just quit hassling me, would ya? Oh, and don't forget you're going to have to cover rent this month, I'm gonna be a bit short."

During these sessions, my mind always raged from beneath my apparently cool exterior. *You know he's wrong, why do you put up with it? Out with his friends? Yeah, right— wonder how many of those are women. You're the only one who's paid rent in almost six months; why don't you just kick him out?*

They were all compelling points. The only real argument my heart had was: *What if he's right? What if I am too fat or too short or too quiet for anyone else to love me?* It was this single fear that kept me clinging by my fingernails to a miserable, failing relationship.

At twenty-two years old, I found myself on a battle-ground, waging war with my constantly drooping self-esteem. To escape, I did animal-rescue work—going to the shelter, as well as fostering numerous cats and small dogs and finding good loving homes for them all, oftentimes maintaining contact through pictures and e-mail. I sometimes thought that my frequent trips to the shelter were really a form of therapy rather than a true offer of volunteerism. Sure, I always had Milk Bones and tennis balls to hand out, but I got just as much—if not more—from the animals' attention as they got from mine.

After our fight that day I headed to the shelter. Walking up and down the rows, I stroked soft noses, saying hi to the more excitable and offering treats to any and all who came forward. It was not uncommon to see four or five dogs in each pen—the sheer number of animals that came through the system every day never failed to blow my mind. While passing out goodies, I came to a pen where there were four large dogs, three of whom were jumping and yipping at the door, wiggling in their excitement, while the fourth, a large black female, remained huddled in the far corner, folded in on herself as if she was trying her hardest to disappear altogether. She looked exactly like I felt.

"Hello, sweetheart, it's okay, I'm not here to hurt you," I murmured, hoping to stir some reaction from her. I received a slow thump of the tail for my effort, but it was apparently not enough to warrant an actual glance. Persisting, I knelt down, speaking softly and offering encouragement.

"Come here, sweetie, come get a treat." I dangled the Milk Bone tantalizingly in front of me, but still just outside the cage door. One chocolate-brown eye peeked at me from the large mass of black fur, and she slowly uncurled, revealing the boxy frame of a startlingly large Labrador.

"That's it. Good puppy, come here and say hi." One of her pen mates took that opportunity to snap at the timid female, sending her scuttling back to her corner in fear. Her current living situation seemed to mirror my own.

Frustrated, I yelled for one of the other volunteers.

"That's Abby," the volunteer offered when I inquired about the Lab. "Her owners moved and dumped her off about a week ago. She's an adult spayed female, probably between three and seven if you want my guess, not terribly friendly, but doesn't cause any trouble. She doesn't seem to want to eat much, just sort of hangs out in that corner all day. Not a bad dog really, just not too much personality if you know what I mean."

"How could you possibly know that?" I snapped at him. "Maybe she's just frightened. Look at the poor thing!" I clamped my mouth shut, my eyes growing large. Oh, for goodness sake! It didn't take a rocket scientist to figure out why I had tried to bite his head off. "I'm sorry, I didn't mean that, just been a bad day so far," I added hastily. "Could I go in and see her?" As I watched the poor dog, my heartstrings were stretching, becoming more and more taut as my conscience eagerly plucked away at them. Though the thick black tail thumped twice at the continued attention, Abby still refused to lift her head or venture toward the door.

My mind was in a whirl: *If you bring this dog home, it's going to be World War III! Just one more thing to fight about. Little dogs are one thing, but a dog this size is a lot of work. Besides, someone will adopt her, and if not, maybe she's better off anyway. Who knows where you're going to be in a month, six months? You can barely make your rent as it is, and the landlord will definitely kick you out if you come home with a big dog like that. It wouldn't be fair to her. Just forget about it.*

The volunteer nodded. "You're welcome to go in, but I doubt you'll get much response. Don't get too close too fast, she might be snappy. Let me get the other three outside for you."

Stepping into the mass of furry bodies, the volunteer pulled Jerky Treats (otherwise known as "bits of heaven" in dog terms) from his ripped jean pocket and tossed them into the far side of the divided kennel. The Mexican jumping beans followed with lightning speed and within seconds they were devouring their treats in the exterior section of the run. In their wake, he slowly dropped the heavy plastic divider, then turned and stepped out, leaving the pen door open for me.

Stepping into the tiny square of space, I squatted across from Abby, offering her my hand as I did so. It was then that she lifted her regal head and looked me full in the face, spearing me with the most heartrending pair of doesn't-anyone-in-the-world-care-anymore? chocolate-brown eyes that I had ever seen. I felt my gut drop to my knees. "Oh, sweetheart . . . you lost your whole family, didn't you? Your whole life. I'm so sorry," I whispered, tilting my head down toward her ear. Uncurling slowly, Abby took a hesitant step forward, then another, and then suddenly she was pushing her large head into the warmth of my jacket, tucking herself up under my arm with her tail thumping wildly. My hand passed over the dusty black coat, picking up flea dirt, malnutrition and heartbreak all in one swipe.

I'd worked in rescue for the better part of six years, had held animals when they breathed their last breaths, had seen what was left of pets who had been abused for years, and yet had never in my life felt as moved as I did with this dog cuddled against me, begging me with her eyes to take her out of this awful, scary place. And somehow, I knew I needed her as much as she needed me. When I shifted my weight, preparing to rise, Abby lifted her head and proceeded to lap at my face with her long pink tongue. "All right, angel, you've convinced me," I murmured, realizing the decision had already been made—whether by me, Abby or perhaps even the Lord himself, I wasn't quite sure. I stepped out of the run with a promise of a hasty return.

Walking into the front office, I cornered the shelter director. "What can you tell me about the female black Lab in pen 41?"

Because of the frequency of my visits, Kelly and I were on a first-name basis, and she knew she didn't have to pull any punches. She watched my face for a moment before reaching under the counter to pull out a clipboard. After flipping through what seemed like an infinite number of sheets, she stopped, pointing her finger at the top of the page. "Her name is Abby, she's a four-year-old spayed female, been here since Wednesday of last week. Dropped off with the moving-and-can't-take-with story. Haven't had a single soul take a second look at her. She's big, she's all black and she's shy, not a good combination for quick adoption. As of right now she's scheduled to be put down on Friday unless a miracle happens. She's also registered, in case any one really cares, previous owners dropped off her papers when they dropped off their responsibility. I know you work with the small dogs most of the time, Jen, but I'm sure you already know that large black dogs are the last to get chosen. If we can find her a foster, she might open up a little, but here she's just not going to make it."

My mind was already made up. "If you can clear her, I'll take her right now. I'll take her home myself . . . she's just got to get out of here."

"You're sure about this?"

"Just show me where to sign, Kelly."

Ten minutes later Abby crept slowly out of the shelter at the end of an old knotted leash Kelly had scrounged up. Surprisingly, she hopped up into the passenger seat of my beat-up, pickle-green Buick with little coaxing and settled in quickly. Curling up in the seat in her usual tight ball, her only concession to her changed circumstance was to stretch her neck across the armrest so her head could rest on my thigh. She slept for the whole drive to the vet's office, heaving deep sighs every so often, and occasionally lifting one sleepy eyelid, as if to confirm that I was still there.

Abby's medical checkup was less than stellar: she was covered in fleas, suffering from a nasty ear infection, and to make matters worse, she was heartworm positive. I left with medication to heal her ear, which had to be done before her heartworm treatment could be considered safe.

Her arrival home brought about the expected blow-up, but her steady form sitting quietly at my side kept me from backing down. When the shouting was over, I packed my things and left. With my family's support, I got my own Lab-friendly apartment and my life started to take a slow turn for the better.

A round of uncomfortable weeks began for Abby with her first heartworm treatment, during which time she absolutely refused to let me out of her sight. She would wait just outside the bathroom door to make sure I didn't accidentally get flushed away and would follow me from room to room, regardless of how exhausted it seemed to make her. Luckily, I was working for the same wonderful veterinarian who was administering her heartworm treatment, and was able to bring her to work with me each day so she could rest and still watch me as I went about my daily activities.

Once her treatment was complete, and after a few months of constant TLC, her coat took on a glorious blue-black sheen, her eyes regained a beautiful twinkle and her personality took a leap for the stars. Abby, or Lady Abigail as her papers dubbed her, proved herself to be a tender and ever-loyal companion. As she started to feel better, she revealed a friendly, inquisitive side and insisted on meeting and greeting everyone she came across. This habit eventually led to Abby's therapy dog certification, and soon we were visiting hospitals and nursing homes in our area, my wonderful dog relishing the attention she received and offering her silent support to all she met.

Five years have come and gone. Abby and I have beaten our demons together. I have come to a whole new understanding of myself as an individual, and Abby knows that she need never worry about being abandoned again. I have recently married the love of my life, a man who respects me as an equal and treats me like the beautiful, intelligent woman that I am. He is also working hard at turning Abby into a spoiled, eighty-pound "daddy's girl." My husband and I recently built a home and are looking forward to starting a family soon.

Through all these changes, Abby remains my steadfast companion. She often sits at my side, laying her head against my thigh and giving me a healthy dose of those powerful eyes as if to say, *Thank you for saving me . . . I'll always love you.* I wish so much that I could explain to her that it was she who did all the saving, and that "always" just isn't going to be long enough for me.

Jennifer Remeta

$\overline{\underline{5}}$

A FURRY R$_X$

I have found that when you are deeply troubled there are things you get from the silent, devoted companionship of a dog that you can get from no other source.

Doris Day

Willow and Rosie:
The Ordinary Miracle of Pets

*D*ogs are our link to paradise. They don't know
evil or jealousy or discontent.

Milan Kundera

In the early morning hours of September 13, 2001, the
Sheraton Hotel in Crystal City, Virginia, was teeming with
military personnel—setting up tables, installing phone
lines, laying computer cables. Chaplains, Red Cross volunteers, FEMA (Federal Emergency Management
Agency), the Salvation Army, everyone had a purpose
amid the controlled chaos.

The hotel was the official assistance center for
Pentagon families waiting for news on the fate of loved
ones. It was less than forty-eight hours since the 9/11
assault on America, and the atmosphere was one of
immense sorrow, bewilderment and tension—hardly the
time or place for dogs. As Sue and Lee Peetoom made
their way through the busy operations with their two
Labrador retrievers, Rosie and Willow, they saw the questioning looks on the faces of people they passed. Several

times, the Peetooms heard, "What are dogs doing here?"

Rosie and Willow, both over ten years of age, were veteran therapy dogs with Spiritkeepers out of Fredericksburg, Virginia. Certified through Therapy Dogs International (TDI), they wore the official insignia on the red bandannas tied around their necks. The volunteer coordinator had never heard of the concept of bringing dogs to comfort people at a trauma site, but she welcomed them anyway and invited them to stay the day. Sue and Lee and their dogs were set up in the path between the hotel ballroom, now dubbed "the briefing room," and all the services being assembled for grieving relatives.

Two big dogs in the middle of a passageway swelling with arriving families could hardly be missed, so before long, people became curious and asked about them. As Sue and Lee explained the purpose of therapy dogs, Rosie and Willow wagged their tails and snuggled in to receive lots of pats and hugs. Soon chaplains as well as military personnel were stopping by to see what it was all about.

That afternoon, hundreds of people gathered in the ballroom for the briefing. When it ended, unimaginable sorrow hung over the place. Silently they filed out—parents clung to their children, elderly couples held hands as they walked in pain. But as the first of the crowd neared the dogs, Rosie and Willow stood up ready to receive them. Kids came over to pet them. Then their families joined in. A military escort leaned down to hug Willow. There were chaplains. Then volunteers. The dogs graciously took them all in.

Across the hall, a serious-looking officer watched. When the crush of people passed, he stepped over to say hello, giving each dog a pat before he moved on.

The officer turned out to be the man in charge, General John Van Alstyne. At his request the dogs were asked to return. And they did—every day for the month the center was active. Backed up by forty-two teams from therapy groups in Virginia and Maryland, the dogs became a symbol of strength and love for all.

According to Sue, no words could express the incredible sadness they witnessed. There was the leather-clad biker who sat on the floor, his tattoo-covered arms draped over Willow and Rosie as he sobbed into their fur. His wife had perished inside the Pentagon. And the woman who became so overwhelmed with grief, not even the chaplains could console her. Rosie was called in and, laying her head in the woman's lap, gently licked her hands. The woman wrapped her arms around the big dog and for ten minutes they stayed like that, Rosie accepting all her sorrow until her tears subsided.

Two women waited to learn the fate of their missing husbands—one with three toddlers and a baby on the way, the second a recent arrival from Central America. Neither one spoke English. The dogs needed no words to comfort them. A child who couldn't face a family visit to the site where his daddy was lost chose instead to find comfort with the dogs.

Hundreds of people with eyes full of pain still stopped with a smile, no matter how small, to say hello and hug Rosie and Willow. General Van Alstyne came by several times a day to give the dogs cookies and take a break from the grief, always expressing his gratitude for the important work of the therapy team. A chaplain confessed to pretending to be a "therapy dog" by barking and acting silly for the children who gathered in the hallway each morning to await their arrival.

Sue has vivid memories of the other gentle "comfort dogs" as they became known—from Yorkies to Newfies, pit bulls to greyhounds and mixed breeds of every size— all putting in fourteen-hour days to ease the pain of those who lost so much and refresh others who gave so much of themselves. A hundred times a day people stopped to thank them.

At the one-month memorial service with President Bush, the therapy teams were honored. In preparation for closing the center, a four-foot-tall plush dog was positioned in a place of honor. Throughout the course of that final day, it became covered with mementos from all the people involved: meal tickets, Red Cross tissues, military insignias, caps, business cards, even a Bible. A dog tag inscribed, "Therapy Dog" was hung round its neck. Willow's official scarf was added, and the "dog" was presented to the general as a symbol of the center's achievements.

Since the tragic events of 9/11, both Willow and Rosie have passed on. One can't help but believe those two gentle angels were greeted with hugs in heaven by the people who perished that day.

Audrey Thomasson

At Face Value

About five years ago I had a recurring dream. The message was clear and precise, directing me to go to a specific shelter and adopt a particular dog. It was obvious from the dream that I would know the dog by something unusual about its face. But when I woke up, I could never recall what the unique facial feature was. I could only remember it was important for identifying the right dog.

I was very curious and felt compelled to follow the instructions in the dream. So early one Saturday morning, I went to the specified shelter to check the available canine adoptees. After looking carefully at all the dogs, I was disappointed that not one dog had anything unusual about its face. There were lots of cute puppies and just as many appealing older dogs, but I didn't feel a connection to any of them.

On my way out of the shelter, I noticed a box of puppies just outside of view from the main area. My attention was drawn to one puppy in particular, and I decided to take a closer look. The one puppy appeared to have no fur on his face, while the rest of the litter were all black with spots of white. I was worried about the strange-looking pup, and hoped he hadn't been injured. The puppies were a mix of black Lab and Chesapeake Bay retriever, called Chesapeake Labs. Each pup was named after a type of pasta. The one who had captured my interest was Fettuccine. On closer inspection, I realized he did have fur on his face, but it was a very odd shade of gray that made it look like skin. Satisfied that he was okay, I turned to leave the shelter.

And then it hit me: *The face—it's the dog with the unusual face!* Immediately, I returned to the puppy and picked him up. As I lifted him from the box, his large and clumsy paws reached over my shoulders to cling tightly to my back. We bonded instantly, and I knew we belonged together. I could not leave without him, so I headed for the adoption desk. In that short amount of time, the gray-faced pup had wrapped his paws around my heart.

Meeting with the adoption counselor, I was informed that a family had already selected him. There was, however, still a slight chance since the family had not made their final decision. They were choosing between Fettuccine, the gray-faced pup, and his littermate, a female named Penne. I decided to wait for their decision. I hung around outside, watching the door. After an anxiety-filled hour, I saw the family leaving the shelter carrying Fettuccine. I began to cry inside. Then I realized a member of the family, the mother, was walking straight toward me. They knew I was awaiting their decision, and I was prepared for the worst. My heart pounded and I stood frozen in place as she approached. For a moment she didn't say a word or give any indication of her decision, then, with a broad grin, she said, "Here's your dog."

I was speechless as grateful tears gushed from my eyes. I hugged the puppy to me and again felt those big front paws securely hugging my back. Although I was thankful to have him then, I didn't know how thankful I would be later.

I took the gray-faced pup home and named him Dominic, keeping Fettuccine as his middle name. From the start, he was not at all a typical, rambunctious puppy. He was very calm, serious and didn't play much. However, he was obedient, intelligent and very attentive. We lived happily together, and as Dom grew into a healthy, robust dog, he became my valued companion.

When Dominic was two years old, I was diagnosed with a seizure disorder. I was having full-blown grand mal seizures as well as milder petit mal types. These seizures caused me to collapse into unconsciousness. Upon awakening, I would always find Dom on top of me. At first I was not at all happy to have a ninety-pound dog lying on top of me, until I came to realize he was preventing me from hurting myself by restricting my thrashing movements.

During mild seizures, Dom stood rock solid, so I could hold onto his front legs until the seizure passed. He was also helpful after a seizure. As I began to regain consciousness, I was aware of his "voice." Focusing on his barking became a means to bring me back to full consciousness. I soon came to rely on Dom to warn me before a seizure would take hold, and we'd work through it together, each of us knowing what we had to do till the crisis passed. Dom was my four-legged medical assistant.

During my worst period, I had five grand mal seizures a day. They came without warning, but the force of the seizures and the physical injuries I received were minimized when the vigilant Dom sprang into action. Dominic, the puppy I was led to in a dream, turned out to be a natural-born seizure-assistance dog—a one-in-a-million pup with astounding instincts.

For about a year I had seizures every day, then they gradually started to subside. I am now well, and seizure-free. Dom has returned to his previous daily doggy activities, though still watchful of me and ready to be of assistance.

He finds ways to help out around the house—and I indulge his sense of duty, since that is what he lives for.

Some heroes wear a uniform or a badge; my hero wears fur.

Linda Saraco

Abacus

The soul is the same in all living creatures, although the body of each is different.

Hippocrates

A lot has been written about what dogs can do for people. Dogs lead the blind, aid the deaf, sniff out illegal substances, give us therapeutic hope and joy, make us laugh with their idiosyncrasies, and give us companionship—to name just a few of their many talents. But what about our duty to dogs—what about their needs, wants, hopes and joys? And what about the ones most people do not want to adopt—the ones who aren't completely healthy or cute? This is a story of just such a dog.

I first learned about Abacus while doing some Internet research on special-needs dogs. I had become interested in special-needs dogs after losing my brother Damon, who was left paraplegic after an accident in 1992 and committed suicide three years later. Damon loved exploring the outdoors and preferred the freedom of driving a truck to working behind a desk all day. Losing those options was difficult enough for him, but the thought that nobody would want him was more than he could deal with. His death made me more aware of the challenges that people—and animals—with disabilities must face.

I knew my husband and I couldn't get a dog because of the no-pets policy at our rental, but I couldn't keep myself from researching them. On *www.petfinder.com*, there was a listing for a very handsome fellow named Abacus who was staying at Animal Lifeline, a no-kill animal shelter located near Des Moines, Iowa. Abacus had originally been rescued as a stray puppy two years earlier by the kind staff at a veterinary hospital in Nebraska after being hit by a car and subsequently paralyzed. Normally, a stray dog with partial paralysis would have been euthanized because few people want to adopt a dog in that condition. But the veterinarian and his staff saw something special and endearing in Abacus. They took him under their wing and eventually entrusted the shelter in Iowa with his care.

The picture of Abacus on the shelter's Web site showed a largish black dog with a rubber ducky in a hydrotherapy tub, enjoying a workout to help improve the muscle tone in his paralyzed hind legs. Through his photograph alone, Abacus cast his spell on me and I was never the same.

I couldn't get the image of Abacus out of my mind and felt compelled to visit him—even though I knew I couldn't adopt him. My husband, John, supportive and understanding as always, drove with me on the nearly two-hour drive to the special-needs animal shelter. When I first saw Abacus in his quarters at the shelter, my breath stopped for a few seconds. It was a little disconcerting to see his atrophied hind legs, the result of his paralysis, but his exuberance and happy-go-lucky attitude quickly masked his physical challenges. I was struck by the sheer joy he radiated. His wide, loving eyes stayed in my mind and heart long after we drove away from the shelter.

Meeting Abacus inspired me to start looking for a house to buy instead of continuing to rent. Soon we found a nice rural home with acreage at an affordable price. I applied to adopt Abacus, and we were able to celebrate his third birthday by bringing him home with us a few weeks later.

Life with Abacus required a few adjustments. I learned daily therapeutic exercises for his hind legs, and how to get his strong, wiggly body into his wheelchair (called a K-9 cart) by myself. His castle, when I am not home, is a special padded room with a comfy mattress and lots of blankets and washable rugs. Often, I wrap his paralyzed legs in gauze bandages to help protect them from the abrasions he gets from dragging them on the floor or from the uncontrollable muscle spasms that occur in his hindquarters.

When Abacus is inside the house but out of his cart, he scoots around using his strong, muscular front legs. At times he can support his hind legs for a while, which looks a bit like a donkey kicking and occasionally causes him to knock things down as he maneuvers around the house. But when he is in his K-9 cart, Abacus can run like the wind. We have to supervise our canine Evel Knievel in his cart since he can tip it over and get stuck when taking curves too fast.

Even though he requires extra care, I have never thought of Abacus as a burden. Living with him is a privilege. Enthusiastic about everything, he treats strangers like long-lost friends. And as much as he loves food, he loves cuddles even more. His zest for life inspires me, as well as others who meet him. Some people who see him feel pity for his challenges, but I always point out that he is not depressed or daunted by his differentness. I am sure if Abacus could speak, he would say that special-needs dogs can live happy, full lives and can enrich the lives of their adopters as much as—if not more than—a "normal" dog can.

The main reason I adopted Abacus was because I wanted to give him the comfort and security of a forever home, but in addition to that, I felt that he could help me give encouragement to others. A principle I have always lived by was shaped by part of an Emily Dickinson poem I learned as a child:

> If I can ease one life the aching
> Or cool one pain,
> Or help one fainting robin
> Unto his nest again,
> I shall not live in vain.

I only wish my brother could have known Abacus. For although animal-assisted therapy is not a cure-all, I believe a seed of hope can be planted in the heart of a physically, mentally or emotionally challenged child—or adult—when he sees a special-needs animal living a full and happy life in a loving home.

To spread this hope, I worked with Abacus to train him to become a certified therapy dog. After passing an evaluation this year, Abacus has begun visiting a school for special children. My employers at Farm Sanctuary—an organization that understands the mutual healing power that people and animals share—graciously grant me permission to take time off work for these twice-monthly weekday visits. Abacus looks forward to these excursions and always wows the kids (and teachers) with his bouncy "Tigger-like" personality. On occasion, his visiting attire includes his snazzy Super Dog cape that flies behind him as he zooms around in his wheelchair. Abacus always leaves happiness in his wake.

Living with a special-needs animal isn't for everyone,

but it is a rare treat for those who choose to take it on. In fact, my experience with Abacus has inspired me to adopt a number of other special-needs animals over the years. All of them have more than repaid my investment of time and energy by being constant positive reminders that life's challenges need not be met with despair and negativity. Their love is healing, their appreciation rewarding, and their quirky personalities add priceless meaning to my life.

Meghan Beeby

Dog Days of School

Teaching second grade is always a challenge. Each student arrives at school with his own needs and difficulties. One particular year a student I'll call Billy challenged me with his behavior as well as his academic requirements. He struggled daily with his overpowering emotions and often became angry—sometimes even violent. I knew that in order to make academic progress, his emotional outbursts needed to be controlled.

One way I tried to help Billy was to have him come directly into the classroom when he arrived at school, rather than playing on the playground. Billy liked the extra attention before school, and I could make sure his school day started out on a positive note. I also found that when Billy came to the classroom early, he avoided the usual playground fights and arguments caused by his volatile temper.

Oftentimes Billy's mom would call me to alert me to a particularly emotional morning at home. On those mornings, I would focus on defusing his anger and calming him down before the other students arrived. Billy's mother loved him and wanted desperately for him to improve and do well. As the weeks passed, home communication, firm boundaries, and love and care were helping Billy make big strides in controlling his own behavior, yet he still lapsed now and then.

One week our class was studying pets. I thought one way to bring hands-on learning into the classroom was to bring my dog Rocky to school for the day. Rocky is a two-year-old shih tzu. A perky, friendly creature, Rocky loves people—especially children. He was raised with my own children, so he is used to being petted, played with and snuggled. I was confident that the class would adore him, and I knew that Rocky would love all the attention from twenty eager, excited seven-year-olds.

The morning of Rocky's big day at school began as normal. Arriving at school early, I prepared activities focused on dog themes. Our math for the day was to measure Rocky in as many ways as we could think of. We were going to measure the length of his ears and body, his weight, and even how much water he drank. The read-aloud story I planned for the day was about a dog. I was looking forward to a fun day.

A few minutes before I expected Billy to arrive, the phone rang. It was Billy's mom. She was calling to tell me that he had a rough morning at home and I might need to spend some time getting him settled. As I was talking to his mom, Billy stormed into the classroom. To Billy's surprise, Rocky immediately ran up to his new "friend," wagging his tail. Billy knelt and Rocky licked Billy's face, slathering him with doggy affection. Billy couldn't resist Rocky's charm. The little boy began giggling and laughing as his anger melted away. The happy sound of his laughter traveled through the phone line to his mother's ears. In a quavering voice she asked me, "Is that Billy?"

"Yes," I replied. "I brought my dog to school today, and Billy and he are getting acquainted."

"It sounds like Billy will be just fine," she said, her voice filled with relief.

I couldn't have chosen a better day to have Rocky at the door.

Throughout the day, Billy showed his caring and loving nature. He never left Rocky's side and took responsibility for Rocky by feeding him, being gentle with him and even shushing the other students when Rocky took a snooze.

Billy was known for doing anything he could to avoid reading. But on this day he found a good dog story, *Clifford's Puppy Days,* and read it to Rocky. Rocky was a good listener and never minded if Billy missed a word. I marveled at the sight of Billy reading happily. My little dog was able to transform Billy's day from one of anger and frustration, to one of joy, laughter, gentleness and unconditional love.

That day Rocky did more than just help me with teaching; he helped to change the life of a child. After that Billy's behavior definitely improved. For, thanks to his mom, Billy soon had a dog friend of his very own at home.

Jean Wensink

Raising a Star

From the very first meeting that I attended, I knew that raising a guide-dog puppy was the project for me. My dad had other ideas. He thought the responsibilities required were too much for a sixth-grader to handle. After months of my lobbying, begging, sobbing and working my tail off to convince him, he finally agreed that I could raise a puppy. And so I began my journey as a guide-dog puppy raiser—a journey that lasted six years.

After I turned in my application, I still had a long time to wait before a puppy would be available. In the interim I began to puppy-sit. When the dogs I cared for dug holes in the yard, I thought, *Oh . . . my puppy will be different.* I was in a euphoric (and definitely ignorant) state. The days seemed to pass so slowly without a puppy to raise.

On Christmas Day, 1992, after all the presents under the tree were unwrapped, I still had the gifts in my stocking to open. I pulled candy, brushes and Silly Putty out of the overflowing stocking, but when I reached the bottom, my fingers closed around something unlike anything I had ever felt in a stocking. It was a piece of fabric. I pulled it out and saw it was a tiny green puppy jacket. Attached to the jacket was half a sheet of paper with a note written on it:

Dear Laura,
  You will need this on January 6 when you come to get me in the Escondido Kmart.
  I am a male yellow Lab and my name begins with B.

When I finished reading the note, I burst into tears. My puppy! I could hardly wait for the day when I would meet the newest member of my family.

On January 6, 1993, I received my first puppy: a yellow Lab named Bennett. He was the first of a series of guide-dog puppies—Hexa, Brie, Flossie and Smidge, to name a few—that I raised over the next six years. Each of the puppies holds a special place in my heart, a place each won as soon as I saw him or her. Who could resist that small, bouncy bundle of fur placed into your arms for you to love and care for?

I found raising guide-dog puppies to be a deeply reward-ing service project, yet sometimes I wondered who was raising whom. Each one of my canine teachers imparted lessons of love, pain, separation, forgiveness and patience. Four legs and a tail motivated me to do things I would have never attempted on my own. And when you know you'll have just 365 days to spend together, you learn to cherish each moment.

During that year, I organized my time carefully, making sure to include all the required training, such as obedi-ence, grooming and socialization. To help these future guide dogs acclimate to many different environments, I had to take each puppy with me just about everywhere I went, sometimes even to school! I admit that at first this special privilege was the main reason I had wanted to raise a guide-dog puppy, but the meaning of the project grew much deeper as time passed.

The many hours I spent in public with each dog turned out to be a fraction of the time and energy I spent with him or her at home. It's then that the individual raiser adds his or her own personality to each dog. In my experience, it was the minute or two that I took before leaving for school or going to bed—just to stop and pet my puppy or tell him that I loved him—that created the strongest bond.

And that love flowed both ways. Every time a puppy would jump up onto my lap and kiss me one last time for the night, I'd forget all about the unhappy manager who threw us out of the grocery store that day, the hole being dug to China in the backyard and the potty calls at three in the morning. It takes so little extra time to raise not just a well-trained dog, but a loving dog—a dog who will bring such light into a nonsighted person's life.

At the end of the year, it is time for the puppy to leave. The day arrives sorrowfully for me, even though she suspects nothing. The whole day I'm filled with memories of the year we spent with one another: long days at school together, hours spent swimming in the pool and cuddly moments watching TV. But the time has come for the puppy to move on, to do what I have raised her to do. Tears fill my eyes and rush down my cheeks as I say the final good-bye, then take off her leash and hand her over to her new school. Before she even leaves, I miss her, wondering if the important work I have done is worth the anguish. The squirming, brand-new puppy placed into my hands cannot be compared to her. I know I will soon be filled with the same love for this new little one, but I will never forget the one that's leaving.

For six long months, I wait for her weekly school reports, opening them eagerly when they arrive. Finally, she has made it: she graduates from school and is matched with a blind person.

The long trek to San Francisco would be worth it just to catch a glimpse of her, but I usually get to spend the whole day with her and the person she will help. Before that day, I feel as if no one could deserve her love and affection, but I always change my mind as soon as I meet her new partner.

Seeing them together, once again my perception of the project is lifted to new heights. The puppy who pulled me across the yard is now a sleek, gorgeous, grown-up dog who guides a nonsighted person across the busiest streets in America. They are no longer a human being and a dog, but a single unit that moves with more grace than a world-class ballerina. To know I have been a part of creating this team is enough to erase the last vestige of the pain of missing her. She has a new job now. She has matured from the puppy who comforted me, loved me and was my best friend, to become a guide dog: a lifeline for someone who needs her. And though a single star is missing from my sky, she has opened up a whole universe for another.

Laura Sobchik

Star Power

Our perfect companions never have fewer than four feet.

Colette

"How much longer can I live with this *loneliness?*" Mom sighed heavily into the phone after her last remaining friend in Florida had died.

For many years, Mom had relied on their daily conversations, filled with laughter, to nourish her soul. She clearly thrived on friendship, but it wouldn't be easy for her to find another friend. Her days were spent homebound, caring for Dad, who rarely felt the need to talk to anyone.

Mom's despair gripped my heart, choking off any coherent reply. My words of encouragement felt thin and grew thinner as they traveled a phone line a thousand miles long. After hanging up, Mom's voice continued to echo in my mind, which was devoid of answers. My thoughts seemed paralyzed, but my feet began to search for a solution as I paced around the house. Eventually, I wandered outside and looked skyward. I asked the heavens to take care of Mom's needs. Each morning and every night, without fail, I repeated the request.

One night after nearly two weeks of this prayer vigil, my dog woke me to go outside. She repeatedly disturbed my sleep that night. Finally, as I opened the door for the third time, I witnessed a star shoot across the southern sky.

Earlier that day, one of my favorite childhood songs, "When You Wish Upon a Star," had played during a television program. The song stayed with me that afternoon as I hummed the tune over and over. Seeing the falling star, I immediately appealed to that action-packed star to deliver the answer to Mom's needs. It felt like an exclamation point to my prayers.

Meanwhile, down in Florida, during those same two weeks that I pleaded for answers, Mom's thoughts turned to her dog, who had died three years prior. He had always listened to her when she had needed to talk to someone. She realized his comfort had carried her through other times of grief. A dog was definitely needed. She contacted the animal shelter about rescuing a dog, but Dad didn't feel that they could afford the seventy-dollar adoption fee. What could she do? She had found the answer, but not the means, to improve her days. Mom drifted back into despair.

Finally, on a Friday morning three days after the falling-star incident, Mom announced with forceful determination to Dad, "I'm taking the grocery money to get fruit, vegetables—and a dog."

At the animal shelter, her bubble of hope burst. All the dogs were too large for her to handle. Bewildered, she wandered through the shelter's kennel area, searching for one small set of ears to whisper into.

At the same time, just outside the front door of the shelter, an elderly couple stood frozen with indecision. A few weeks earlier a sweet dog had strayed into their yard. The couple had tried tirelessly, but in vain, to find the owner.

They already owned a dog and were unable to keep this one. Still, they found it difficult to release her to the unknown fate that awaited her inside the building.

Then suddenly the man went into action, telling his wife, "I'm going inside to find someone to take this dog home."

He walked through the kennels, around a man petting a German shepherd and a child peering in at a Labrador retriever. His path continued until he directly faced Mom.

He asked hopefully, "Are you looking for a dog?"

Dispiritedly she replied "Yes, but I want a *small* one."

The man smiled warmly and replied, "Come with me. My wife is outside with your dog."

As Mom walked out the door, she saw the dog: a Boston terrier. She held out her hand. The dog greeted Mom with wiggles and licks. She opened her arms and the dog stepped into her heart. Mom offered to pay the couple.

The woman laughed as she told Mom, "Payment in full is the smile on your face."

Mom and the couple exchanged names, handshakes and the dog they called Fancy Face.

Later that day, Mom's voice beamed across the miles as she phoned to tell me about her new furry friend. Mom confided that she had always wanted that breed of dog. She thought this one was perfect in every way, except for the name. I suggested that since the dog had only been called Fancy Face for a few weeks, Mom could certainly give her new dog a new name.

Mom thought about it for a minute, then replied in an excited voice, "Well maybe I will. The dog has very nice markings but most obvious is a partial star on her forehead—"

I broke in, "Mom, you won't believe this!" I proceeded to tell her the story of my two-week prayer vigil with its shooting-star finale.

"Well," my mom replied, "that settles it. I'm going to call her Star!"

Mom's shooting star has continued to shower her with blessings. After twenty-plus years of living in Florida—for Dad's sake—my father suddenly agreed to move to Colorado where my mom's sister lives. They have been looking at a home there that has been sitting empty for over two years. Mom thinks it's been waiting for her. It even has a fenced-in backyard for Star.

When I talk to my mom now, she is bubbly and excited about the future—so different from the despairing woman who just a few short months ago was feeling so unbearably lonely. Now that's what I call, "Star Power!"

Mary Klitz

Max

A dog is one of the few remaining reasons why some people can be persuaded to go for a walk.

O. A. Battista

Over the past few years, depression has become a common topic; even TV commercials advertise the latest drugs to treat it. This was not the case in 1986. People knew about depression, but it was not really accepted as a legitimate illness. Like alcoholism, depression fell more into the category of a "character flaw." It was not something people talked much about, and it was certainly not something you wanted anyone to know that you had.

By 1986, I had suffered for five years with the terrible illness known as depression. I had become a shell of the person I'd once been, going through the motions of life but not really living anymore. Despair was my daily companion. Each day was a struggle to survive the darkness that made me want to end it all and seek peace in death. I had been to doctors who prescribed drugs, and I had been in therapy. Nothing had worked. My family loved me and tried to help, but still I couldn't make my way out of the awful pit I found myself in. I was so ill that my once-a-week trip into town for groceries was an ordeal that I dreaded all week and that afterward left me unable to function for the rest of the day. My five-year-old son was all that kept me hanging on—though I was so numb I could hardly feel my love for him or his love for me. Yet I knew that ending my suffering would cast a terrible shadow on this innocent little boy's life, and so, even though I didn't want to, I kept what was left of myself alive day after day.

That was my situation when I walked into the Wayne County Humane Society one sunny October day. Although it was unusual for me to be able to leave my home, I was there on an errand for my landlady, who wanted me to find a dog for her.

I should explain. All my life I have loved dogs and lived with dogs, but during my pregnancy and the years following, we lived in a rental and the landlady wouldn't hear of our having a dog. Despite my begging and promising to take excellent care of a dog and not let it destroy the apartment, my landlady steadfastly refused. Though by nature I am not a hateful person, in the midst of my depression it was easy to sincerely hate this woman who seemed bent on depriving me of the one thing I thought might give me a small bit of pleasure in my otherwise painful existence.

Hate is a terrible thing; I knew this. When my hate continued to grow, I sought therapy. I also prayed, asking God to help me love my enemy, to truly feel some measure of love for this woman. Over a period of weeks and months, I made progress and we became friends of sorts. I found out that she actually liked dogs as much as I did. She didn't have one herself because she thought it wouldn't be fair to her renters if she had a dog while not allowing us to have any. My heart went out to her. She was old and didn't have many years left to enjoy a dog. I assured her no one would care if she got a dog; that, in fact, I thought she should get one right away, and I would be glad to help her find one.

So when I walked into the shelter that day, I was looking for a dog for my landlady—now my friend—to share her golden years. I looked at them all. A long, low, brown and white dog in particular really appealed to me, but I quickly passed him by because of his size. He was about fifty pounds, much too big for my frail landlady. I did find a sweet little dog who I knew would be perfect for her. When I got back to her house and told her about him, she said she'd been thinking and had decided that getting a dog was a bad idea because of her failing health. She had few relatives and fewer friends, and didn't want to end up in the hospital or nursing home with no one to take her dog. I was disappointed for her but I understood.

That night, my depression was still very much with me, but I did feel a little bit better just from trying to help someone else. And the fact that my hate had been turned into love by the grace of God was something I knew was wonderful—even though I couldn't *feel* the wonderfulness of it because of my illness.

The next day my landlady called and told me she had reconsidered letting me have a dog. She said I could have one providing I brought it over to visit with her. I was so shocked I couldn't speak. I came as close to having happy feelings as I was able. I actually got into the car without stopping to be afraid to go somewhere, and drove straight to the shelter to find the brown and white dog I'd seen before.

All the dogs were jumping and barking except for the one long, low, brown and white dog. He was just standing and slowly wagging his tail, looking up at me with the kindest eyes I had ever seen. I started to open the door of his run to get better acquainted, but then decided to be cautious because the back door of the building was wide open, letting in the glorious sunny fresh air of the October day. This dog looked like he had a lot of basset hound in him. I had no doubt he would try to make a break for that door and the outside delights well known to all hunting dogs, especially pleasant on a crisp autumn morning like this one.

So as I opened his gate, I quickly squatted down and held my arms out wide to be able to head him off if he bolted. This dog had no thoughts of that. With great deliberation, he waddled straight into my arms, sat down and leaned against me, fastening those kind eyes on mine and giving a great sigh of contentment. The very tip of his tail wagged ever so gently.

As he continued to gaze at me, I felt something miraculous taking place inside me. Looking into the dog's loving gaze, I saw myself as I had once been, before my illness, before the darkness overtook me and drained me of myself. This dog's gaze looked past all that. He saw the real me, the healthy me that was still in there somewhere. And looking into his eyes, I saw it, too. I remembered who I was!

I began to cry. Holding the dog in my arms I cried and cried—with joy, with sorrow for the wreck I had become, but mostly with relief—because I knew who I was again and knowing that was a way out of the pit I had been in for five very miserable years. It was like seeing the Promised Land or being handed the key to open a prison cell. It was a miracle. The dog sat there and never moved while I held him and cried. He took my tears and all the pain of my five-year illness in exchange for a few minutes of human contact. Truly this dog was a gift from God to me. I believed it at that moment, and I came to know it even better in the years that followed.

Max came home with me. (And yes, we made regular visits to my landlady, who always had a cookie for him.) Max became my best friend, my brother, my teacher and, most of all, my healer. With Max at my side, I was eventually able to leave my home without feelings of fear and panic. Instead of worrying if my depression was showing, I concentrated on people's reaction to Max—which was always positive since Max, being mostly basset hound, was not only very friendly but also amusing to look at.

Together Max and I attended obedience classes, and also took many rambling walks in the country where our bond became even stronger and our delight in and understanding of each other continued to increase. After a year or so my depression was over. I was out of the pit. It was unbelievable to me. I could love my son and my husband and feel their love for me. I was *me* again: able to love and laugh and live my life once more.

I grew to depend on Max's constant loving gaze, and many times over the years his devotion was a great comfort to me—on hot days he could always make me laugh just by lying on his back on the couch, with all four paws in the air, soaking up the A/C.

Max had a good life. He was much loved by me, as well as by all my friends and family, until the day he left me. When he took his last breath, I held him in my arms and whispered in his ear the words I had told him a thousand times in our fourteen devoted years together: "Best dog in the universe."

At times I wonder if I would have recovered from my depression without Max. I don't know. I do know that the moment I looked into his loving eyes, something inside me began to shift. Do I believe that angels can come to us in our darkest hours wearing funny, furry, brown and white dog suits? You bet I do!

Susan Boyer

A Lesson from Luke

One bright, sunny afternoon in September our golden retriever, Luke, rose from a nap to go for our usual walk to the park. I should say he attempted to rise, because as he stood, he wobbled, tried to get his balance, then collapsed. My heart did somersaults as my husband and I carried him to the car and sped to the vet's office. After hours of blood tests, exams and an ultrasound, we learned the grim news: Luke had hemangiosarcoma, an inoperable cancer of the blood vessels.

"How long does he have?" I asked through my tears, my arms wrapped around Luke, hugging him to my heart.

"I can't say for sure," the vet told us. "Weeks. Maybe only days."

I barely made it to the car before I broke down in uncontrollable sobs. My husband didn't handle the news any better. We held on to each other and bawled. How could Luke have gotten so sick without our realizing it? Sure, he was ten years old, but you'd never know it. He ate every meal with the gusto of a starving piglet, and just that morning he'd chased his tennis ball as if it were filled with his favorite doggy biscuits. He couldn't have cancer, not our Luker Boy, not our baby.

For the next several days we hovered over him, studying him diligently. We took slow walks around the neighborhood, and instead of throwing the ball, we tossed it right to his mouth and let him catch it. One day while dusting the furniture, I picked up his blue pet-therapist vest—Luke had been a volunteer with the Helen Woodward Animal Center pet therapy department, and had visited centers for abused and neglected children. I held the vest to my cheek and started to cry. Why Luke? He was such a sweet dog; he deserved to live.

As I started to put the vest away in a drawer, Luke trotted over, wagging his tail. He looked at me expectantly, his ears perked up and his tongue hanging out.

"You want to put on your vest and go to work, don't you?" I knelt and scratched behind his ears. I could swear he grinned at me.

Although there could be no running or jumping, the following day Luke joined the other pet-therapy dogs on a visit to the children's center. I'm often envious of Luke's ability to light up kids' faces just by being himself. They giggle and clap their hands when he gives them a high ten or catches a cookie off his nose. But the best reaction by far comes when the children ask him, "Do you love me?" and he answers with an emphatic, *"Woof!"* The kids whoop and holler, continuing to shout, "Do you love me?" He always answers them.

On this particular day I wanted to make sure that Luke enjoyed himself, so I wasn't paying as much attention to the children as I usually did. A girl about nine or ten years old inched over to us. Her narrow shoulders slumped and her head hung down; she reminded me of a drooping sunflower. Luke wagged his tail as she neared us and licked her cheek when she bent to pet him. She sat next to us on the lawn and smiled at Luke, but her large brown eyes still looked sad.

"I wish people would die at ten years old the way dogs do," she said.

Stunned, I could only stare at her. None of the kids knew that Luke had cancer. Luke rolled over on his back and the girl rubbed his belly.

Finally, I asked her, "Why do you say that?"

"Because I'm ten, and I wish I would die."

Her sorrow curled around my heart and squeezed it so tightly, my breath caught. "Are things so bad?"

"The worst. I hate it here."

What could I say to her? I couldn't tell her that she shouldn't feel that way, or that she had a wonderful life ahead of her. What good would that do? It wasn't what she needed to hear. I put my hand gently on her back and asked her name.

"Carly."

"Carly, you want to know something? Luke here has cancer. He's dying. And he wishes more than anything that he could go on living. You're perfectly healthy, yet you want to die. It just isn't fair, is it?"

Carly snapped her head up and looked at me. "Luke's dying?"

I nodded, swallowing back tears. "He doesn't have much time—a week, maybe two . . . or just a few days . . . we don't know for sure."

"Shouldn't he be at home or in the hospital?" she asked.

"He wanted to visit with you kids, to bring you some happiness. Just like you, things aren't good for him either. He probably hurts a lot inside." I paused, wondering if she was old enough to understand. "But by coming here, it's as if he's trying to make every minute of his life count for something."

Carly sat silently, looking at Luke while she softly rubbed his belly. "Poor Luke," she said, almost in a whisper. When she raised her head and met my gaze, her eyes looked wary, almost accusing. "You think I should be glad I'm alive and not wanting to die, don't you? Even if I'm stuck here."

I took a few seconds to try to gather my thoughts. "Maybe you could make it sort of like a game. Every day try to think of at least one good thing about being alive."

The counselors began calling the children back to their classrooms. I looked straight into Carly's eyes, trying to reach her. "If nothing else, there's always hope things will get better."

"Come on, Carly," a counselor called out.

Carly stood. "Will you come back and see me?"

"Yes, I will. I promise. And you'll tell me lots of reasons to live, right?"

"Right." She gave me a big nod, and then ran off to join her classmates.

The next week, though Luke's walk was slower and more labored, we visited the children's center again. Carly didn't show up. Alarmed, I asked one of the counselors where she was. They told me that she'd gone to live with a foster family. My heart settled back into place. *Good for you, Carly.*

Twelve days later, Luke lost his battle with cancer.

When I think of him now, I try to focus on what I told Carly: that Luke made every minute of his life count for something. Perhaps he inspired Carly to do that, too. I hope that she, and all the other children we visited, benefited from being with Luke. I know I did.

Christine Watkins

Honey's Greatest Gift

Like most families with a dog, we loved our yellow Lab and treasured the gifts she brought into our lives. From the time she joined our family at the age of seven weeks, Honey enlivened our household with her boundless enthusiasm, happiness and love. Her powerful "helicopter" tail wagged in a circle; she loved to play hide-and-seek with us and readily allowed visiting children to crawl all over her—and to play with her tennis balls and squeaky toys.

When our oldest son, Josh, began kindergarten, our youngest son, Daniel, found an eager playmate in Honey. When Daniel began school, she became my companion, often sitting next to me, head resting on my lap as I did paperwork for our fledgling business. But it was her companionship with my mother that led to what was, perhaps, her greatest gift.

Growing up in Germany, Mom's life had been difficult. A stern older couple adopted her when she was about three years old. At sixteen, the town she lived in, Wuerzburg, was leveled during a World War II air strike. She fled from town to town on her own, trying to survive and suffering repeated rejections by people who could

have helped her, but instead looked after their own interests. Then she married my father, an American soldier.
Their marriage was not a happy one, and Mom struggled
in her role as a mother of four. Between my mother's
unhappiness and my father's quiet and distant nature,
there wasn't a lot of emotional nurturing in our family.

When Mom—a widow—moved to our city as a senior
citizen, I was concerned. Would we relate? Could I deal
with the emotional distance between us? To top it off,
once again Mom felt lonely and displaced. In an effort to
ease her loneliness, Mom often drove the mile to our
house to walk Honey. They were perfect for each other.
Mom walked slowly, and by this time, so did Honey, also
a senior citizen. Together they explored the trails that
interlace our neighborhood. The gentle yellow dog
brought out a softness in Mom. My mother babied Honey,
sometimes sneaking her forbidden foods despite my
protests. Although I considered Honey a family member,
to me she was still a dog, but to Mom she was nearly
human; as a result, we occasionally clashed over our dif-
fering "dog-parenting" styles.

It was about a year after Mom's arrival that my husband, Steve, and I knew Honey's end was near. Honey,
now fourteen, could no longer curl up to sleep. Her joints
were stiff, and though we gave her daily anti-inflamma-
tory drugs, we suspected she continued to suffer. But we
didn't have the heart to put her to sleep. In spite of her
physical ailments, Honey still fetched the paper daily and
turned into a puppy at the prospect of a walk. Her enthusiasm for life masked what should have been obvious.

Then one sunny Tuesday in March, I finally understood
that our stoic pet had had enough. She was clearly suffering, and I knew it was time. Before I could change my
mind about doing what we had put off for too long, I
called the vet. They made arrangements for Honey's

favorite veterinarian, Dr. Jane, to come in on her day off. Steve met me at the vet's office and together we comforted Honey as she slipped away from this world.

Her loss affected me far more than I could have imagined. I moped around the house, restless and overcome by sudden bursts of tears. My grieving was heightened by the fact that just a few months before we had also become empty nesters. Without Honey to fill her customary space in our kitchen, our house now seemed bigger and emptier than before.

I resisted telling Mom that we had put her walking buddy to sleep. How could I cope with her emotional reaction, which I anticipated would be greater than my own? So, I hatched a plan: Steve had to work late on Thursday night. Mom and I could have dinner together; after dinner I would reveal my secret.

"Okay," Mom said when I telephoned. "I'll come over."

"No, no," I countered, realizing she would wonder where Honey was as soon as she walked through the door. "Why don't you cook for us? I'd like to eat at your house."

Mom agreed. I don't remember the conversation we had or what we ate because the whole time I was distracted by the secret I was keeping. Finally, it was time to leave, and I still couldn't tell Mom about Honey. Mom made herself cozy on her sofa. I said good-bye, pulled on my coat and was at the door when I forced myself to turn around.

Sitting stiffly near Mom with my coat on, I blurted: "Mom, we put Honey to sleep on Tuesday."

"Oh, no!" Mom cried out. "I didn't get to say good-bye."

To my surprise, *I* was the one who started to cry. Through my tears I explained why we had put Honey to sleep. With more honesty and vulnerability than I had ever shown to my mother, I blubbered, "I miss her so much."

"But you carried on with her so," she said, referring to our differences concerning Honey's "parenting."

"I know, but I loved her. We did so much together."

Mom scooted closer to me on the couch. "I'm so sorry," she said, wrapping her arms around me. Then she cradled me while I rested my head on her chest and sobbed.

For the first time in forty-six years I experienced the calm reassurance of a mother's love. Soaking up my mother's tenderness, I marveled that it had its root in her relationship with Honey. And, although crying in my mother's arms didn't take away my pain, I was deeply comforted. I lost a loving companion that week, but I also gained something rich and beautiful. My mom and I finally made an emotional connection, which has continued to expand— thanks to Honey and her last and greatest gift.

B. J. Reinhard

Puppy Magic

Since I began incorporating animals into my child psychotherapy practice fifteen years ago, my life as a clinician—and as a person—has been turned upside down. Surrounded by my dogs, birds, lizards and fish, I feel like a modern-day Dr. Dolittle. Though in my case, it's not that I talk to the animals, but that the animals help me in my work communicating with children in need.

Diane,* a dark-haired five-year-old, small for her age, came to me with a problem. Although she was a chatterbox in the house and with her family, no one had ever heard Diane say a word to anyone outside her home environment. Not one word.

For years her parents had simply told themselves that Diane was shy. But after her first week at kindergarten, her teacher called her parents into school for a conference and informed them that Diane needed professional help. Not only was the little girl unwilling to speak, but also she appeared terrified.

Diane's parents, concerned and upset by this evaluation, tried to work with Diane to overcome her selective mutism.

Name has been changed to protect privacy.

Yet nothing they said or did seemed to make any impression on her. Diane refused to talk—in fact, seemed incapable of speech—when she was outside her family circle.

Diane's parents contacted me and I agreed to see her. It was a Friday afternoon when Diane and her parents arrived for Diane's initial session. They were all seated in the waiting room when my six-year-old golden retriever, Puppy, and I walked out to greet them. I noticed right away that Diane sat with her head down, her eyes directed toward the floor in front of her. She made no move to look up or acknowledge our entrance.

Puppy, walking ahead of me, made a beeline for Diane. Because Diane's head was bowed, Puppy was just three feet from Diane when the girl finally caught sight of her. Startled by the unexpected sight of a large golden dog, the girl's eyes became huge and then her mouth curved slowly into a smile. Puppy stopped directly in front of Diane and laid her head in the girl's lap.

I introduced myself and Puppy, but Diane didn't respond. She gave no indication that she had even heard me. Instead, Diane began to silently pet Puppy's head, running her hands softly over Puppy's ears, nose and muzzle. She was still obviously nervous and apprehensive at being at my office, but she was smiling and seemed to be enjoying her interaction with Puppy. I was speaking quietly with Diane's parents when an idea hit me.

I turned back toward the girl and the dog and spoke Puppy's name quietly. When Puppy looked up at me, I gave her a hand signal to come toward me and continue back into the inner office. Puppy immediately started walking toward me. As Puppy walked away, I watched Diane's face fall and her eyes take on a sad and disappointed look. I said, "Oh, I'm sorry. I didn't realize you wanted Puppy to stay with you. All you have to do for her to come back is say, 'Puppy, come.'"

Diane's parents stared at me, their expressions skepti-cal. For a few tense seconds, Diane sat debating what to do, her lower lip quivering. Then, in a soft voice, she called, "Puppy, come; please come, Puppy."

Her parents' gaze flew to their daughter and their jaws dropped in surprise. I gave Puppy the signal to go and she whirled around and ran over to Diane who slid off her chair to the floor, and kneeling, hugged Puppy tightly around the neck. We watched, Diane's parents in tears, as Diane and Puppy snuggled happily together.

I knew that I had to seize the moment and sent Diane's parents back into the office to wait for me. Sitting on the floor beside Puppy and Diane, I began to talk to Diane. I told her that I knew how hard it was for her to talk to people she didn't know and how happy we were that she had been brave enough to call Puppy. Hoping to keep the miracle going, I asked her what she liked about Puppy. She hesitated a moment and then answered, "That she is soft. That she is funny." As we talked, Puppy sat leaning against Diane, the little girl's fingers laced through Puppy's fur.

It was time for the session to end; I asked Diane to say good-bye to Puppy. She hugged Puppy again and said, "Good-bye." Her voice was soft, but it was clear. She had made a remarkable breakthrough and had taken the first step in her journey toward being able to interact with the world outside her home. I was deeply pleased.

When Diane and her parents left, I sat in my office, stroking Puppy's soft golden head. I knew that without her, the session would have gone completely differently. Puppy had worked her magic again.

Aubrey Fine, Ed.D.

An Angel in the Form of a Service Dog

He has told me a thousand times over that I am his reason for being: by the way he rests against my leg; by the way he thumps his tail at my smallest smile.

Gene Hill

The start of my life in a wheelchair was the end of a very long marriage.

In 1989 I had a serious truck accident, which shattered my lower back. Though I was considered an incomplete paraplegic, as the years passed, my back got progressively worse. At the end of 1999, my doctor ordered me to use a wheelchair at all times. My wife walked out.

Suddenly on my own, I decided to relocate to California where the weather was warmer, there was more to do, and, most important, things there were more handicapped-accessible than in the rural area where I was living. Even so, adjusting to life in a wheelchair, alone in a new place, was no picnic. After six months in California, my doctor felt that a service dog would be an immense help to me and put me in touch with Canine Companions for Independence (CCI).

I went through the application process, but when I was finally accepted I was told that I was looking at nearly a five-year wait. Disappointed but determined to make a life for myself, I continued to struggle through each day, at times becoming so tired that I'd be stranded somewhere until I found enough energy to continue.

So the call from CCI only three and a half years later came as a complete surprise. They'd had a cancellation for a class starting in two weeks—would I be available on such short notice? Without hesitation I said, "Yes!" I felt a rush of emotion. I'd pinned all my hopes on this, and now it was finally happening, almost too fast.

The very next day I headed to the CCI campus as requested, just to be sure they had a possible match for me. This preliminary session was to test my handling skills and to see which of three potential canine partners might "click" with me. I was taken into a dog-filled room, and was surprised when a very fat black-and-white cat, threading his way calmly through the dogs toward my wheelchair, decided my lap was the perfect resting spot.

A trainer brought the first dog, a petite black Lab named Satine, to meet me. We had only a minute to get acquainted before starting basic commands such as "heel" to see how she would respond. Despite the feline riding shotgun on my lap the entire time, Satine responded amazingly well to everything.

Next, a much larger dog, a black Lab-mix called Hawk, took Satine's place—and the cat left my lap in a rush. But Hawk didn't give chase. In fact, he ignored everything to focus on me. Although his headstrong personality initially tested my commands, I held to my guns and soon Hawk started working for me—opening doors, picking up dropped items and a long list of other things. I was awestruck by his sheer presence, not to mention his skills and obedience.

The third candidate was a lively golden retriever named Tolarie. She was very pretty and smart, but no matter what I did, she didn't want to work for me.

When asked which of the three dogs I would choose, I named the more easygoing Satine as first choice, but really, I wanted Hawk. I was totally in love with that dog from the word go!

The next day, CCI called to tell me that I had impressed the trainers with my handling skills with Hawk and that they hoped to place me with him. My heart soared! I thanked them profusely and made arrangements to attend the two-week training course at CCI's campus in Oceanside, California.

I arrived early and spent the first day doing paperwork and meeting the three trainers and five other people in my class. When we entered the classroom, I immediately found Hawk. He came to the door of his crate and licked my fingertips as if to say, "Hi there, I remember you." I could hear his tail thumping in eager anticipation.

Then came the moment we all were waiting for: working with the dogs. The trainers brought Hawk to me, and we spent the first few minutes in a joyful exchange of greetings.

The next four days were nerve-racking. Pairs wouldn't be assigned until Friday, after we'd each worked with enough dogs for the trainers to determine the best matches. By the second day, though, most of us had already chosen our favorites and felt jealous if "our" dog was working with someone else. On Friday, Hawk was paired with me, but the match still wasn't permanent. Trainers needed to be satisfied that the dogs had bonded with us, and that we felt comfortable with each other and worked well together. By then, I couldn't imagine having any other dog but Hawk—especially after what happened the first night we spent together.

Since my accident I'd always had a very hard time sleeping at night. Every time I moved, the pain roused me, and falling back to sleep was next to impossible. For me, three hours was a good night's sleep. The first night with Hawk, I was supposed to crate him while I slept. But as Hawk and I lay on the bed watching TV together, I dozed off. I woke at five the next morning—and Hawk was still there. He had stretched himself across my body in a way that was comfortable for me but kept me from painful motion. I had slept the whole night through!

I was amazed. With the renewed energy and sharpness that comes with a full night's sleep, I realized Hawk had done similar things all week that I'd written off as part of his training. He'd bonded with me from the start, and in a remarkably short time, had figured out my abilities and limitations and adjusted to them to make the whole training process easier on me. Every time the pain got unbearable, he had done something silly or sweet to take my mind off the pain and help me get through that day. He had done all this with no instruction—just his innate love for me and his desire to please me and make my life easier.

Hawk and I passed our final test with flying colors. We returned home and started a new and very different life—together.

Now when I go out in public, people no longer avoid me or give me weird stares. When people hear the jingle of Hawk's collar and see this team on the move, they smile and come over to meet us. Hawk does so many different things for me: he pulls my wheelchair when I'm feeling tired, opens doors and picks up things I might drop. People love to see my beautiful black dog rear up on a counter and hand a cashier my cash or credit card—what a crowd-pleaser!

Hawk's "fee" for all this? A simple, "Good boy." He loves

to hear those words because he knows he is doing something that makes me happy.

His other rewards come when we get home. We both enjoy our nightly cuddle on the floor, followed by a favorite tennis-ball game. It still amazes me that Hawk, who can pick up a full bottle of water and not leave a single tooth mark, can pop a tennis ball in no time flat.

I would never have believed that I could feel this way about my life again. Each day I look forward to getting up after a full night's sleep, grooming Hawk, going out somewhere new and being a part of the world around me, then coming home to cuddle, play and relax for the evening.

Thanks to this wonderful dog and all the people who worked so hard raising and training him, my life has started all over. Hawk, my angel in the form of a service dog, truly shares his wings with me.

David Ball

6

DOGS AS TEACHERS

*I think dogs are the most amazing creatures.
They give unconditional love. For me they
are the role models for being alive.*

Gilda Radner

Good Instincts

If your dog doesn't like someone, you probably shouldn't either.

Unknown

The wind whistled round the corner of the house, thunder rolled and rain slashed against the windows—not a night to be outside but rather to sit by the fire, thankful for the solid walls and roof overhead. I could imagine Dr. Frankenstein's creation being abroad on such a night. I was alone, my husband away and the nearest neighbor a quarter mile down the road. Alone, that is, except for Lassie, a shaggy, black-and-white border collie, who sat with her head in my lap, her intelligent, brown eyes gazing up at me as if to say, *Don't worry, we'll be all right.*

Lassie had arrived at our front door four years earlier by her design, not ours. Throughout the eighteen years she was with us, she proved time and time again to be a superb judge of character. We never knew if it was as a result of her sense of smell or sound—or some sixth sense—but, whatever it was, she definitely possessed a talent we humans lacked. On first meeting she would either wag the tip of her tail a couple of times to indicate that the visitor was acceptable, or slightly curl her top lip, which told you to be wary. Always accurate, her gift was never more apparent than on this night.

The doorbell rang. I decided not to answer it. It rang again, more insistently this time. Whoever was there was not going away. Still I hesitated. On the fourth ring, with Lassie by my side, I finally answered the call. My stomach lurched and my mouth went dry, for there, silhouetted by the porch light, stood the monster himself. Not as big as I imagined but equally menacing. A twisted body under a heavy overcoat, one shoulder hunched higher than the other, and his head leaning slightly forward and to one side. Gnarled fingers at the end of a withered arm touched his cap.

"May I use your phone?" The voice came from somewhere back in his throat and, although the request was polite, his tone was rough.

I shrank back as he rummaged in his pocket and produced a piece of paper. Shuffling forward he handed it to me. I refused to take it. Believing he might try and force his way in, I looked at Lassie to see if she was ready to defend the homestead. Surprisingly, she sat by my side, the tip of her tail wagging.

You're out of your mind, Lassie, I thought. But there was no denying the sign and, based on past experience, I trusted her instincts.

Reluctantly, I beckoned the stranger into the hallway and pointed to the phone. He thanked me as he picked up the instrument. Unashamed, I stood and listened to the conversation. From his comments, I learned his van had broken down and he needed someone to repair it. Lassie always shadowed anyone she mistrusted until they left the house. Tonight she paid no attention to our visitor. Instead, she trotted back into the living room and curled up by the fire.

Finishing his call, the man hitched up the collar of his overcoat and prepared to leave. As he turned to thank me, his lopsided shoulders seemed to sag and a touch of sympathy crept into my fear.

"Can I offer you a cup of tea?" The words were out before I could stop them.

His eyes lit up. "That would be nice."

We went through to the kitchen. He sat while I put the kettle on. Bent over on the stool, he looked less menacing, but I still kept a wary eye on him. By the time the tea had brewed, I felt safe enough to draw up another stool. We sat in silence, facing each other across the table, cups of steaming tea in front of us.

"Where are you from?" I finally asked, for the sake of conversation.

"Birmingham," he answered, then paused. "I'm sorry if I frightened you," he continued, "but you've no need to worry. I know I look strange, but there's a reason."

I said nothing, and we continued to sip in silence. I felt he would talk when he was ready, and he did.

"I wasn't always like this," he said. I sensed, rather than heard, the catch in his voice. "But some years ago I had polio."

"Oh," I said, not knowing what else to say.

"I was laid up for months. When I managed to walk again, I couldn't get a job. My crippled body put every-one off. Eventually, I was hired as a delivery driver, and as you know from my phone call, my van broke down outside your house." He smiled his crooked smile. "I really should be getting back so I'm there when the mechanic arrives."

"Look," I said. "There's no need to sit outside in this weather. Why not leave a note in your van telling them where you are?"

He smiled again. "I'll do that."

When he returned, we settled by the fire in the living room. "You know," I said, "if it hadn't been for Lassie here, I wouldn't have let you in."

"Oh," he said, bending forward to scratch her head. "Why?"

I went on to explain her uncanny ability to judge people, then added, "She sensed you for what you really are, while I only saw the outside."

"Lucky for me she was around," he said, laughing.

After two hours and several more cups of tea, the doorbell rang again. A man wearing overalls under a hooded raincoat announced the vehicle was repaired.

Thanking me profusely, the stranger headed out into the night, and a few minutes later, the taillights of his van disappeared down the road. I never expected to see him again.

But on the afternoon of Christmas Eve I answered the door to find the rainy-night stranger standing there. "For you," he said, handing me a large box of chocolates, "for your kindness." Then he placed a packet of dog treats in my other hand. "And these are for Lassie, my friend with the good instincts. Merry Christmas to you both."

Every Christmas Eve, until we moved five years later, he arrived with his box of chocolates and packet of dog treats. And every year he got the same warm welcome from our wise Lassie.

Gillian Westhead
as told to Bill Westhead

A New Home

"Mom, watch out!" my daughter Melissa screamed as a drenched brown pooch charged under our van. Slamming my foot on the brakes, we jerked to a stop. Stepping out into the freezing rain, we hunched down on opposite sides of the van, making kissing noises to coax the little dog—who, miraculously, I hadn't hit—to us. The shivering pup jumped into Melissa's arms and then onto her lap once she sat down again in the heated van.

We were on our way home from Melissa's sixth-grade basketball game. Her once-white shirt with the red number 7 was now covered in dirty black paw prints. I stared at the mess as she wrapped her shirt around the small dog.

"That shirt will never come clean!"

"Well, at least we saved his life," she frowned as she cuddled him. "Running through all those cars he could have been killed."

She continued petting him. "He's so cute. And he doesn't have a collar. Can we keep him?"

I knew how she felt. I loved animals myself—especially dogs. But I also knew the mess they made. Dogs dig through the garbage. They chew up paper, shoes and anything else they can fit in their mouths. Not to mention the little piles and puddles they make when you're trying to housebreak them. I didn't need a dog. I loved the clean, bright house we had recently moved into, and I wanted to keep my new house looking just that—new.

I glanced at the ball of brown fur and the black mask outlining his wide, wondering eyes. *She's right. He is cute.*

The smell of wet dog escalated with the burst of heat coming out of the vents, bringing me to my senses. I turned the heat down and shook my head. "Melissa, we've been through this before. I told all four of you kids when we moved into the new house: absolutely no pets."

As we pulled into the drive, she said, "But Mom, it's the middle of February. He'll freeze out here."

I glanced at the pup licking Melissa's fingers. "Okay," I decided. "We'll give him a bath, keep him for the night and call the animal shelter tomorrow."

Still frowning, Melissa nodded and slid out of the van. Carrying the dog in her arms, she entered the house. By the time I reached the door, the news was already out.

"We've got a new puppy!" Robert, Brian and Jeremiah chorused.

"I'm afraid not," I said, as I took off my shoes. "We're only keeping him overnight."

Wiggling out of Melissa's arms, the pup scampered across the room and jumped up on my couch.

"Get down!" I shouted, pointing my finger at him and toward the floor.

He licked his nose remorsefully and sat there shaking.

"Mom, you're scaring him." Melissa scooped him into her arms. "C'mon, boy, I'll take you to my room."

"Ah-ah," I corrected, "bath first."

All four kids crowded around the puppy in the bathroom. I listened over the running water as each became excited over every splash the dog made. Their giggles brought a smile to my face. *Maybe it wouldn't be such a bad idea to have a dog.*

I glanced around the kitchen with its shiny black-and-white tile floor. Picturing a dog dish, with food and water heaping into a sloshing puddle of goo, I turned toward the living room. With this messy weather, I envisioned my pale-blue carpeting "decorated" with tiny black paw prints. Not to mention the shedding, fleas and all the other things a dog can bring. I shook my head. *A dog will ruin this place.*

After his bath, Melissa brought him out wrapped in one of our good white towels. He looked like a drowned rat, except for his big, brown puppy-dog eyes. The boys raced around the kitchen getting food and water.

The water sloshed back and forth in the bowl. "Be careful, Jeremiah," I warned. "You're gonna spill—" When Jeremiah heard my voice he stopped with a sudden jerk. Water splashed onto his face and down the front of shirt and blue jeans, soaking the floor.

I ran to get towels. When I returned, I watched in horror as the pup tramped through the water. Even after his bath, his feet were still dirty and left muddy little prints all over my kitchen floor. "Wipe his feet and put him in your room, Melissa. *Now!*"

Melissa snatched the dog up, with the boys traipsing at her heels. I sighed as I wiped up the mud and water. After a few minutes, the floor shined like new, and laughter erupted from Melissa's bedroom.

My husband, John, came in from work moments later. "What's so funny?" he asked after he kissed me on the cheek.

"A dog."

"A dog?" he asked, surprised. "We have a dog?"

"Not by choice," I explained. "It ran under the van. And of course I couldn't just leave him in the middle of the street."

John smiled. "What happened to no pets?"

"I told them he's going tomorrow."

After John joined the kids he came back out. "You know, he is really cute."

"Yeah, I know." He didn't have to convince me; my resolve was already slipping.

The next morning, the kids mauled the dog with hugs and tears. "Can't we keep him?" they sobbed. I watched how he gently and tenderly licked each one as if to comfort them.

"I promise we'll take care of him," Melissa said.

"Yeah, and I'll water him," Jeremiah added. I smiled, remembering the incident the night before. "But I won't fill his dish so full next time."

How could I say no? *He's housebroken. He's cute. And he's great with the kids.*

"We'll see," I said, as they scooted out the door for school. "But first, I'll have to call the dog pound to make sure no one is looking for him."

Their faces lit up as they trotted down the drive. With John already at work, the pup and I watched from the door as the four kids skipped down the street. Once they turned the corner, I grabbed the phone book and found the number for the animal shelter.

The lady at the shelter informed me that no one had reported a brown dog missing. However, she instructed me to put an ad in the local paper about him for three days, and if no one responded, we could legally keep him for our own. I called the newspaper and placed the ad. Although I had mixed feelings, mostly I hoped his owners would claim him.

Each day, the kids would ask the same question, "Did anyone call?" And each day it was always the same answer: "Nope."

By the third day, the dog and I had spent so much time together that he followed me around the house. If I sat on the couch, he'd jump in my lap. If I folded clothes, he'd lie by the dryer. If I made dinner, he'd sit by the refrigerator. Even when I went to bed, he'd follow, wanting to cuddle up with me.

"Looks like we have to come up with a name," I said Sunday morning at breakfast.

The kids cheered and threw out some names. When we returned from church, I played the messages on our answering machine, my heart sinking when I heard: "I think you may have my dog."

After speaking with the lady, I realized that Snickers was indeed her dog. She explained she'd be over to get him within the hour. As we sat around the table, picking at the pot roast, tears flooded our plates like a river. Even I had grown attached to this sweet little dog.

When the lady arrived, I met her at the door. I clenched a wet tissue in my hands and invited her in. She took in the scene: four mournful children sitting in a huddle around the little dog and petting him, while Snickers, perched on Melissa's lap, licked her tears away.

After a long moment, she said, "I want you to have him. I can see you love him and we already have another dog."

I gave her a hug while the kids cheered in the background.

Snickers has definitely left his mark on our house. Still, I wouldn't trade his muddy paw prints for anything—not even the nicest-looking house in the world! For, although he makes little messes sometimes, he has filled our hearts with love. Before Snickers came into our lives, we had a new house. Now we have a new home.

Elisabeth A. Freeman

"It might help Skippy's feelings if you said he needed improvement instead of calling him a bad dog."

Judgment Day

On Judgment Day Saint Peter stands,
A list of virtues in his hands.
As all the souls in silence wait
To see who'll pass through heaven's gate.
"You'll enter first," he says, "if you
can swear your heart was always true.
And you were constant to the end,
A steadfast, loyal, devoted friend.
Never spiteful, never mean,
Unchanging through good times and lean.
With no desire but this: to be
allowed to love eternally."
And this is why Saint Peter's hand
Throws wide the heavenly portals, and
With wagging tails and shining eyes
The dogs walk into paradise.

Millicent Bobleter

Mound of Dirt

The year I was in first grade I ended my prayers each evening with a plea to God to send me a dog. It was a plea that did not go unnoticed by my parents, who knelt beside me. Two weeks before my seventh birthday, which was in May, they told me that they wanted to get a load of dirt for our backyard. I didn't realize something was up until Dad parked the car in front of a ranch house in a suburban neighborhood.

"This doesn't look like a place for dirt," I said, eyeing the surroundings.

While my parents exchanged nervous glances and whispered to each other, a woman named Martha ushered us inside the house.

"I bet you are a very good student," said Martha. I didn't know what to say. I was anything but a good student. As hard as I tried to do well in school, I was failing first grade.

Sensing my discomfort, Martha asked, "Well, I guess you probably want to see the 'dirt,' don't you?"

"Yes," I answered, eager to get off the subject of school.

Martha set a large box in the middle of the living room floor. I padded up and peeked inside. Six black dachshund puppies clawed at the inside of the box, each begging for my attention. Snoozing at the bottom was the runt. I rubbed my fingers on a tuft of hair that stood up in the middle of her back.

Martha said, "That one will never be a show dog."

It didn't matter to me whether she'd ever be a show dog. Her brown eyes looked up at me with such hope. When I picked her up, she snuggled against my heart. There she stayed on the long ride home. I named her Gretchen.

As Gretchen grew, she loved to chew on bones, bury them in the backyard and chase squirrels that dared to disturb her burial mounds. Watching Gretchen's determination and persistence in protecting her bones was a learning experience for me. I saw that because Gretchen never gave up in her battle against the squirrels, they finally left her alone.

As unwavering and fierce as she was with the squirrels, she loved children, especially my neighborhood friends. If I played mud pies with Sally, Gretchen was right there with us. If Markie and Joanie wanted to walk to the corner drugstore, Gretchen begged for her leash. If the neighbor kids put on a play, Gretchen had a part. If Gretchen slipped out of the gate, all the kids in the neighborhood helped chase her down. She was not a dog to us. She was a playmate—a friend.

Gretchen was the only friend I told about my troubles with learning. While we sat underneath my father's workbench, I told her about my failure in school, about feeling like a dummy because I couldn't read and about how the other children made fun of me. I believed Gretchen understood my problems because as the runt of the litter she had struggled from the moment of her birth. The closer we snuggled in our secret little space, the more I came to believe that maybe things weren't as bad as they seemed. Maybe there was hope for me. She seemed to understand how much I needed her. And I needed her a lot that summer before second grade. I wanted to get smart, and I figured the best way to do this was to read every day.

"Which book?" I'd ask her as she jumped up on my bed.

Gretchen, who used her nose to move *anything* I set on the bed, would nose toward me one of the books lying on the coverlet, and I'd read it aloud. It wasn't easy for me to read, but Gretchen was patient. Sometimes she'd sigh when I fumbled with the words. Once I made it through a rough spot, she'd nestle against me and lay her snout on my heart. It made me feel better to have her with me as I read. My fears about being a dummy melted away with her beside me.

The summer passed—book by book—until it was time to go shopping for school clothes. Since it was such a hot day, my mother felt Gretchen should stay home. Gretchen whined about being left behind. She hated it when I went someplace she couldn't go. And no amount of trying to explain to her that dogs can't go shopping would stop her whining. I looked back just in time to see her head pop up in the window before we drove off, but when we came back from shopping, I didn't hear her claws clicking against the hardwood floor to greet me.

My mother noticed the hall closet door ajar.

"Oh, no," she whispered upon closer inspection. On the floor we found chewed up containers of poison that Gretchen had dug out from the dark recesses of the closet. We found Gretchen behind the living room sofa. She beat her tail in slow motion as I approached. We rushed her to the vet.

"Gretchen is very sick. The vet says she is not responding to treatment," said my mother at the dinner table.

"She's going to get well," I said firmly.

"It's best we prepare ourselves for the worst," my father said.

"No," I cried. "She's going to get well. She's going to come home."

I thought about how lonely Gretchen must be. *She probably thinks I don't love her anymore. She probably thinks she'll never see me again.* Gretchen had always been there to comfort me when I was sad and hurt.

"I want to go and see her," I told my parents. "If she could see me, I know she'd get well."

"Wake up, Gretchen," I said, after following the vet to a back room in his office. Hearing the sound of my voice, her tail beat the bottom of the cage, again, in slow motion. The vet couldn't believe it when Gretchen stood up in her cage and whined for me to open the door to hold her. It wasn't long before she recovered and came home to stay.

Gretchen and I continued reading together for the whole following year. My reading definitely improved, but it was third grade that was the turning point of my life. That year I became the best reader in my class. My third-grade teacher understood that I was a bright child who had a learning problem. She told stories about people like me who struggled successfully to learn despite obstacles.

Although I appreciate everything my teacher and parents did for me, I feel I owe so much to that little "mound of dirt" my parents bought me on my seventh birthday. Persistence and determination were only a part of the story. The runt who would never be a show dog taught me that love is a healing and nurturing soil in which a broken spirit can grow whole once more.

Paula Gramlich

The Last Puppy

There is only one smartest dog in the world, and every boy has it.

Louis Sabin

It had been a very long night. Our black cocker spaniel, Precious, was having a difficult delivery. I lay on the floor beside her large four-foot-square cage, watching her every movement. Watching and waiting, just in case I had to rush her to the veterinarian.

After six hours the puppies started to appear. The first-born was black and white. The second and third puppies were tan and brown. The fourth and fifth were spotted black and white. *One, two, three, four, five,* I counted to myself as I walked down the hallway to wake my wife, Judy, and tell her that everything was fine.

As we walked back down the hallway and into the spare bedroom, I noticed a sixth puppy had been born and was now lying all by itself over to the side of the cage. I picked up the small puppy and lay it on top of the large pile of puppies, who were whining and trying to nurse on the mother. Precious immediately pushed the small puppy away from rest of the group. She refused to recognize it as a member of her family.

"Something's wrong," said Judy.

I reached over and picked up the puppy. My heart sank inside my chest when I saw the puppy had a cleft lip and palate and could not close its tiny mouth. I decided right then and there that if there was any way to save this animal, I was going to give it my best shot.

I took the puppy to the vet and was told nothing could be done unless we were willing to spend about a thousand dollars to try to correct the defect. He told us that the puppy would die mainly because it could not suckle.

After returning home Judy and I decided that we could not afford to spend that kind of money without getting some type of assurance from the vet that the puppy had a chance to survive. However, that did not stop me from purchasing a syringe and feeding the puppy by hand—which I did day and night, every two hours, for more than ten days. The little puppy survived and eventually learned to eat on his own, as long as it was soft canned food.

The fifth week after the puppies' birth I placed an ad in the newspaper, and within a week we had people interested in all the pups—except the one with the deformity.

Late one afternoon I went to the store to pick up a few groceries. Upon returning I happened to see the old retired schoolteacher who lived across the street from us, waving at me. She had read in the paper that we had puppies and was wondering if she might get one from us for her grandson and his family. I told her all the puppies had found homes, but I would keep my eyes open for anyone else who might have an available cocker spaniel. I also mentioned that if someone should change their mind, I would let her know.

Within days all but one of the puppies had been picked up by their new families. This left me with one brown and tan cocker, as well as the smaller puppy with the cleft lip and palate.

Two days passed without my hearing anything from the gentleman who had been promised the tan and brown pup. I telephoned the schoolteacher and told her I had one puppy left and that she was welcome to come and look at him. She advised me that she was going to pick up her grandson and would come over at about eight o'clock that evening.

That night at around 7:30, Judy and I were eating supper when we heard a knock on the front door. When I opened the door, the man who had wanted the tan and brown pup was standing there. We walked inside, took care of the adoption details, and I handed him the puppy. Judy and I did not know what we would do or say when the teacher showed up with her grandson.

At exactly eight o'clock the doorbell rang. I opened the door, and there was the schoolteacher with her grandson standing behind her. I explained to her the man had come for the puppy after all, and there were no puppies left.

"I'm sorry, Jeffery. They found homes for all the puppies," she told her grandson.

Just at that moment, the small puppy left in the bedroom began to yelp.

"My puppy! My puppy!" yelled the little boy as he ran out from behind his grandmother.

I just about fell over when I saw that the small child also had a cleft lip and palate. The boy ran past me as fast as he could, down the hallway to where the puppy was still yelping.

When the three of us made it to the bedroom, the small boy was holding the puppy in his arms. He looked up at his grandmother and said, "Look, Grandma. They found homes for all the puppies except the pretty one, and he looks just like me."

My jaw dropped in surprise.

The schoolteacher turned to us. "Is this puppy available?"

Recovering quickly, I answered, "Yes, that puppy is available."

The little boy, who was now hugging the puppy, chimed in, "My grandma told me these kind of puppies are real expensive and that I have to take real good care of it."

The lady opened her purse, but I reached over and pushed her hand away so that she would not pull her wallet out.

"How much do you think this puppy is worth?" I asked the boy. "About a dollar?"

"No. This puppy is very, very expensive," he replied.

"More than a dollar?" I asked.

"I'm afraid so," said his grandmother.

The boy stood there, pressing the small puppy against his cheek.

"We could not possibly take less than two dollars for this puppy," Judy said, squeezing my hand. "Like you said, it's the pretty one."

The schoolteacher took out two dollars and handed it to the young boy.

"It's your dog now, Jeffery. You pay the man."

Still holding the puppy tightly, the boy proudly handed me the money. Any worries I'd had about the puppy's future were gone.

Although this happened many years ago, the image of the little boy and his matching pup stays with me still. I think it must be a wonderful feeling for any young person to look at themselves in the mirror and see nothing, except "the pretty one."

Roger Dean Kiser

7

FAREWELL, MY LOVE

A good dog never dies, he always stays; he
walks beside you on crisp autumn days
when frost is on the fields and winter's
drawing near, his head is within our
hand in his old way.

Mary Carolyn Davies

Dad's Right Knee

We had gathered from our distant homes to be with my mother as she kept her heartrending watch at my father's bedside. He had suffered a series of strokes at Thanksgiving, lingered through the holidays and was loosening his tenuous hold on life as the New Year dawned. The stages of our grief had been punctuated by moves from a hopeful bed in the ICU, to a bargained-for stay in a long-term ward, and a final spiral downward to the cold, cruel equations of a move to hospice. Dad's strong body had become a skeletal frame, silent and unmoving, as his essence fled. His stroke-destroyed and disintegrating brain had left him flaccid and limp.

There had always been a dog in my parents' hearts and home; the one at the time was an elderly golden retriever named Randy. We used to call him "Dad's right knee" and marvel at the precision and military bearing of those two impressive males as they marched their deliberate path around the neighborhood. Dad always walked with one glove on; Randy proudly carried the other one for him. After the walk, Dad would hold his hand out and Randy would return the glove to him and be rewarded with a stroke on his golden forehead. His immense, feathered plume of a tail swept grandly back and forth as his eyes radiated love.

Randy's laundry-sized basket of toys sat next to my father's chair, and each evening Randy would lovingly place each treasure in his mouth and repeatedly offer them to my father to be admired. By bedtime, both the toys and my father's lap were liberally bedewed with saliva. My father called it liquid diamonds, laughingly proclaiming that Randy was giving him jewelry again.

When Randy developed arthritis and could no longer climb into the van for trips around town, my father built him a ramp and carpeted it to match the van's interior. He installed a bed in the back with a built-in water bowl and they resumed their jaunts. Randy had special water in the refrigerator waiting for those trips. "Car water" my father called it. Pity the visitor who accidentally tried to drink any of Randy's water; he was soon set straight by vigorous complaints from both Randy and Dad.

After my father's stroke we took turns sitting in Dad's chair, trying to interest Randy in his toys. But he just fixed his eyes on us, mutely demanding to know where Dad was. A dog who had always taken an avid interest in all food, his rotund form was melting from round to slender as he waited for his person to return. His fire-kissed hair carpeted the floor and sunset was in his eyes. Inconsolable and stolid in his grief, he was willing himself to death before our eyes. We kept promising Randy he could go see Dad, and he'd look at us as if to say, "When?" He missed Dad with every fiber of his being.

As the hospice allowed pet visits, we were determined that Dad and his right knee would be together again. The day Dad was moved to hospice, we coaxed a reluctant Randy away from the empty chair he guarded and loaded him into my parents' van for the trip across town. Randy insisted on carrying my father's glove in his mouth. After checking to see if Dad was in the van, he collapsed in the back and softly moaned. Even though I kept telling him we were going to see Dad, he just lay there and never even looked at his car water.

By the time we got to the hospice, the van's dog bed was covered with grief-shed hair. It took all my powers of persuasion to get Randy to reluctantly leave the vehicle that smelled of his beloved master's Old Spice aftershave for the illness-imbued odor of the hospice entryway. It was obvious he knew he was in death's waiting room. Lagging behind, he dragged himself down the hall, head drooping and plume-like tail dragging.

As I turned the corner into the main hallway, the end of the leash froze behind me. Then a whimpering golden streak with upturned nose began dragging me rapidly up the corridor. Randy was heading for his master, his massive tail no longer dragging, but sweeping frantically from side to side. He lunged around the door and into my father's room. I lost the leash and Randy headed immediately for the right side of the bed to rest his large head next to my father's limp hand. He dropped the glove next to Dad's hand and stood looking at the still form on the bed. I moved forward to take the glove and spare Randy the impossible wait for a caress that could never come again.

Suddenly, Dad's heart monitor shrieked an alarm. My knees gave out, dropping me to a sprawl on the floor and I watched in amazement as my father's long fingers twitched and moved, coming to rest on Randy's head. Randy sighed deeply, happy once more.

Over the next few weeks, Randy's daily visits held together the lingering remnants of Dad's warm spirit. Every morning Randy would prance down the corridor carrying Dad's glove and tenderly place it on the bed. Then resting his head next to Dad's hand, he waited for the caress that never came again. The nurses commented that Dad rested easier with Randy beside him. In the evening, Randy would hesitantly accept the glove from us and then go home to guard it until the next day.

At the end, we gathered in a circle at Dad's bedside and read the Prayers for the Sick. My mother's strong faith held grief at bay, allowing only love to stay. My father's last breath was accompanied by a deep, low moan from Randy. The family huddled together in misery and then reluctantly prepared to leave the room for the last time. Through tear-filled eyes, I saw Randy pick up Dad's glove and carefully carry it out of the room without being asked.

As we walked down the hall, Randy's eyes looked up and followed something only he could see as it vanished into the light. His tail wagged as he gazed, his silky golden head bobbing under an unseen caress.

Carol M. Chapman

Just Like Always

Blessed is the person who has earned the love of an old dog.

Sydney Jeanne Seward

For as long as I could remember, Ivan had always been at the door when I came home, wagging his brown tail in greeting. Tonight when I walked in after my classes, he wasn't there.

"Ivan?"

Silence was my only answer.

Then my mother appeared from the kitchen. "Ivan is not feeling well, Lori. He's downstairs in the family room. He's getting old."

"Old? Mom, he's only eleven or twelve."

"Fourteen," Mom corrected. "He's been with us a long time."

"When did he get sick?"

"He hasn't been himself for quite a while. He hasn't had much of an appetite. And he sleeps a lot more."

"But this is the first time he hasn't been at the door to meet me just like, well . . . always."

"He's made an effort to be up here every night lately because he loves you so much."

"He's going to get better, isn't he?"

Mom avoided my eyes. "I took him to the vet today. The doctor gave me some medicine to keep him comfortable, but nothing else can be done."

I couldn't breathe. A fist grabbed my heart, squeezing tightly. "You . . . you mean he's . . . going to die?"

"While you were growing up, honey, he was growing old."

I could have cried. But when you're almost twenty . . . well . . .

The phone rang. "Hi." It was my girlfriend Cathy. "What time do you want me to pick you up for the movie?"

"Ivan is sick."

"Ivan? Who's Ivan?"

"Ivan. My dog."

"Oh. I haven't heard you mention him, have I? Anyway, I'm sorry, but what time shall I pick you up?"

"Well, Cath, I . . . I don't think I can go. I want to stay home with Ivan."

"What? Lori, we've been waiting weeks for this movie to open, and now you're not going on account of a dog?"

"Ivan isn't just any dog, Cath. He's my friend, once-upon-a-time playmate, and—"

"Okay, Lori, I get your drift." I could tell by her voice how upset she was. "Are you going or not?"

"No. I'm staying home with Ivan."

The phone went dead in my hand. Some people just didn't understand.

As I went downstairs, I thought about what Cathy had said. "Who's Ivan?" Had I really never mentioned him? It wasn't that long ago that we went everywhere together. In the last few years, though, my interests had changed. Still, my love for him hadn't. Only how would he know that if I didn't take the time to show him? Ivan seemed happy, so I hadn't thought that much about it.

Ivan's tail wagged weakly as I sat down beside his bed. He tried to raise his head, but I leaned closer so he wouldn't have to, my hand caressing his brown body. "How's my buddy? Not too great, my friend?"

His tail flopped again, his black eyes gazing into mine. *Where have you been?* they seemed to say. *I've been waiting for you.*

Tears filled my eyes as I stroked his back. What had Mom said? I'd grown up while Ivan had grown old. Although I always petted him in passing, I couldn't remember when we'd last done anything together.

I shifted my position and Ivan tried to get up. "No, no," I whispered. "I'm not leaving you. We have a little catching up to do." He settled down again, nuzzling my leg.

"Remember when you were a puppy, Ivan, and how on Mother's Day you brought home a dead mouse and placed it at Mom's feet? Remember how she screamed? You never brought her another one." He was trying to watch me, but he was getting sleepy.

"And remember the time we all went camping and you flushed out that black-and-white kitty that turned out to be a skunk?"

His eyes were closed, but his tail wagged and his feet moved. Maybe he was remembering in his sleep.

Mom tiptoed in with a sleeping bag. "I thought you'd want to spend the night with him."

I nodded. It was like old times—our sleeping side by side—my arm around him.

His tongue licking my ear woke me up the next morning. I hugged him and his tail waved like a feeble flag in the wind. Work didn't seem important, but I knew I'd better go.

"Ivan will be waiting for you when you get home," Mom assured me.

And he was—right at the front door.

"I found him trying to climb the stairs to get up here to meet you," Mom said. "I don't know how he made it as far as he did. I carried him the rest of the way."

"It's like the old days, buddy," I scooped him into my arms and hugged him to my heart. I carried him downstairs and held him until he fell asleep.

He died that night in my arms. I told him over and over what an important part he'd played in my life. And in the end, we were together . . . just like always.

Lorena O'Connor

A Smile from Phoebe

Old dogs, like old shoes, are comfortable. They might be a bit out of shape and a little worn around the edges, but they fit well.

Bonnie Wilcox

About to begin my first teaching job, I moved out to Colorado completely alone, ready to reinvent myself in a new place. At the school where I was teaching, I soon met warm, friendly people with similar interests, but I found myself returning to my empty apartment each night with a keen sense that something was missing. Another teacher suggested that I get a pet—an older dog who would not need to be trained and would be ready to be a devoted companion. I scheduled a visit to a local animal shelter, eagerly picturing how wonderful life would be with a loving face to greet me every night.

The shelter was large and loud. I briskly walked up and down the aisles, stopping in front of one of the last kennels. I felt my throat squeeze tight with emotion when I saw her staring up at me from the cement floor: a beagle with a completely white face and a tail running on a motor. Her shiny eyes met mine as her head tilted back at an angle that caused her ears to hang straight out on either side. When I smiled at her, it sent her into a foot-to-foot shuffle. That was all it took. In no time the paperwork was completed and I was on my way home with an eleven-year-old beagle with no name.

Phoebe, a name I had never thought much about, seemed to fit the old girl all too well. My new friend nestled herself comfortably into my life. Often I would return home stressed by my work as a first-year teacher, but Phoebe knew how to change my mood instantly. She would stretch her neck backward and balance her head just so, until her ears stretched out perfectly on both sides of her white face. My little old beagle would suddenly become a plane ready for takeoff, and I would smile and forget my bad day.

In the light of the happiness that was spilling out of this eleven-year-old dog who had been bounced from home to home, my own small annoyances faded away. I resolved that it was only right for me to spoil her to the best of my ability. Phoebe was no stranger to the occasional table scrap, and her dog bed seemed to go empty when she realized mine was bigger and warmer. We were a perfect pair, each finding exactly what we needed in the other.

Our new life together was blessed in so many ways, but soon I began to notice that Phoebe was struggling to climb stairs and to run. Our visit to the vet brought news that twisted my stomach: Phoebe had severe arthritis in her spine that could not be reversed. The vet consoled me, and we discussed a plan to keep Phoebe comfortable and in as little pain as possible. On the ride home, Phoebe sat in the front of the car with me, a look of intense concern on her face as she watched me fight back the tears.

I resolved to make the best of the time Phoebe had left. We walked to her favorite park every day, and I massaged her ears whenever she pulled on my hand with her paw. I also took many pictures of her around our home and at her favorite places, though I never managed to capture her perfectly balanced "ready-for-takeoff" ears on film.

Unfortunately, none of this guaranteed me more time with her.

One fresh spring afternoon I returned from work, excited to take Phoebe to the park. We couldn't even make it down the stairs. I called the vet, who asked me if she was still having more good days than bad. Once off the phone, I looked into Phoebe's eyes as if to ask her. Our eyes locked and the answer was clear.

I took the following day off from work and spent that time petting Phoebe. I felt numb during the trip to the vet. As the vet prepared to put Phoebe down, I whispered all the thanks I had into my dog's ears. I told her how much joy she had given me. She sighed in relief just moments before her head became a weight on my lap. As a look of peace came over her, an emptiness swelled inside me.

Every day brought new reminders of Phoebe's absence. Whether it was a hidden bone or a paw print on the kitchen floor, it left me helpless with grief and in need of comfort. I tried to focus on how peaceful she had looked, but I still agonized over whether I had made the right decision.

I found solace when I started making a collage of photos of Phoebe. To complete my project, I picked up the photos from the last roll of film that I had taken of her. When I opened the envelope, the picture on top of the stack made the corners of my mouth twitch. It was a terrific shot of a white-faced beagle with her head tipped back, ears hanging to the sides in perfect symmetry. It was my Phoebe, asking me to smile.

Beth McCrea

Legacy of Love

The best thing about being a veterinarian is helping welcome new puppies and kittens to a family. The absolute hardest thing is helping someone say good-bye to a family member. Because pets' biological clocks tick faster than ours, few pets live past their teens. Over a career, a veterinarian can be involved with tens of thousands of pets dying. It has no parallel in any other profession—second place is not even close.

In order to cope with the high number of deaths and the difficulties in dealing with grieving clients, veterinarians sometimes find their hearts hardened to death, their souls callused against yet another tearful good-bye. Although surveys show that the public appreciates the visible care, compassion and concern that veterinarians express, the fact remains that, as a veterinarian, you can become numb to saying good-bye to a pet or helping ease its passage. Until it's *your* pet.

I was a senior in veterinary school when we got a spunky, salt-and-pepper miniature schnauzer. My wife, Teresa, named him Bodé (pronounced *bo-day*) after a favorite college professor of hers. Bodé became our first child. We called Bodé our son, and ourselves his mom and dad, another example of our generation's philosophy that "pets are family."

We spoiled Bodé rotten. He ate with us in the kitchen, munched on the best pet foods, rode with us in the car (yapping his way around town like a canine siren), sat with us on the couch to watch TV at night, slept in our bed and went on vacation with us. He wore handmade sweaters, received the hot-oil treatment at the groomer's and got the very best medical care available. We did anything and everything to pamper our beloved first child.

Sadly, because of a very weak immune system, Bodé had medical problems—a lot of them. First, he got a severe case of pancreatitis and went blind. Then, he developed incurable, greasy seborrhea that left his skin oily and smelly. Over time, his teeth went bad, which caused his breath to smell horrible; he lost his hearing and he limped on a bad hip joint. Despite his bad breath, smelly skin and the need to be lifted on and off the bed, he *never* missed a single night sleeping in our bed.

On December 10, 1985, our "second" child was born: our first daughter, a beautiful two-legged, blond-haired girl named Mikkel. When we brought Mikkel home, we, like a lot of first-time parents, were worried about what would happen between Bodé and our baby. Would Bodé be jealous of the lost attention and try to bite Mikkel?

As Teresa sat with Mikkel on the couch, the two sets of grandparents and I watching intently, Bodé walked over to check out this wrinkled, weird-looking alien with a baby-bird-like tuft of hair on her head. Bodé opened his mouth and made a sudden movement toward Mikkel. I sprang to my feet. But Bodé wasn't going to bite the baby! Instead, he started licking her, giving Mikkel a canine version of a sponge bath. Forget worries about disease transmission, we were delighted a powerful affection-connection had been born.

Almost exactly a year later, close to Mikkel's first birthday, Bodé was stricken with a fatal condition called autoimmune hemolytic anemia. Simply put, Bodé's red blood cells were being destroyed by the thousands as his immune system attacked the very thing that kept life-sustaining oxygen flowing to every cell in his body.

Refusing to accept the finality of this diagnosis and with a dogged determination to save Bodé, I ran tests, called specialists at various veterinary schools, consulted with other veterinarians with whom I worked, pored over textbooks, ran more tests. Sadly, all roads led to a dead end.

I remember delivering the news to Teresa. She sobbed as she held Bodé in her arms, gently rocking his body, which was becoming increasingly lifeless due to the lack of oxygen. She couldn't imagine life without Bodé. Neither could I.

She looked to me for guidance in making the right decision, and suddenly it hit me. I wasn't counseling another client about options; I wasn't preparing for the passing of another precious pet; I wasn't gearing up for my standard lectures on what happens when a pet is euthanized or what the options are for memorial services and remains. This wasn't another pet; this was our child, the greatest dog in the world.

Although the weight of that realization crushed my soul, it also succeeded in breaking through the heavy callus around my heart, a barrier built up from participating in thousands of pet passings. I began to cry—releasing not only the tears of a grieving family member, but also tears that had been subdued and submerged as I'd struggled for years with the sadness of saying good-bye to hundreds, thousands of my clients' and friends' family members and beloved pets. My heart was reawakening even as my four-legged child was slipping away.

Finally, Teresa said to me, "You know Bodé won't get better and is in a lot of pain. We love him so much; you know what we need to do." Then she handed me Bodé's warm, limp body.

Overcome with grief, she couldn't go with me to my veterinary clinic, so I gathered up his favorite toys and held him in my lap as I drove to the clinic. "Your journey is almost over, my boy," I said to Bodé as I stroked the full length of his body. *We'll miss you, we'll miss you, we'll miss you,* echoed my aching heart.

Sobbing, almost unable to see or catch my breath, I walked in the back door of the hospital and told my veterinary-practice partner that it was time. He put an experienced, caring hand on my shoulder and nodded his head in agreement.

As my partner prepared the injection that would end Bodé's suffering, I cradled Bodé's head and looked deep into his eyes. I told him how much love, laughter and loyalty he had blessed us with. I whispered to him that where he was going, his body would be new again: He would have sparkling white, razor-sharp teeth, eagle-eyes able to spot the most distant bird, ears that could detect the treat drawer being opened from across the ranch, glistening Howly-wood hair, four good wheels able to not just keep up, but lead the way on our frequent horseback rides in the mountains and sweet smelling breath for sleeping nose to nose at nights.

As the solution left the syringe and entered Bodé's body, his stub-of-a-tail hesitated, then stopped. It was over for our first child, only six years old. His body was still there but his essence had left him.

That night Teresa and I sat in the yard at home holding Mikkel and reflecting on what special gifts Bodé had brought to our lives. We decided to return him to the soil at the family farm. We knew he was gone physically, but in memory he would be with us forever.

Bodé's passing brought me a new understanding of the grieving process. When we lose a pet, it breaks our hearts—but when our hearts mend, they expand some-how to accept another four-legged family member, a process to be repeated many times during a pet lover's lifetime. So the pain of loss—however great—is just one step in the journey of making our hearts capable of expe-riencing more and more love.

There was one more important part to Bodé's legacy: The callus around my soul never came back. From that day forward, I lost the numbness to other people's pain at losing their pet. This was Bodé's most precious gift to me: He gave me back my heart.

Marty Becker, D.V.M.

Tears for Sheila

It was a regular, busy afternoon at the vet clinic where I worked as a vet tech. The morning surgeries, spays and some dental cleanings were finished, and we were now taking care of afternoon appointments. Some puppy shots here, suture removal there, itchy skin in room three. I moved along to the sound of dogs barking, doors shutting and the wobbly centrifuge finishing a cycle.

As I drew up a rabies vaccination for a beagle puppy, one of the receptionists came out of an exam room and handed me a file, saying in a low voice, "It's a Labrador in for euthanasia. The owner wants it done in his vehicle, because the dog is large and it'll be hard for him to carry her out afterward."

"Sheila, nine years old, cancer found in June, inoperable," I murmured to myself as I flipped through the file before setting it down. And here it was October. The Lab had lived four months longer than I would have expected. Usually cancer takes its toll very quickly.

I finished with the little beagle's shot, soothed the puppy and the nervous owner a bit, and then slipped to the back of the clinic to find the technician who had been there the longest. I knew she would have some information on the Labrador.

"Doc told him in June that Sheila had cancer. She had a lump on the back of her neck that he brought in to have Doc check, and it turned out to be carcinoma," she told me as she drew up the pale-pink fluid for the euthanasia and handed it to me. "She wasn't suffering and he wasn't ready to put her to sleep then, but now he's had four months to prepare."

I gathered up the syringe and some alcohol swabs and went to find the doctor. I explained to him that we would be performing the euthanasia outside, and we walked outside the clinic together.

Sheila's owner, a burly man named Mike, had parked his pickup under some shade trees on the far side of the parking lot. As we approached, I saw that Sheila was in the back, lying behind the cab, her head resting on her front paws. At one time, she had been a beautiful chocolate Lab. Now the cancer had dulled her magnificent coat to a dusty brown. Her sad brown eyes were half-closed, and she sighed deeply as we walked up to her. Sheila had been to the vet many times, and I'm sure she expected that some sort of painful test or needle sting was coming.

As I prepared the syringe for the doctor, Mike called softly to her, "Come on, Sheila. Come here, girl."

My eyes welled up with tears as I saw her struggle to rise. That Sheila was in a lot of pain was obvious. When she finally managed to climb to her feet, I saw the cancerous lump. It stuck out grossly from the back of Sheila's neck, larger than a grapefruit.

"Come on, Sheila," the man called softly again. With nothing but trust and love in her tired brown eyes, Sheila hobbled over to the three of us at the tailgate of the pickup. As Mike lowered the tailgate, he said softly, "It's been real hard for her these past three days. Her neck is bothering her pretty badly, and she can't eat or sleep. I guess I knew it was her time." He gently cupped the big dog's face in his hands and slowly stroked the graying brown muzzle.

Doc quietly asked Mike if he was ready.

"Yes. Go ahead," came the whispered reply.

At Doc's imperceptible nod, I carefully picked up Sheila's front leg and applied light pressure. Sheila's eyes never left Mike's face, even as Doc deftly slid the needle into her vein. After only a few cubic centimeters of the fluid had been injected, I helped Sheila lay down as the drug began to take effect. With one final glance at her dear friend's face, Sheila's sweet brown eyes closed for the last time. The last of the injection in her bloodstream, Sheila slipped away, Mike's hand on her grizzled head.

Slipping the needle out of Sheila's leg, Doc handed it to me and pulled his stethoscope from around his neck. After listening intently for several minutes, Doc turned to Mike and uttered just one sentence: "She went very peacefully."

The man simply nodded, his head down. I could see the tears streaming down his face.

I gathered up the items we had used as Doc walked back into the office. I lingered for a moment, wanting to say something, anything, to comfort the grieving man. I wanted to say, "Sheila was beautiful. She was so brave and strong to have fought this cancer for so long. I could see how much she loved you. I could see it in her eyes, the way she trusted you."

In the end, I couldn't bring myself to say any of that. Putting a hand on his shoulder, I whispered, "I'm sorry for your loss."

He didn't move or respond, and his eyes never left Sheila. There was nothing I could have said that he didn't already know—how wonderful Sheila was in life, and how dignified she was in death.

As I walked into the building, I stole one last glance at him. The sun glinted off the tears pouring down his face as he sat on the tailgate of the truck, his hand methodically stroking Sheila's still body.

I let the door close softly behind me, wiped my own eyes and slowly made my way to the front of the clinic. My heart ached for quite a while as I went about my tasks. I've been through many such scenes, but it never gets any easier. There's no question: love hurts. Still, I felt grateful— and honored—to have been in its presence.

Laurie MacKillip

Harry and George

Every year, starting on the day after Christmas, my sister and I looked forward to the fifteenth of June. That was the day our parents loaded up the car, and we moved to a ramshackle cottage on the bay for the rest of the summer. It was a child's idea of heaven on earth—late nights fishing on the wharf; barefoot days in bathing suits, sunning on boats; meals on a big, screened porch under lazy ceiling fans. Every summer seemed better than the last—until the summer we lost George.

George and his brother Harry were golden retrievers, and you never saw one without the other, whether they were crashing through tall saw grass or chasing bait-stealing herons off neighboring wharves. When they did get separated, Harry would bark until George found him. We all loved those dogs as if they were our own, but they really belonged to an old salt known to everyone as "the captain."

One afternoon during this particular summer, Harry and George lay down for a nap under some hydrangea bushes. After an hour or so Harry woke up, but George didn't. All the children, most of the mothers and even a few of the fathers could be seen sniffling and wiping away the tears when they heard Harry barking for his brother. The captain was almost as pitiful as Harry. Finally, Harry gave up barking altogether. Unfortunately when he quit barking, he also stopped eating. He wouldn't touch dog food, ignored his favorite doggy treats, even turned his nose up at a cheeseburger.

My sister and I were so worried that on the fifth night of Harry's fast, as we ate our supper of fried speckled trout, corn steaming on the cob and fresh tomatoes, I asked Mama what to do. She said to pray for an angel to help Harry.

That night I lay in bed under the slumber-inducing, back-and-forth breeze of an oscillating fan and pondered Harry's plight. I was pretty sure that angels dealt only with people and had certainly never heard of them involving themselves in dogs' problems. But just in case, I prayed myself to sleep: *Please, God, send an angel to help Harry.*

The next morning after breakfast Mama gave me a sausage with instructions to take it to Harry. I found him and the captain sitting morosely on the end of their wharf. I waved the sausage under Harry's nose, but he didn't blink. *There's never an angel around when you need one,* I thought. Harry got up and started toward the house. His huge head was so low it almost dragged on the wharf boards, and I could tell he was weak from not eating. The captain, watching Harry make his slow progress to the house, shook his old head and sighed.

A sudden splash in the water made us turn to see what kind of fish it was. It wasn't a fish, but the smiling face of a dolphin that broke the dark water, and even the captain had to smile back at her. She made a little dolphin squeak. A deep growl made me look up toward the house. Harry was on the deck, his ears all perked up. The dolphin rolled and splashed—as all dolphins do—then did something you often see trained dolphins do, but rarely get to see a wild bay dolphin do. *Whoosh!* Up she went like a rocket, silver and shining against the deep blue of the summer sky. The captain and I were clapping and cheering, we were so overcome at the sight. The next thing I knew, Harry came flying down the wharf barking his big, golden head off. When he was finally quiet, the dolphin looked the dog straight in the eye, said something in dolphin and swam away.

In all the excitement, I had dropped Mama's sausage. I watched in delight as Harry gobbled it up. The captain and I took him back to the house and fed him a giant bowl of dog food, then loaded him up with doggy treats.

The next morning Harry was waiting, and sure enough, the dolphin came by. She blew air out of the top of her shining, gray head and smiled her dolphin smile. Harry began to bark like he had the day before and got a quick dolphin reply. Then off she went again, a smiling silver rocket.

Although I heard that the dolphin returned to visit Harry all through that summer, I never saw her again. But it hardly matters, since it was her very first visit that set Harry on the mend. When I told my sister the story, she decided that this qualified the dolphin as a pet and decided to name her Fishy. But I knew better: I called her Angel.

Margaret P. Cunningham

Gentle Giant

Several years ago, after losing our Doberman mix, Turnpike, to colic, I stood on my front porch and publicly announced that I was now officially *not* looking for a St. Bernard—in hopes that one would magically materialize. This had been my standard MO: If I wasn't looking for something, it would always appear.

For once, this approach didn't work, so I called a rescue buddy who worked with an all-breed rescue group called ARF (Animal Rescue Foundation) and said, "How 'bout putting us on the waiting list to adopt a St. Bernard?"

Mary Jane just laughed. She told me that they hardly ever got St. Bernards here in Tulsa, Oklahoma. She laughed and then laughed some more. I said, "Okay, now. I charge extra if I'm funny, so just please put us on the list!"

I then called another rescue friend and said, "Put us on the waiting list for a St. Bernard." She laughed and laughed. Same song, second verse.

One week later, none of us were laughing when a St. Bernard's dad had to go overseas with the military and couldn't take his 140-pound dog. They called my husband, Dale and me, and we adopted Bart.

We were one week into loving Bart when—you guessed

it—the phone rang! It was the other laughing rescue buddy. She asked me if we had found a St. Bernard to adopt. I told her, "Yes, we have, thank you very much. Why do you ask?"

She said that a one-year-old Saint was about to be shot by a country sheriff in a small town forty minutes north of Tulsa.

"*Shot?*" If you want to get me moving in high gear, all you have to do is mention the words *shot* and *dog* in the same sentence. I can flat out *move* when I have to!

It seems that the Saint's owners couldn't keep Bogey in their fenced yard, and the local animal control had already given them three tickets for complaints filed against them. And since this Saint was running loose again, the animal control officer was planning to shoot this gentle giant.

I called the sheriff and told him that I was on the way to pick up Bogey for ARF.

He answered, *Chomp, chomp* (chewing tobacco), "Lady, you have thirty minutes to get here—or I am shootin' him."

I answered back, *Chomp, chomp* (sugarless gum), "Mister, you will give me however long it takes to get there—or you will see your face and your name in every newspaper from here to Arkansas, telling how a back-woods country sheriff shot a loving pet while a rescue group frantically tried to get there in time. By the way, do you have any good black-and-white glossies?"

Bam! He slammed down the phone.

I grabbed my purse and ran to find Dale. "TRUCK!" I screamed. "GET IN THE TRUCK! NOW! DRIVE!" I began grabbing leashes and collars and bacon (you never know when you may need a good slab of bacon), and off we raced while I relayed the story to Dale, who reminded me that we already owned one St. Bernard and he was certain we didn't need two of them.

We got to the address I'd been given. There was no sign of any sheriff, backwoods or otherwise, but there was a *beautiful,* starving St. Bernard pup. He had been "confined" by a simple piece of chicken wire. He only had to step over it to gain freedom to search for food.

A very poor couple owned him, and the guy said, "He eats like a horse, and we can't afford to feed him."

Of course, Dale thought we were picking up Bogey for ARF, but this boy was mine and I knew it. I failed Fostering 101 before I even began.

We took Bogey home to live with us. He especially loved Nicholas, our small something-a-poo, and the feeling was quite mutual. Each morning Bogey and Bart would run with Dale in the neighborhood. There's something about two St. Bernards that attracts children of all ages. Bogey looked just like Beethoven, the movie star, complete with flopping jowls and drooling slobbers that he could sling a good twenty feet.

The years sailed by. Our two beloved poodles, Fred and Munchie, passed on, as well as little Nicholas. New dogs joined our pack.

When Bogey was thirteen years old, he began to fail. He was having trouble going up and down the steps, moving his 180-plus pounds to stay in our air-cooled garage during the day when the temperatures reached over 70 degrees. I worried that the time was coming when we would have to make the dreaded "decision."

One night I returned home from a five-day trip. When I got out of the car, Bogey came over to me, wagging his tail. I put down my bags and leaned over to give his bear-sized head a hug. Bogey seemed 100 percent normal and happy to see his mama coming home. How could I have known that it would be his last night with us?

Dale woke me up the next morning with tears streaming down his face. I knew someone had died, and I instinctively began searching frantically for the bichons. Both were in bed with me, still asleep.

Dale managed to mouth the word, "Bogey."

I flew out of our bedroom and raced out to the garage. There lay Bogey, on his tummy, with his back leg kicked out behind him and his head resting on his front paws. It was the same position he slept in each and every night. He truly had just slipped away peacefully in his sleep.

What I did next may be surprising to some, but if you've ever been forced to make the loving, last decision for an older, failing pet, you will certainly understand. Through my tears, and in my nightgown, I walked outside the garage, just to the beginning of the driveway. I raised both hands into the air and wept openly, saying, "Thank you, Lord. Thank you."

You see, my prayers had been answered for Bogey: to die peacefully in his sleep when it was time for him to go, when the bad days outnumbered the good. Dale and I didn't want to have to take Bogey for that final trip to the vet.

I had prayed this prayer many times in my life for several of my dogs as their days drew to an end, but this was the only time in forty-seven years that it had been answered. All the other times we had to help our dogs cross the Rainbow Bridge. Our poodles, Fred and Munchie, had been put to sleep on the same day, May 19. Then, six years later, strangely enough on May 19 again, we'd had to say good-bye to Nicholas, our once-in-a-lifetime heart dog. With a start, I realized that today was May 19! Our Bogey had gone to be with God on the very same date—another six years later.

Coming back inside, I knelt beside Bogey, "Godspeed, my gentle giant," I whispered. "You are so loved. Run to your Nicholas now. You always did love him so." I smiled through my tears. There was such peace knowing without any doubt that it had been Bogey's time to go.

Robin Pressnall

A Familiar Road

Dog ownership is like a rainbow. Puppies are the joy at one end. Old dogs are the treasure at the other.

Carolyn Alexander

I slowly run the tips of my fingers over the nerve-rich compass of Joe-Dog's nose, eliciting no reaction. Still warm, it feels lustrous as silk. In our ten years together, it's been the single place he's consistently reserved as too sensitive for human contact—patiently shaking off all attempts with a gentle head butt or sneeze.

A second guarded touch again meets with no response. His eyes are closed, broad Labrador chest still. My beloved best friend, who for eighteen months fought back cancer with a tenacious spirit, and from whom I have sought—and received—boundless solace and joy, is gone.

What began a decade ago, as an effort to teach my children the responsibilities of caring for a pet, has instead become for me an achingly rich lesson on the fleeting gifts of life.

I bundle up his body in a well-used wool blanket, but

not before sinking my face one last time into the soft fur of his shoulders, inhaling deeply the familiar comfort of his scent until my lungs threaten to explode. I want to remember this smell forever. I take care to leave his head uncovered, as if wrapping an infant, leaving in place his azure-blue collar with the worn metal ID tags that tinkled a melody with each step.

While my husband prepares a burial site along the cool shaded edge of a pasture still verdant with spring, I wander numbly through the house, ambivalent about this last task of choosing which of Joe-Dog's belongings to send with him. I have known this day was coming, and chastise myself for being so unprepared. With a sigh, I settle on a white porcelain kibble bowl sporting the words "Dog from Hell" lettered in gold, a gift from family after Joe-Dog once underwent emergency surgery to remove an ingested pair of underwear hopelessly twisted in his belly. In the bowl I place three of his favorite chew toys, including a star-shaped fleece one, nicknamed "chemo-baby," not for its missing threads of rainbow hair, but because it often accompanied us on our drive to the vet's office for chemotherapy treatments. To the pile I add a half-eaten box of Milk Bones, and last, a photo of the three of us at Silver Falls, taken in the light of an icy, bright February day.

Outside, I stand nearby as my husband gently lowers the bundle with Joe-Dog into the freshly prepared grave, handing him the items I have chosen when he finishes. He adds these, too, in silence. Offering him a hand up, we are drawn together in a momentary embrace. The ensuing knock and rattle of the tractor's diesel engine as it labors to return the scoops of black earth isn't enough to cover the sound of my sorrow. It pours out of me in gulping sobs. My husband wipes his face with a checkered shirt-sleeve between working the tractor's levers. With a last pat of the machine's bucket, the job is done.

Navigating through grief in the only way we know how, we later plant a rose bush with petals the color of peaches at Joe-Dog's burial site. As a gesture we add a small concrete tile that is imbedded with his paw print and three smooth round stones, the tile originally made for the butterfly garden in happier times. In the still moments of daybreak, we place an occasional offering of waffle, Joe-Dog's favorite morning treat, to feed both the birds and our souls.

Several months pass; my husband and I travel to the county animal shelter, seeking an unsure measure of relief for our loneliness. We agree Joe-Dog can never be replaced, but still, we have much to offer a homeless new companion, and we know he would understand. After an emotional visit, we bring home a nine-month-old female shepherd mix—full of love, energy, and soon, bits of rubber from the sole of my favorite dress shoe.

Already a Frisbee expert, she willingly chases many a misdirected spin as I work at mastering this fast new game. We name her Josie, and she takes a quick interest in squirrels, all manner of human breakfast fare and the warm comfort of our king-size bed. Before I realize it, she has led us down a familiar road, tugging all the way.

Pennie DeBoard

Saying Good-Bye to Dingo

My daughter Ella had a unique and remarkable relationship with my parents' loving but irascible poodle mix. As a rule, Dingo didn't like children. He would simply move away from them, or, if necessary, growl for them to keep their distance. But he loved Ella. She was always very gentle and kind and he trusted her. She trusted him, too. Trusted him to always be there for ball-fetching, raspberry picking or just for softly stroking his ears.

When Ella was eight years old, Dingo was seventeen and in very poor health. My parents delayed the inevitable as long as they could, but one bright spring morning my mother phoned me to let me know the time had come. I held the phone tightly and looked out the window, my welling eyes making the daffodils and tulips in my garden blur.

"Dingo's in a lot of pain. We've made an appointment with the veterinarian for this afternoon," my mother said, trying to keep the choking emotion out of her voice. "It's against my better judgment to tell you," she said. "But I wanted to let you decide how to handle it with Ella." My mom always wanted to protect her children and grandchildren from any and all heartache; her way to do that was to only tell us about painful events after the fact, or not at all. But for whatever reason, this time she included us. I will be forever grateful to my mother for that phone call. It was a generous gesture, and ultimately, it would have repercussions beyond what any of us could have guessed at that time.

I agonized for a while, thinking that maybe my mother was right, just let it happen and we'll tell Ella afterward and "spare" her the heartache. By phone, I talked at length to my husband and a couple of close friends about whether to offer Ella a chance to say good-bye to Dingo in the comfort of his own home. Was she too young to choose for herself how, or even whether, to say good-bye? I looked at our own aging wheaten terrier mix, Petey, sprawled across our kitchen floor, and our spunky Persian cat, Albert, snoozing in the morning sun on the couch. When their time came, we would certainly want to be able to say good-bye. Could I deny that choice to my daughter with her adored Dingo? I decided to trust my mothering instincts, which dictated that we pick out the important "eight-year-old" points of this sad event, and help her to decide for herself.

My husband took the afternoon off from work and we walked to her elementary school. Ella's teacher allowed our daughter to leave the classroom with us. My husband and I sat with Ella on the deserted playground and spoke softly, all holding hands.

"Sweetheart," I said, grateful that I could control my own voice at the moment. "As you know, Dingo is very old. And you know that he often doesn't feel well, right?"

She nodded solemnly, looking from me to my husband and back again.

"Well, the past few days he has felt very bad. He hurts all over and the vet says he's going to die soon. Nana and Da don't want him to hurt anymore, so they are going to take him to the veterinarian and he's going to help Dingo die and not be in pain anymore. Do you understand?"

Ella's eyes welled up with tears but she nodded.

The emotion began to creep into my voice now. "So, even though it's very sad, if we want to, we can go visit Dingo right now and talk to him and tell him we love him and say good-bye. Your teacher and the principal say it's fine. But only if you want to. If you'd rather write Dingo a letter or draw him a picture, we can do that."

Her feelings revealed only by the tears falling down her cheeks, Ella said in a strong, clear voice, "I want to go say good-bye to Dingo."

We took her out of school, with the full support of her principal and second-grade teacher, both of whom knew that this old dog would likely teach Ella a more powerful life lesson than any they could offer that day.

So the three of us went to visit Dingo at Nana and Da's house one last time. My parents graciously arranged to be absent when we arrived. Ella sat next to Dingo on his round, plaid bed. The old guy couldn't lift his head, but when she put her hand near his mouth, his soft pink tongue gently kissed her. Her tender eight-year-old voice and the ticking kitchen clock were the only sounds in the otherwise silent house.

"Remember how I would throw the tennis ball and you used to chase it, Dingo?" she asked him. "Remember when you helped me hunt for Easter eggs?" She held his paw with one hand and stroked his ear with the other. "Remember going up to the cabin and walking across the bridge? I was always afraid to go across that bridge but you waited for me. Remember?" A tiny tip, tip, tip of his tail. She fed him his favorite treats and gently hugged him, told him how much she loved him, her warm tears falling on his gray fur. My husband and I both said our good-byes and cried, too. The three of us hugged around his bed, Dingo in the center of our love. We all knew together when it was time to leave.

Ella wanted to return to school. As she entered her classroom, several friends rushed to her with comforting words and hugs. Her teacher later told us that she had then read to the class *The Tenth Good Thing about Barney*. Then they had all talked about love and loss and the many different things we learn from our pets. The teacher said it was a remarkable day.

Although I knew then how important and loving that good-bye experience was for all of us, especially Ella, I had no idea what lay ahead for our family in dealing with death. I knew in my heart that we were wisely seizing a "teachable moment," but my head wanted reassurance that we didn't make too big a deal of it. Had I known that in the next twenty months our family would say good-bye to Ella's loving grandfather "Grampi," her wonderful great-uncle "Gruncle," and then our beloved Nana herself, I wouldn't have questioned our response to Dingo's death, not even for a moment.

Saying good-bye to Dingo helped us all to know how important and helpful it is to say good-bye, in any and every way opportunity presents. Grampi died suddenly, with little warning and a thousand miles away. There was no chance to say good-bye before he died, so we wrote letters and drew pictures and put them in the ground with him so he could read them in heaven. Gruncle, too, was far away, but he was able to read our missives of love before he died.

Thankfully, because she lived just three miles from our home, we were able to say good-bye to Nana in person. Over the course of many special visits, we hugged her and kissed her, we talked about special times, we cooked her favorite meals for her. We told her over and over how much we loved her, as she died of cancer in her home. We knew how to do all this because we'd had a wonderful teacher: a little gray poodle mix named Dingo.

Elizabeth Wrenn

8

RESCUE ME!

*Saving just one dog won't change the world ...
but surely the world will change for that
one dog.*

Unknown

Just an Old Golden Retriever

She was just an old golden retriever. Her name was Brandy, and for eleven years she was the sole companion of an elderly woman who lived in a bungalow colony in the country. Neighbors often saw the two of them together in the garden. The woman would be hunched over picking flowers and there was that old dog, close at her heels or lying in the middle of the grass watching her pull weeds. When the woman died, some relatives came and collected anything they thought was valuable and put a "For Sale" sign on the front lawn. Then they locked the dog out and drove away.

Some of the neighbors left food out for Brandy, but mostly the dog stayed near the house that she knew and waited for her owner to come back. A young mother who lived next door noticed the old retriever, but she had never been around animals before and while she thought the dog was friendly enough, she didn't feel it was any of her concern.

However, when the dog wandered into her yard and began playing with eighteen-month-old Adam, she wanted to shoo the dirty thing away. Adam was her only child and the light of her life. But he was having so much fun feeding

Brandy cookies she decided to let her stay. After that, whenever Adam had cookies Brandy came by to visit.

One afternoon, the boy's mother left Adam in the soft grassy yard to play while she answered the phone. When she returned he was gone. Just gone. The mother was frantic. Neighbors came over to help in the search. Police arrived and looked for three hours before calling in the state police and helicopters to do an extensive aerial search. But no one could find the child, and as the sun set over the horizon, whispers of abduction, injury or even death crept into conversations.

The search had been going on for six hours when a neighbor, who'd just returned home, wondered where Brandy was. Adam's mother, hysterical with worry, didn't understand why anyone was asking about the old dog at a time like this.

When someone suggested she might be with Adam, a trooper recalled hearing a dog barking deep in the woods when they were doing a foot search. Suddenly, everybody started calling for Brandy.

They heard faint barking and followed the sound until they found the toddler, standing up fast asleep, pressed against the trunk of a tree. That old dog was holding him there with one shoulder as one of her own legs dangled over a thirty-five-foot drop to a stream below.

Brandy had followed Adam when he wandered off. When she saw danger, she'd pushed him out of harm's way and held him safe for all those hours, even as the child struggled to get free.

As soon as the rescue team picked up Adam, the old dog collapsed. A trooper carried Adam back home, while his mother, sobbing with relief, carried Brandy. She was so grateful to the old golden retriever that Brandy spent the rest of her days with them. Brandy lived to the ripe old age of seventeen.

But this story doesn't end with just one life saved. In Brandy's honor, Adam's mother, Sara Whalen, founded Pets Alive, a rescue sanctuary in New York that takes in unwanted animals, including those designated to be euthanized because they are old, blind, incontinent or perhaps not cute enough to be adopted. While she can't save them all, Sara feels comforted that she can help at least some of them. She knows that if someone had put that old retriever to sleep, she could have easily lost the light of her life: her son.

Today, thirty years later, there are more than three hundred animals in her care, including birds, potbellied pigs, old horses retired from the carriage business and unadoptable pets from rescue groups across the country. The woman who used to think an old, abandoned dog wasn't any of her concern found that every life has value and has become a beacon for thousands of animals in need.

Audrey Thomasson

Nothing That Can't Be Fixed

"Oh, no! Look out!" I shouted as I watched the truck in front of me narrowly miss the little black dog on the high-way. Startled, my children, ages one and two, looked at me from their car seats.

Cringing, the dog ran away, limping on one leg. It made it to the shoulder of the road and then turned to stare hopefully at my car as I drove past. I didn't feel that I could stop with the children in the car, but something in that earnest stance stayed with me well after the stray was out of sight.

Stray dogs were a problem in the rural community where I lived. My husband, a veterinarian, often spoke about the plight of these forgotten animals. Most did not survive long. If they were not killed on the roadways, they died of starvation or disease.

I kept thinking about the black dog as I drove home. Then I made a decision to do something I'd never tried before. I dropped the children off at home, asking a neigh-bor to watch them, then drove to my husband's veteri-nary clinic. I found him inside and began to tell him about the injured dog.

"If I can catch it, would you put it to sleep?" He didn't

seem very pleased with my plan, but he knew the dog was probably suffering. There were no animal shelters in our area, and we both knew there was no way for us to keep the dog—besides having two small children, we had no yard or place for a pet. My husband thought for a moment, then answered quietly that he would do what I asked.

Armed with a blanket and some dog biscuits, I drove back along the highway. I found the dog once again on the shoulder of the road. I pulled over and parked, grabbed some biscuits and stepped out of the car. When I walked to where the dog lay, I got my first good look at just how miserable such an existence can be.

The little black dog was painfully thin. Its hair was missing in patches and roughened, raw skin showed through the bare places. A tooth caught on an upper lip gave the dog's face the appearance of a snarl. One eye seemed to be gone, and the dog's leg had been injured. It was so hungry that it was gnawing on the bottom half of an old turtle shell it held between its paws.

Kneeling down in front of it, I fed it the treats until they were gone. Then I carefully picked up the dog and set it on the blanket in my car.

During the drive back to the veterinary clinic, I kept telling myself that what I was doing was the right thing. This animal was badly injured and starving. A quick, painless euthanasia was better than the fate that awaited it otherwise.

I glanced down at the dog and saw it studying me. The look in that one brown eye was unnerving.

Just don't think about what's ahead, I told myself.

My husband was waiting for me when I pulled back into the parking lot. He opened the car door, picked up the dog and carried it into the clinic. Reluctantly, I followed him inside.

Instead of taking the dog to the kennel area, he carried

it into the exam room. There, he started looking over his newest patient.

"It's a young female, about a year and a half old. She has mange, that's why her skin looks so bad. Probably hit by a car, but this leg's not broken. Her jaw is fractured, though, and starting to heal itself. This eye needs some corrective surgery and the other eyelid needs to be closed . . ."

While my husband continued to examine the black dog, she sat quietly on the table. Her gaze never left my face. Why was she staring at me? Did she understand why I had brought her to this place?

His examination completed, my husband turned to me. He looked at me meaningfully and said, "There's nothing here that can't be fixed."

I looked once more at the dog. She was still watching me with her single brown eye. I felt heartsick about this dog's sad life, but the decision had to be made, and I was the one who had to make it.

* * *

It's been twelve years since that day. I think about it often, especially on days like today when I'm sitting in the yard watching my hens peck around in the grass. My orange cat stretches lazily in a sunny spot on the patio. The summer's last hummingbirds are fussing about the feeders.

An old dog leans against my leg. She lays her gray muzzle, once so black and shiny, on my knee and looks up at me. I give her silky head a pat. Now I understand the expression in that solitary brown eye. And I answer her, "I love you, too, Daisy."

Pamela Jenkins

Ana: From Rescued to Rescuer

Ana's early life was a long series of painful—and unfortunately, all-too-common—experiences. Like many golden
retrievers, Ana started out as an adorable high-energy
puppy, but when her energy and high prey drive began
to take a destructive turn, it soon drove her human family crazy. Instead of training her, they eventually booted
her out of the house to a doghouse in the backyard. This,
of course, made things worse. She was the type of dog
who desperately needed a job to do. Now, with even less
attention and direction, Ana began to dig and bark. When
she destroyed the irrigation system for the plantings in
the family's backyard, that was it! Ana was given away
and soon was passed from one home to another.
Fortunately, she was rescued by a responsible woman
who recognized Ana's need for a job. This special dog
eventually found her way into my life, starting the train of
events that would lead to the creation of one of the most
successful disaster search-and-rescue training programs
in the country.

When I retired after a long career as a physical-education
teacher, my husband and I moved from the suburbs of
Los Angeles to a small town in the mountains of Southern

California. There I decided to pursue all the interests and dreams I had put on hold during my working life. One of these was to have a highly trained dog for rescue work. I started in wilderness search and rescue, but soon decided that, given my age and personality, disaster search-and-rescue work suited me better: The search area in a disaster situation is clearly defined, the need is certain and heavy packs are not necessary.

Immediately after the bombing in Oklahoma City, my canine partner, a black Lab named Murphy, and I were deployed there. Working at the Murrah building, I saw first-hand how vital search-and-rescue teams were. Unfortunately, there simply weren't enough trained teams available. When I returned home, I decided to do something about the shortage.

At that time search-and-rescue dogs took between three and five years to train, and the expense was prohibitive. An idea began to percolate in my head: if assistance dogs could be trained in nine months to a year, why couldn't a search-and-rescue dog be trained in the same amount of time?

I began making inquiries and eventually found a trainer who I believed could take a year-old dog and within a year turn the pup into a search-and-rescue dog. The next hurdle would be to find appropriate dogs to train. After a phone call to my friend and mentor, Bonnie, who was deeply involved in assistance dog training, the whole thing really started rolling. When I told Bonnie that I needed dogs for this new program, she said, "Oh! I think I have the perfect dog for you."

Ana had been given to Bonnie in the hope that the highly intelligent dog could be trained as an assistance dog. Bonnie knew quickly that Ana wouldn't make a good assistance dog—she was a fast learner and had the right attitude, but wasn't mellow enough. When I asked Bonnie where I could find dogs to train as search-and-rescue dogs, it clicked in her mind: Ana would be perfect!

And she was.

When I drove to Bonnie's to pick up Ana, Bonnie led me out to a large fenced paddock where at least twenty-five golden retrievers were all playing happily together. She opened the gate and let the dogs into a big barn area where they began to run together in an enormous golden circle around the barn. I noticed that one, and only one, of the dogs had stopped to pick up a stick and now galloped merrily around us holding the stick firmly in its mouth. Bonnie smiled at me and said, "Wilma, can you pick out the dog I have in mind for you?"

I hazarded a guess. "The one with the stick?"

Bonnie's jaw dropped. "That's her!" she said. It was a lucky guess, but my stock sure went up with Bonnie that day.

I took Ana home with me. She was a *wild* thing! As Ana flew around the room, leaping over the couch and the coffee table, my three sedate Labs watched her, then looked at me with expressions that said, *You've got to be kidding.* She's *going to live* here?

It took the next month for me to teach Ana basic manners. During this time I found two more goldens for the program. The three dogs started their training. Ana was superb. Everything was there: She loved to learn, and her intensity, which had spoiled her chance of success as an ordinary family pet, was one of her strongest traits. She never gave up, but would try, then try again—and keep on trying until she mastered something. When their training was complete, the dogs were ready to be matched with handlers.

Ana was matched with Rick, a Sacramento firefighter who was one of three handlers selected by the California Governor's Office of Emergency Services, Fire and Rescue branch. Rick was a precise man, physically quick, strong and wiry. Ana had the same agile quickness, and the trainer felt that their personalities would work well together.

Back in Sacramento, the two learned to live with each other. Ana's need to *always* have something in her mouth—dirty laundry being her item of preference—didn't sit well with Rick, who loved neatness and order. Eventually, the two worked it out: Ana learned to restrict her "mouth item" to one of her own toys, and Rick made sure the toys were always available.

Rick and Ana earned advanced certification from the Federal Emergency Management Agency (FEMA) within seven months—an amazing accomplishment. As the years passed, dog and handler continued their training and bonded closely as a working team.

Rick and Ana were members of California Urban Search and Rescue Task Force 7 deployed to the World Trade Towers on September 11, 2001. Here is an excerpt of the journal Rick kept of his experiences with Ana at Ground Zero:

> *Tethered to our sides as they moved through the dust and smoke twelve hours a day, the dogs were full of energy. These canines more than proved their value as a vital tool in the search efforts at Ground Zero.*
>
> *The firefighters were amazed at the canines' skill . . . at one point, we had to walk down an I-beam that was at a steep angle. Ana had no problem. We then had to make our way across the twisted steel and metal that had once been the World Trade Towers. Ana gracefully maneuvered the twisted terrain as if it were another day in the park. I know that her trainer would have been very proud to see her student fly across the debris.*

Reading these words, it's clear that Ana was a special gem—she only needed polishing and the right setting to shine.

The little idea I had so many years ago has developed into a successful disaster search-and-rescue dog training foundation. Many dogs have followed the trail Ana blazed. More than sixty of them have gone through our program and have been placed with handlers all across the country, including at the Capitol in Washington, D.C., and in Mexico as well.

Many, like Ana, who were doomed to unhappy lives or worse, have instead gone on to become an invaluable resource to their communities and to the nation. The rescued have indeed become the rescuers.

Wilma Melville

Scouting Out a Home

We didn't have the space or the energy to take in any more animals. Richard and I and our three dogs and three cats were already cramped in our small, rented home. The last year had brought the deaths of my father and grandmother, a move to a new city, the start of my career as a veterinarian, the purchase of our first house and plans for our wedding. I was exhausted and emotionally drained, which explains how Annie ended up at the shelter that first day.

Richard, a park-service employee, arrived at work to find two dogs—a young golden retriever and a small, black terrier—gallivanting around outside the old house in the woods that served as his office. Both dogs were very friendly, readily coming to him for an ear rub and a check of their collars. They didn't have any kind of identification, so Richard decided to give them a little time to see if they would head home on their own. For several hours he kept an eye on them through his window, but they showed no inclination to leave. The dogs could only get into trouble if they hung around for much longer, so Richard brought them into his office and called me at the veterinary clinic.

"Hi, honey, we've got a situation here." Richard went on to explain.

At the other end of the line, I groaned. "Look," I said. "The kennel is completely filled with patients and boarders, and we're still having trouble finding homes for our available adoptees. My boss will kill me if I let you bring them here, and you know that we can't handle any more dogs at home."

"Well, what do you think I should do?"

"The best place for them is probably the shelter," I replied, feeling a little frazzled. "If their owners want them back, that would be the first place they'd look."

Richard could tell I was in no mood for an argument and agreed to make the call to animal control. The officer told him that it would be afternoon before she could pick up the dogs. Several hours and a shared lunch later, Richard shepherded them out of his office and reluctantly handed them over.

That evening over dinner our conversation centered around the two dogs. Richard had grown attached to them in the short period of time that they had spent at his office. I was beginning to feel a little guilty for not trying harder to find a way to fit them in at the clinic. We concluded that we had probably done the right thing under the circumstances but hated to think about what the future could hold for the two good-natured dogs.

A week later I was wrapping up the morning appointments at the clinic when the receptionist called to the back, "Dr. Coates, there are two dogs waiting at the front door."

I sighed. *Walk-in appointments at one o'clock. There goes my lunch break.*

"Okay, Royann, please put them in room one and tell the owners that I'll be right in."

"No, Dr. C, you don't understand. It's just two dogs, no

people, and now they're starting to head for the road."

"Go get them," I shrieked through the intercom as we all went running for the front door. The clinic is situated on a busy four-lane road that has been responsible for many of our trauma patients. Thankfully, before I could even make it past the reception area, Royann was steering the dogs through the front door. I stopped short. Before me was a golden retriever and a slightly scruffy black terrier.

"I may be crazy," I said "but I think these are the dogs that were at Richard's office last week." The clinic staff was aware of the story, and looks of disbelief passed all around. If these were the same dogs, what had happened to them at the shelter? I guessed that they had somehow escaped. But what were the chances that they could have found both Richard and me, in a town of thirty-four thousand people, when our offices are separated by five miles?

Needing to know if these were the same two dogs, I brought them home with me after work. As I pulled to a stop in the driveway, my own three dogs, Owen, Duncan and Boomer, sensed that I was not alone in the truck. The sounds of five dogs barking brought Richard to the kitchen door.

"Hey, babe," I hollered over the din. "I've got some folks here I think you might know."

He made his way to the back of the truck and peered through the fogged-up window of the shell. "What? How?" His stunned expression gave me my answer.

We let them out of the truck to investigate their new surroundings, and they scampered around the yard, tails wagging. I smiled with relief thinking how lucky they had been to escape harm during their recent escapades. The circumstances were too eerie to ignore, and Richard and I decided that they could stay with us until we figured out a long-term solution.

The next morning I left for work with the newcomers still in the fenced yard. Our three dogs stared forlornly out of the front windows of the house as I drove away. I promised to come back at lunch for some supervised introductions and play.

Returning home a few hours later, I could hear dogs barking but was a little surprised when nobody greeted me at the gate. As I pulled up to the kitchen door, I could hear that all the noise was coming from inside the house. A search of the yard proved that the gates were just as I had left them—the two dogs must have gone over the fence. My heart sank as I realized that they had vanished. We had been given a second chance to help, but now that opportunity was gone along with the dogs.

Several weeks passed, during which time we started moving to the farm that we had recently purchased in a nearby town. All our free time was spent traveling between the two houses to renovate and clean. Memories of the two itinerant dogs were beginning to fade, and I no longer expected to see them around every corner.

One Saturday morning, I began to pull away from the house with a load of boxes and furniture. I stopped the van at the base of the driveway and glanced to the left to check for traffic. In the distance I could just make out a small black dog trotting purposefully down the side of the road. Not wanting to get my hopes up, I slowly got out of the van for a closer look. As she got nearer, she picked up speed and ran to a stop in front of me. Jumping up, she put her front feet on my thighs and gave me a look as if to say, *I choose you.* This amazing little dog had somehow made her way back to us for the third time, and I was elated! But where was her friend? The two had been through so much together; I couldn't imagine that anything but the worst would have caused their separation.

Although Annie's friend never did return to our home,

he did show up again at the clinic a month later. I had no idea that this was going to be anything but a routine appointment. Walking into the exam room, I glanced at the chart—a golden retriever, one of our most popular breeds. I petted the high-spirited dog as I asked his new owner, "So how'd this beautiful boy come into your life?"

"It's a funny thing, Doc," she said. "He showed up at our house a couple times but always left within a day or two. He was hanging around with another dog, but when he came back to stay this last time he was alone."

I started to laugh as I finally recognized my old friend. Crouching in front of him for a more appropriate hello, I said to his new owner, "Let me guess: the other dog was about so high, shaggy and black with a gray muzzle."

Astonished, she asked, "How could you possibly know that?"

We compared our stories and were both thrilled that, in the end, the two nomads had each found themselves a loving and permanent home.

Jennifer Coates, D.V.M.

Brooks and
the Roadside Dog

Normally, a dead animal would not have caught Brooks's eye. The old man was used to seeing them on the side of the gravel road near his home in rural West Virginia. However, the dead dog lying partially in the road looked so much like his own Labrador, Jake, that he was compelled to pull the truck over to get a closer look. Jake didn't leave the yard, but Brooks wanted to be sure. As he opened his door, motion near the tree line caught his eye. It was a smaller dog, definitely a mixed breed of some sort, carefully eyeing Brooks.

"Come here, boy," Brooks called, but the timid mutt scampered a few yards farther. "All right. Have it your way." Clearly the dead Lab was not Jake, so Brooks moved the dog to the soft earth of the shoulder and then continued in his truck the half mile down the road to his house.

The next day Brooks was returning home from church when he noticed the dead dog still on the side of the road. This time, the mutt was lying beside it. As Brooks slowly pulled up, the skittish dog scampered back to the tree line, his ribs clearly visible from lack of food.

"Come on, boy! Get in this truck and come get a meal!" Brooks shouted, but the mutt once again moved away from him and toward the forest.

"This must have been your buddy. Pretty broken up over it, ain't cha?" The mutt slowly took a few more paces backward into the cover of the trees. "Dern you, boy. You gonna starve to death."

As he drove his truck home, Brooks muttered to himself, "Dern dog."

Later that afternoon Brooks sat at his kitchen table trying to concentrate on the newspaper. "Dern dog," he said, unable to get his mind off the mutt. Thinking chores might help distract him and ease his frustration, he headed out the back door to the woodpile. Every stroke he made with his ax, he grumbled, "Dern dog. Dern dog."

He finally made one last, heavy stroke of the ax into a large log. "Dern it!" he yelled. He stormed back to the house and grabbed his truck keys. He knew what he had to do.

Driving back to the spot, he saw the mutt was lying in the same place next to the dead Lab. Once again, he scampered to the tree line when he heard the truck pull up. Brooks got out holding a can of dog food. "Come on, boy. Come eat! You gonna die, boy, if you don't eat!" But the dog again ran at the sound of the booming voice.

"You stubborn dog!" Brooks called after him. "You don't want nothin' but your buddy here to come back to life, do ya?"

Brooks looked at the miscellaneous equipment in the back of his truck. "You gonna make me do somethin' silly, boy," Brooks said as he grabbed a tarp and some work gloves out of the bed of the truck.

The dead dog's body was heavy as Brooks hoisted it into his truck. "Come on, boy. Come with your friend," Brooks said as he slowly drove the truck with the Lab's paws hanging over the tailgate. The mutt kept a careful eye on the scene and then reluctantly followed the Lab, making sure to stay a safe twenty yards back. "That's it," Brooks whispered. "You come with your buddy."

It took a while to get to Brooks's home. The mutt followed the entire way, trailing at a cautious distance. As the truck reached the driveway, Jake, as usual, began barking and ran to greet Brooks.

"Be down, Jake! You gonna scare off our friend here!" Brooks called from his truck window.

To Brooks's surprise, the mutt saw Jake and ran like a racing greyhound straight for him. Jake was caught off guard by the sudden rush of an unfamiliar dog. However, Jake had a gentle nature and he assumed an apprehensive stance as the mutt licked him again and again, playfully pawing him.

"You think that's your old buddy come to life!" Brooks laughed loudly. He continued laughing, so hard, in fact, that he had to support himself on the truck. He watched with delight as the ecstatic mutt jumped all around Brooks's old Lab. Jake stared at his owner in complete confusion.

"Dern dog!" Brooks bellowed with laughter.

Loyal, as the mutt came to be known, never left Jake's side after that moment. Jake warmed to him and eventually the two wove a tight bond. The dogs served as Brooks's faithful companions for many years. Friends and family swore it was the happiness these two dogs brought Brooks that kept him healthy and happy into his later years of life.

Shannon McCarty

Can't Help Falling in Love

A good dog deserves a good home.

Proverb

Every once in a while an animal enters our shelter and touches hearts in a special way. Tino was that kind of fellow.

He came to the Humane Society Silicon Valley (HSSV) as a stray on July 5 sporting an ID tag in the shape of a purple bone. Repeated efforts to contact his human companion failed. After completion of his legal holding time, Tino was checked for health and behavior and deemed adoptable. He settled into his new home: kennel nine.

At first the large black and tan Siberian husky/German shepherd mix didn't turn heads. Understandably. He was a rather plain-looking guy, a little paunchy and rarely sought the attention of passersby. His salt-and-pepper muzzle and yellow teeth didn't help either. Flecks of gray, coupled with his quiet manner, suggested to all that this guy was eight years old and counting. Since the majority of customers who visit HSSV are looking for puppies or small dogs, Tino's prospects for a quick turnaround were slim at best.

As his stay extended throughout the month of July, a funny thing happened. Both staff and volunteers alike began to take note of this sweet old guy and wanted to spend quality time with him. Tino's life skyrocketed from ho-hum to sizzle as dog socializers began scheduling community outings and adoption counselors advised customers to view the special boy in kennel nine. Unfortunately, all this additional PR did nothing to move Tino into a loving home. Potential adopters continued to voice various reasons why Tino wasn't quite right: too big, too old, too something or other.

Tino's fate looked bleak.

Upstairs, someone else was becoming the object of shelter PR. Laura, the new communications manager, joined the staff on July 9. After several weeks of settling into her busy new job, she found herself darting downstairs several times a day to visit our animal guests. And it wasn't very long before she noticed the cutie in kennel nine. Laura always had a soft spot for older dogs—they are loving, easy to train, and unlike puppies, there is no second-guessing as to how big they are going to get. Laura's job as communications manager allowed her to champion Tino's cause in a special, very public way. She featured his photo and bio in several community newspapers. She also featured him as a cyberpet on our Web site. She was sure someone would see his smiling face and fall in love, just as she had.

But despite Laura's continuing efforts, nothing happened. Even though it is HSSV's policy that adoptable animals can stay on as long as they are happy and healthy, the Tino Fan Club worried. Mid-September was approaching and he had already racked up more shelter days than any dog in recent memory.

Around that time, a bolt of lightning ignited Laura's imagination. Maybe a little flash and dash might call attention to this low-key canine. With that insight, Laura made an executive decision: Tino's name would be changed to Elvis. On September 19—Tino's seventy-seventh day at the shelter—fate stepped in.

Laura was in the kennels dispensing her daily ration of doggy treats when a kindly seventy-six-year-old gentleman named Maurice approached her. "I'm an old guy looking for an old dog," he said. "I want a gentle dog who won't sit on the furniture and is smart enough to use a doggy door."

With Maurice close behind, Laura marched up to kennel nine. "Meet Elvis," she said.

Laura held her breath, waiting for sparks to fly.

Nothing. Elvis stayed focused on Laura and her treat sack.

"He seems a lot more interested in you than in me," Maurice announced, disappointed.

Laura's hopes were dashed. No sparks. No fireworks. The attraction so crucial for the human/animal bond to take hold just wasn't happening for Maurice and Elvis.

A saddened Maurice left the adoption kennel and walked around to the courtyard. He glanced back at kennel nine. There was Elvis. For some reason, Elvis had run out into the open and stood at the fence. Their eyes met. In that moment Maurice knew he couldn't leave him there. And that was that.

A few days after the adoption, Maurice took Elvis to the vet for a general checkup. He had a few things wrong: a little lump that needed to be removed and a sty on his eye, but nothing major. The vet cleaned his teeth and said that Elvis was in pretty good shape—for an old guy. In keeping with the spirit of his namesake, Elvis boasts one more attribute. The vet told Maurice that Elvis "has hips to die for."

So now Elvis and Maurice's days are filled with three long walks, visits to the Las Palmas Dog Park in Sunnyvale and quiet evenings sitting together. They even share treats every now and then.

Maurice told me that last week he prepared a nice banana split for himself. He left it on the counter and went into the garage for a minute. When he returned, it was nowhere in sight. Elvis, who was sitting nearby, had a smirk on his face. It was the whipped cream on his nose that gave him away.

Elvis touched many hearts during his lengthy stay here— our dog socializers, adoption counselors, Maurice—but most of all, our communications manager, Laura. Her tireless efforts paid off on the day her special ward was adopted. In order to spread the good news, she wrote a memo to her colleagues that day. It read: "Elvis has left the building."

Patricia Smith

The Miracle of Love

When there is great love, there are always miracles.

Willa Cather

If ever there was a dog in need of a miracle, it was this dog. Cast off on the side of a busy street in the spring of 2002, the older pit bull mix had lost everything important in her life, even her name. Things only got worse when she ran into the road and was hit by a car. Left with a shattered leg and eyes full of pain, she was dropped off at the local animal control facility. If a rescue volunteer from a private shelter had not noticed her, her life might have come to an end the very next day. Instead, she was welcomed at Little Shelter Animal Rescue and Adoption Center in Huntington, New York, where she was given a new name: Foxy.

That summer was a season of rebirth for Foxy. After three surgeries and physical therapy, Foxy learned how to walk again, but because of her age and breed mix, the shelter staff felt that Foxy was probably unadoptable. They went out of their way to make her life at the shelter a pleasant one. The staff noticed right away that Foxy wasn't like the other shelter dogs: she seemed to be more interested in people than in dogs. So they made her their unofficial mascot. By day, she enjoyed walks on a leash, while the other dogs wrestled and chased one another; and by night, she snuggled in a little blue bed in an office, while the others slept in cages.

Yet somehow Foxy knew that the shelter was not her forever-home. Every weekend she looked on as people walked over to the big wall with pictures of the available dogs and cats. Patiently, she waited sixteen long months. But no one ever asked to see her.

Just when it seemed that fortune had forgotten Foxy, Mrs. Maguire and her son Kevin arrived. Kevin saw the older dog limping by. He thought she might be a good match for his elderly mother. Foxy agreed. She put on the show of her life. She rolled on her back and waved her paws toward Mrs. Maguire as if to say, *You've come for me at last!* Mrs. Maguire knew that there was no need to meet any other dogs. Foxy was her girl.

Whether taking long, slow walks around the neighborhood or putting her long, black snout into the stream that ran behind the house, Foxy was home. Sitting side by side on the couch, Mrs. Maguire would stroke Foxy's silky fur for what seemed like hours at a time. From one floppy black ear to the other, joy was written all over Foxy's face. Mrs. Maguire would tell her, "From the moment I saw you, I thought you were beautiful." She and Mrs. Maguire had truly become the best of friends.

Every night at eleven o'clock, Mrs. Maguire would take out her flashlight and bring Foxy outside for the last walk of the day. They would walk carefully down the steep flight of steps outside the front door, especially when the winter's ice and snow blanketed the ground. This routine continued until a bitterly cold January night, when Mrs.

Maguire slipped and went crashing down the stairs.

"Help! Oh, dear God. Please help me," cried out Mrs. Maguire, as pain from a broken hip left her unable to move. The frozen ground began to numb her body, and all Mrs. Maguire could do was wave her flashlight around in the darkness. As if answering her prayer, Foxy moved beside her and then pushed her body on top of Mrs. Maguire.

"Now it's just the two of us," the woman whispered, as Foxy tried her best to keep Mrs. Maguire warm. Before long, this otherwise quiet dog began barking frantically into the night sky.

Over an hour and a half later, Mrs. Maguire's neighbors— after shutting off their TV—heard Foxy's cries for help. Investigating, they immediately called for assistance. By the next day, Foxy's face was splashed across the front page of the newspaper and TV news. The cast-off dog had become a hero!

During the months following that fateful night, Foxy received many awards and honors. The grandest one of all resulted in Foxy's being escorted into New York City for a weekend celebration. Upon checking into her luxurious hotel room at the Ritz-Carlton, Foxy made herself right at home as she stretched out on the lounge and enjoyed the dog food that was presented by room service, complete with a silver tray and china bowl. After her meal, Foxy was escorted down to the grand ballroom at the Ritz, which had come alive with music, flowers and 250 guests, some of whom attended with their own pets. Mrs. Maguire, Foxy and the president of Little Shelter stood side by side as the CEO of the Hartz Mountain Corporation presented them with the 2003 Heroes of Hartz Award. Mrs. Maguire's eyes rarely left Foxy. The love in the older woman's eyes was impossible to miss: that love had created a miracle in Foxy's life, and now it had been repaid a thousandfold.

Valery Selzer Siegel

The Dumpster Dog Finds a Home

Hear our humble prayer, O God, for our friends the animals, especially for animals who are suffering; . . . for any that are hunted or lost or deserted or frightened or hungry; . . . and for those who deal with them we ask a heart of compassion and gentle hands and kindly words. Make us, ourselves, to be true friends to animals and so to share the blessings of the merciful.

Albert Schweitzer

It was a bitter cold winter day in Michigan when the call came from Midwest Boston Terrier Rescue (MWBTR). "Can you take a senior girl in bad shape?" Gwen, cofounder of MWBTR, asked. "She is a little old lady who is very nonthreatening, and I think she would get along with your dogs." I said yes. It was the start of our journey with a small, sick, frail dog whom we named Lacey.

When I met her, I whispered the same thing to her that I have whispered to all the dogs we have fostered in our home. I hold them and tell them, "You are safe now; you have been rescued. No one will ever hurt you again." It may sound strange, but I can tell that they understand. They breathe deeply and relax—some of them almost collapse. It never matters where they come from, whether I have picked them up on their last day of life at a shelter, or they come from an owner who no longer has a place for them. When I am handed a confused soul at the end of a leash, my response is always the same: I give them a little piece of my heart, and they begin to heal.

Lacey's story had a sad start. She was found one February day, half dead, in a Dumpster by the local animal control. They decided that she was unadoptable—too sick and too old. A volunteer from another rescue group happened to visit the shelter a few days later. Although she didn't usually go there, the volunteer asked to go to the back area—where the unadoptable dogs are housed. She asked about the frail little Boston terrier and was told Lacey would be euthanized. The kindhearted volunteer said, "Oh, no, I will take her. I know someone who has a place for her." She called MWBTR and with that call set Lacey back on the road to life.

Lacey was taken to the vet, who said that her blood levels were dangerously off, she was malnourished and most of her teeth were decayed. She weighed barely thirteen pounds. Her coat was very thin, and it was painfully obvious that she had produced many litters of puppies. She had to be placed on antibiotics for several weeks until she was well enough to stand surgery.

Lacey came to our chaotic household to regain her strength before her surgery. The little dog had very nice manners and was completely housebroken. At first, all she did was sleep. When she was strong enough, her surgery was performed. All her teeth, except her four canines, had to be extracted. She was spayed and given all of her shots—this is done for most rescue dogs because, unfortunately, there is no record of prior health care. And although she had worms, thankfully, she tested negative for heartworm. For several months, Lacey rested, healing her body and her spirit. It was interesting to watch our other dogs take care of her. Our pack can be a rowdy bunch, but with Lacey, they were as gentle as if she were a child.

That spring, a six-month-old large male boxer was turned into Mid Michigan Boxer Rescue, and he stayed with us for about a week. By then Lacey's health had improved greatly. She had gained weight, her coat shined and she danced with newfound energy. I have a wonderful photo of our old girl in bed, sitting with the young boxer pup. The old and the young—two lives saved.

When a rescue dog comes to our house, we make the same commitment to each one: You have a home here for as long as it takes. You will always be safe, have food to eat and be loved.

Of course, in order to find her a permanent home, she was listed on *www.petfinder.com*, and on the MWBTR site for adoption. However, when time passed and no one seemed interested, it was okay with us. We thought no one would ever adopt a senior like Lacey, so she became part of our family. She asked for very little and gave us so many blessings in return.

Then, in early June, a call came from MWBTR. This time Gwen said, "I have a lady who is interested in your Lacey." I was surprised, pleased and devastated all in an instant. It happens that way. When it is right and it is meant to be, somehow you know—but your heart breaks anyway. There is joy and sadness in one fell swoop.

All three of the rescue groups we belong to have similar procedures for adopting a dog. Foster parents always have final say in the adoption because the rescue group feels foster parents have come to know the dog best.

Carol, our Lacey's prospective adopter, submitted an

application. I called her veterinarian and her references. They were fabulous, which is not always the case. Then a home check was completed. Carol passed with flying colors. As much as I wanted this home for Lacey, she still needed to meet Carol to see if they were a good match.

Two weeks later Carol and a friend traveled to Michigan from Wisconsin to meet Lacey. It was love at first sight. Carol and her friend pulled out of our driveway with Lacey, her special bed and food in the car, and headed for home.

That's when it hit me. I had been holding it together, and then I realized just how far away Wisconsin was. The bittersweet tears came. For days all our dogs looked for Lacey, and I asked myself for the thousandth time, *Why do I do this?*

Then a call came from Carol. Her voice was filled with joy as she told us: Lacey loves her new Boston terrier sister Suzie Q and has adopted the two-year-old special-needs kitty as her own, along with two other cat siblings. She goes for walks to the Dairy Queen to get free doggy ice-cream cones. Carol said that Lacey had also just become part of a new program where dogs visit HIV patients.

Lacey, the Dumpster dog who should have died in the back of a cold animal shelter, was home. This, I reminded myself, is why we go through it—because when they leave us, their broken hearts have healed forever.

Debra Jean-MacKenzie Szot

[EDITORS' NOTE: *Carol, Lacey's owner, read this story and sent Debra the following: Thank you so much for sending me a copy of your story! I get so wrapped up in what Lacey means to me and to her friends here that I forget she ever lived anywhere else. It amazes me that an animal so ill used for most of her life has nothing but love and concern for everyone around her.*

I took Suzie and Lacey to the HIV hospice the other day. Suzie has been there before, and she entered the common room and started to make the rounds. Lacey stopped directly inside the front door and began walking in circles. Finally, she walked across the hall and sat down by a closed door. Both Sister Marion and I tried to convince her to move but she refused. She lay down and began to softly cry. Sister explained to me that the resident in this room was nineteen years old and had taken a turn for the worse early that morning. The family had been called, but they were several miles away and were still en route. By now Lacey was really distressed and began pawing at the door. Since this patient had reacted positively in the past to Suzie, we decided to open the door and let Lacey go in. Deb, it was the most incredible thing I have ever seen in my life. Lacey went straight to the bed and jumped up on the chair next to it. She wiggled her head and front paws through the side rails so she could touch the patient's arm, and she stayed there! The patient became less restless. When the family arrived thirty minutes later, Lacey jumped down from her perch and left the room. She went back to the front door, sat on the rug and promptly fell asleep as though exhausted. The power of the human-animal bond never fails to amaze me. Carol]

The Parking-Lot Dog

It was just a routine trip to the drugstore but it changed my life.

As I got out of my car, I noticed a scared, starving, mangy dog with rusty red fur in the store parking lot. He looked as though he was waiting for someone. I learned from a store clerk that a man in a pickup truck had dumped the dog in the parking lot and had driven away. Obviously this dog was waiting for the man's return. By the look in the dog's sad eyes, I knew he needed help.

For the next several days I returned to the drugstore parking lot and tried coaxing the dog with food. Like clockwork, the dog would appear from the woods but wouldn't approach the food until I drove away. I realized that if I were going to help this dog, I needed to use a humane trap. But the next day when I pulled into the lot with the humane trap in the car, the dog was gone. I searched the woods and the surrounding area, but the dog was nowhere to be found.

I decided to hang "Lost Dog" posters in the area. The only information I could put on the poster was a description of the red dog and my phone number. I didn't even know the dog's gender. I don't make a habit of rescuing

dogs, and I already had two dogs of my own—why was I
looking for a dog I knew nothing about? I couldn't explain
it, but I was determined to find this dog.

Within a day I received a phone call from a clerk at a
convenience store located about a mile from where I had
first seen the dog. He said a red dog fitting the description
on the poster had appeared at the convenience store and
had been running up to pickup trucks in the parking lot.
He explained that animal control had picked up the dog
and had taken him to the county shelter. Although it was
almost an hour away, I drove to the shelter to see if it was
the same dog. There he was, crouched in the back corner
of his cage growling, barking and very agitated. The shelter must hold dogs for ten days to allow owners time to
claim them, so I would have to wait and see what happened with this dog.

Even though I had no plans of adding a third dog to our
family, I felt compelled to help this dog. So over the next
ten days I checked on him regularly. The people at the
shelter told me the dog was very aggressive. They said no
one would adopt him, and he would be destroyed when
his time was up. On the tenth day I made the long drive
back to the shelter to see the red dog. The receptionist
asked if my name was Deborah Wood. I didn't pay much
attention to her question; just simply replied "no" as I followed her back to the dog's cage. There was the red dog,
just as scared and agitated as before.

Intimidated by the dog's behavior, but still determined
to save him, I asked the kennel assistant to bring the dog
out to my car and put him into the crate that I had
brought for him. I had no idea if I would be able to handle
the dog once we reached home, but I knew he couldn't
stay at the shelter. As I followed the assistant and dog
through the lobby area to my car, the receptionist
stopped me. She said there was a Deborah Wood on the

phone. She was inquiring about the red dog and wanted to speak to me.

I picked up the phone. The woman named Deborah told me that she had been at the convenience store talking to the clerk about the dog when animal control had picked him up. For some reason, she had been drawn to the red dog, too. Over the past ten days, Deborah had made several visits. She had tried coaxing the dog out of his cage for a walk, but the fearful dog had snapped at her. Despite the dog's behavior, Deborah never gave up on him, and now she wanted to know what I was going to do with the dog. I explained to her that I was taking the dog to the veterinarian for a checkup and that I would call her once I got home. It turned out that Deborah and I lived within five minutes of each other. Both of us had traveled almost an hour to visit the "unadoptable" red dog at the shelter— both of us not completely sure why. I was struck by the lucky timing of her call. If Deborah had called the shelter a moment later, we might never have made a connection.

I was nervous about the dog being in my car and anxious to get him to the vet. Surely I would be able to figure out what to do with him after that. *I must be crazy*, I thought, as I backed my car out of the shelter's parking lot. *Why am I doing this? I have an aggressive dog crated in my car, and I have no idea what I'm going to do with him.*

Just as I thought this, the red dog looked at me with his expressive eyes and stuck his paw through the crate for a "handshake." I reached over and tentatively closed my hand around the outstretched paw. It seemed to me that the red dog was thanking me. This melted my heart. I held his paw in my hand for the entire forty-five-minute ride to the vet's office. When we arrived, we were both smiling!

The red dog spent about two weeks at the vet's recovering from mange, worms and other health problems.

While the red dog was being treated at the vet's office, Deborah came often to visit him, and although she had never had a dog before, when the dog was well enough to leave the animal clinic, she offered to foster him until we could find him a permanent home. It didn't surprise anyone that Deborah quickly fell in love with her foster dog and decided to adopt him, naming him Redd. The moment Redd realized that he was safe, he became the perfect dog: affectionate and sociable—loving everyone he met. He never again showed any sign of aggression.

It has been five years since Deborah adopted Redd. Initially drawn together by our concern for Redd, Deborah and I have become close friends. And Redd has *two* families that adore him. He also frequently visits his "uncle," the clerk at the convenience store who responded to my poster.

Today, Redd is surrounded by people who love him. When I see this contented dog, lying on the sofa and getting belly rubs, I find it hard to believe that he is the same dog with the haunted eyes I saw in the parking lot five years ago. That routine trip to the drugstore brought a very special dog and a dear friend into my life.

Wendy Kaminsky

Two Good Deeds

I was planting flowers in my garden one day, when I spotted a battered old boxer with a broken chain around his neck, staggering up the road. He had the look of a dog who had been abused. Without any hesitation, he proceeded to walk down my driveway and lie down next to me. Exhausted, he just lay there, his eyes following me as I ran inside to get him a dish of water. Returning with the water, I looked into his dark, soulful eyes. A ripple of shock ran through my body: I knew this dog!

About eight years earlier I'd been in the center of town one morning, when a beautiful, fawn-colored boxer puppy ran up to me. Bending down to pet him, I noticed his beautiful eyes—and the ID tag around his collar. The tag said he belonged to Mrs. Reynolds and gave a local telephone number. She lived not too far away and came to pick him up in a matter of minutes. After a few wet kisses, the boxer went home. That was the last time I had seen the dog.

My husband came out of the house. I told him I was sure this dog was the one I'd found in town years ago. He thought I was crazy. "How can you be certain? He doesn't have a collar on and there's no way to identify him. It has to be another dog. This one is so abused; it couldn't belong to that nice family. Besides, do you even remember the name of the family?"

Somehow, I did. "It was Reynolds," I said. "I know it sounds crazy, but I'm sure this is their dog!"

Running inside, I grabbed the telephone book and called the first Reynolds listed. Mr. Reynolds answered and told me he didn't have a boxer. However, just as he was about to hang up, he said that his brother once had a boxer, and gave me his brother's number.

When I called the first Mr. Reynolds's brother, he said it couldn't be his dog because his dog had been stolen six years before. I convinced him to let me bring the dog over so he could look at him. I put the dog into my car. He collapsed in the backseat and lay very still. Crossing over the main highway going into the town, he started to move around. As we passed through the center of town, he started jumping and bouncing around in the backseat.

When I pulled into the Reynolds' driveway, there was no containing him. Three teenagers ran out of the house, and when I opened the car door, the dog bounded out and raced to them, whining and yelping in his excitement.

As the dog licked them, they looked him over. Suddenly, one of the boys yelled, "It's him, it's him! Look, here's the big scar he got over his eyebrow when he went through the sliding glass door."

I stayed a few minutes longer, watching the entire family hug and kiss the old dog, now rejuvenated by joy. They proceeded to run into the house with him.

Backing out of the driveway, I thought again of that morning so many years ago when I had first helped the lost boxer find his family. I went home happy, knowing I had been part of a miracle—for the second time in one dog's life.

Rosemarie Miele

The Promise

*You become responsible forever for what you
have tamed.*

Antoine de Saint-Exupéry

For the past twelve and a half years, I have been an animal control officer (ACO) for Polk County, Iowa. In this profession, you learn early on to toughen your skin, otherwise the stress and emotional drain that come with this job will bring you down. There have been a lot of dogs over the years that I would have loved to take home and make a part of my family, but in this line of work, it's not realistic to believe you can do that with each one—there are just too many dogs in need of good homes. Still, there is always that one that gets through your defenses. For me, that dog was Buddy.

Buddy was the most elusive dog I ever encountered in my years as an animal control officer: I spent an amazing sixteen months trying to catch the big black dog.

I first received a phone call in November 2002 from a lady who said, "There is a dog lying in a field near my home. He has been there for a couple of days, and it is supposed to get really cold tonight. Could you try to catch him?" I told her I would head out there and see what I could do.

As I drove up to the area, I could see that the dog was lying on his side next to a small hillside that served as a sort of break from the cold wind. I got out of my truck with a leash in hand and walked toward him. The dog was asleep and did not hear my coming, so as I got within twenty feet of him, I whistled because I did not want to startle him. He immediately got up and started barking at me. Then he turned and ran away, into the middle of the snow-covered field where he lay down to keep a watchful eye on me. I knew there was going to be no catching him that day, so I left to answer another call that had come in.

That night it did get very cold. I just couldn't keep my mind off the black dog and wondered how he was doing out in that large, cold field all alone.

The next morning I headed to the Animal Rescue League of Iowa. This is where the county sheriff's department houses the animals I pick up, and it is the largest animal shelter in the state. I wanted to check the reports to see if anyone had called in saying they had lost their black dog. I hoped that someone was looking for this dog, so I would be able to ask the owners to come out to the field; I figured if it were their dog, the dog would come to them. There were no such lost reports.

On my way home that night, I couldn't help but drive by the field. There he sat, right in the middle of it. Again, he wouldn't let me get close to him or come to me when I called.

We played this game for a few weeks. I would get calls from different people reporting that a black dog was sitting in a field. I could not get this dog out of my mind, and even on my days off, I would drive by the field to leave food and see if I could get a look at him. He was always there, usually lying right out in the middle so no one would be able to sneak up behind him. I tried over and over to gain his trust with no luck. I could not get closer than a hundred yards from him—too far to use a tranquilizer dart. If I tried to come any closer, he would get up, bark and move to an adjacent field. I wondered sadly what could have happened to this dog to make him so fearful of people.

Finally, I spoke to Janet, one of the animal-care technicians at the Animal Rescue League. She had a reputation of being able to get close to dogs that would not let anyone near them. I told her about the black dog and asked her if she would try to catch him. She agreed, and she did try—to no avail.

It was now late December and the nights were very cold, dropping to ten or twenty degrees below zero. The woman who had called me originally about the dog continued to call, checking in to see what I was doing to help him. I assured her I had been trying to catch him and that I was leaving food for the dog. At this point I told her I was pondering a way to set a live trap to capture the dog. Privately, I worried how he would live through the nights given the bitter cold temperatures of Iowa winters.

The weeks passed. I checked on him regularly, driving by in the morning on my way to work, cruising by during the day and making my final round on my way home at night. It was odd—just seeing him out there made me smile. I was thankful he had made it through one more night and was still alive.

Janet and I talked constantly about this dog. A live trap hadn't worked. We simply could not come up with a way to catch this dog. One day we decided that we would take some shelter out to the fields, line it with blankets and put some food beside it; perhaps he would use it. We got an "igloo" type of doghouse and went out to the field to set it up. The dog watched us intently but wouldn't come near. That was the day that I named the dog Buddy. Looking at him, I made a promise to myself and to him: "Buddy, if I ever catch you, I'm going to adopt you and show you what 'good people' are like."

We went through the rest of the winter like this, as well as the following spring and summer. One day Buddy just seemed to vanish. No more sightings, no more concerned calls about him. I continued to think about him, fearing the worst: that he had been hit by a car and was no longer alive.

That fall, however, I received a call about a black dog standing by the road close to the field where I had first seen Buddy. I couldn't believe it. It had been seven months since I had last seen him, but I immediately hopped into my truck and drove to the area. There, standing by the road, was my friend Buddy. He looked just as he had the last time I saw him. I stopped my truck and got out. I tried to approach him, but as usual he started backing up and barking at me. This time, however, when I turned to walk away, instead of turning and running, he just sat down. He was letting me get closer.

We started the game all over again. I kept leaving treats for him in the same spot. This went on for months until one day he did something he hadn't done before—he slept next to the spot where I had been leaving his treats. I decided I would leave a live trap for him on that spot along with some barbecued pork. When I went back first thing the next morning, it looked like he'd tried to get the food out by digging around the trap, but he was nowhere to be seen.

I tried again the next night. This time I put a slice of pizza in the trap, hoping it would do the trick. I couldn't sleep that night and rose early to go check the cage. It was still dark out, and as I approached I heard Buddy bark. I figured he had heard me and was already retreating, but as I squinted my eyes I could make out the outline of a black dog caught in the cage of the live trap. Overwhelmed with relief and joy, I started to cry. Then I called my wife. "I got Buddy," I told her. "I got him!"

Buddy growled at me as I loaded the cage into my truck and drove to the Animal Rescue League. As I drove in, Janet was just coming into work. I yelled to her, "You are never going to guess who I've got!"

Janet replied, "Buddy?" and started to cry.

Janet and I unloaded the cage and took Buddy to a kennel. I crawled into the kennel with him, keeping my distance. Once I realized he wasn't going to bite me, I just started petting him and loving him. I spent the next few hours trying to build the bond that I knew would last a lifetime. To everyone's surprise, after running from us and being alone for sixteen months, he was a very affectionate dog. All Buddy wanted at this point was to be petted, and if you stopped too soon, he'd let you know by gently nuzzling your hand until you started petting him again.

Over the next few days, I spent almost every free moment with Buddy. I would go to the Animal Rescue League before work, during lunch breaks and after work just so I could spend time with him. A few days later I brought my yellow Labrador, Hershey, to the shelter to meet Buddy. From the moment they met, they got along just fine.

Soon I was able to take Buddy home. Buddy fit amazingly well into our family. He had no "accidents" in the house and didn't destroy anything. Then one day my wife called me and told me that Buddy had gotten into the refrigerator. At first, I didn't believe her, but I suppose all that time scavenging for food had made him highly resourceful. Because it's true—I now live with a dog that can open a refrigerator!

We have to use bungee cords to prevent Buddy from opening the refrigerator door. There have been a few occasions when we have forgotten, only to come home to find that he's emptied the fridge. We've nicknamed him "Buddy, the Fridge King."

It's been four months now since I adopted him, and he is truly a bright spot in my life. I still can't believe this dog survived for sixteen months on his own, through two Iowa winters! He is an example of the true spirit and determination of the species we call "dog."

My long days at work are still challenging, but I am comforted by the thought that I get to go home and lavish Buddy with the love I wish all dogs could have. I kept my promise to Buddy and have shown him that people can be good. It was a happy ending worth waiting for.

Bill King

9

DOGGONE WONDERFUL!

My idea of good poetry is any dog doing anything.

J. Allen Boone

"Do it again! Make her talk in that goofy high voice."

Canine Compassion

A rather unusual overnight guest stayed at our home recently. When I was asked to provide overnight accommodations for a rescued dog being transported to her new home in Boston, I readily agreed. Though I was a tad worried that my own two dogs might not like this new intruder in our home, I wanted to help and figured I could manage if it became a problem.

The visiting dog's name was Meadow, and she was an extremely sweet old canine soul. She had been rescued from an abusive animal-hoarding situation, and a kind-hearted person had agreed to adopt her, even though she was a special-needs dog. Poor Meadow had suffered some type of severe head trauma before being rescued, and when our guest arrived at my front door that afternoon, her acute neurological ailment was painfully obvious. She teetered precariously on four wobbly thin legs, and her aged, furry brown face incessantly wobbled back and forth, as if she were suffering from Parkinson's disease. Immediately, I thought of the great actress, Katharine Hepburn, who had also suffered from Parkinson's. Katharine Hepburn had not allowed her illness to get the better of her, and obviously, neither had this sweet old girl.

As Meadow gamely tottered into my unfamiliar living room, she heard my two dogs growling, snarling and scratching incessantly at the inside of the closed bedroom door upstairs. Stopping, she peered nervously in that direction. I was afraid that the getting-acquainted canine ritual that was coming might be extremely painful for our already stressed overnight visitor. While I contemplated the best method to introduce my two dogs to our special guest, they somehow managed to pry open the bedroom door themselves. Before I could stop them, they both came charging down the steps with only one thought in their collective canine minds: the urgent need to rid their home of this unwanted intruder. But then, instead of witnessing a vicious canine attack, I witnessed something truly remarkable.

Suddenly, both my dogs stopped in their tracks on the long wooden stairway and gazed wide-eyed at the quivering, wobbly-kneed stranger below. Instantly, they instinctively knew that this new guest of ours was not a threat to anyone. They came down the stairs and stood looking at the unfamiliar dog. Blanca, my tiny female Chihuahua/spitz mix, who can be quite mean to other female dogs at times, approached Meadow first. She slowly walked up to our elderly visitor, sniffed her and quickly planted an affectionate kiss of greeting on Meadow's tremulous left cheek. I was immediately reminded of the kisses I, as a child, had lovingly set on my aged grandmother's quivering cheek so many years ago. My large male dog, Turbo, soon followed suit—although his wet slobbery kisses on Meadow's chin were much more exuberant than Blanca's had been. After all, our overnight guest was a female. I was delighted that my dogs had so readily accepted our guest, and I felt a little sheepish that I had been so worried about it.

Soon it was afternoon nap time, that part of the day

when both my dogs always find a comfortable piece of furniture to do their snoozing on. Today, however, they had other plans. They both had watched in silence as Meadow wearily plopped down on the blanket I'd set out for her on our cold living-room floor. They seemed to know that our special guest could not crawl up onto any comfortable bed or sofa as they so easily could. To my utter amazement, my two pampered pooches immediately plopped down on the blanket next to her, one on each side. And soon three tired, newly acquainted canine comrades were dognapping and snoring away on my living-room floor—together.

I was extremely proud of my two lovable mutts that afternoon, but there was more to come.

When bedtime finally arrived, my two dogs sped upstairs to their usual cozy spots in our bedroom: Blanca perched next to my pillow, Turbo at my wife's feet, gently mouthing and licking his beloved teddy bear, just as he does each and every evening before falling fast asleep. As I was about to crawl into bed myself, Turbo suddenly jumped off the bed with his teddy in his mouth. Curious, I followed him out of the bedroom.

There he stood in the dark, at the top of the long staircase, silently gazing down at our overnight guest below. After several seconds Turbo silently carried his favorite teddy bear down that long flight of stairs. He slowly approached Meadow and then gingerly dropped his prized possession next to Meadow's head, as if to say, *This teddy comforts me at night; I hope it does the same for you.*

Our canine guest seemed to sense how truly grand a gesture this was on Turbo's part. She immediately snorted her thanks and then, quickly placing her wobbly head on the teddy bear's plush softness, she let out a loud contented sigh. As my generous pup turned to head back upstairs to bed, he stopped abruptly, turned around and looked back at Meadow once more. Then he walked back to her and plopped down on the floor at her side. My gallant Turbo spent the entire night huddled there with Meadow on the cold living-room floor. I know that our overnight visitor, somewhat stressed and frightened in yet another strange new place, must have been extremely grateful for both his noble gift and for his comforting overnight company.

The next morning, as we all watched Miss Meadow happily departing in her new loving owner's car, I bent down and gave each of my dogs a big hug. *Why had I ever doubted their canine compassion?* I knew better now.

Ed Kostro

Busted!

Our beagle, Samantha, was a real clown. She kept us laughing all the time, making it hard to scold her when she got into mischief. That dog had us wrapped around her finger—or should I say paw?

Samantha was really my husband Al's dog, or more accurately, he was her human. I was the one who fed her, walked her and took care of her, but as far as Samantha was concerned, the sun rose and set on Al. She adored him. The feeling was mutual; when she gave him that soft beagle "googly-eyed look," he melted.

We lived in a place called Yellowknife in the Northwest Territories, three hundred miles from the Arctic Circle. Al was in the army and away a lot. I managed on my own and was thankful for good friends, an enjoyable working environment and, especially, Samantha to keep me warm at night. She would crawl under the blankets and curl around my feet—what bliss.

It had been a long arctic winter and Samantha had waited patiently for the sunshine and warm weather to come and was raring to get out and about. A typical hound, she loved running, chasing rabbits and squirrels, and swimming in the lake. When the first warm day of spring finally arrived that year and we went out for a walk, in her exuberance, Samantha overdid it—running at top speed over the rocks that are the landscape in Yellowknife. By the time we reached the house, she was limping quite pronouncedly and appeared to be in significant pain. Her injury was diagnosed as sprained ligaments, and she was ordered to keep still: no running for several weeks. It was not welcome news for this beagle. Now she was confined to the porch while I was away at work, and then took short, quiet walks on a leash when I was home. As the weeks passed, her limp slowly but surely diminished; I was pleased with her progress.

During that period, Al was away from Monday to Friday. On his return Friday evenings, there were hugs and kisses all around, and Samantha would be plastered to his lap. She followed him everywhere all weekend, lapping up the attention she received because of her "hurtie." It was clear to me that her limp became even more pronounced when Al was home.

By the end of the summer her leg was all healed and she was back to normal. She ran and played and chased her ball for hours on end—during the week. When Al came home, her hurtie mysteriously came back, and she was placed on the sofa for the weekend with lots of hugs, a blanket and treats.

I told Al that this was just an act for his attention. "Of course it isn't," he said. "Can't you see her leg is still bothering her? How come it's not healing like the vet said it would?"

I sighed but let it drop.

The following weekend when Al returned, Samantha's limp was as bad as ever. Friday and Saturday, Al pampered his little injured princess while I tried not to roll my eyes.

Like most people, Al and I love to sleep in and snuggle on Sunday morning. We chat about the events of the past week, reload our coffee cups, chat some more, nap and generally laze around. Samantha lies at the bottom of the bed enjoying this special time as well. Eventually, we get up, shower and head to the kitchen to start making breakfast. It was our routine to cook an egg for Samantha, too. She usually waited on the bed until it was ready and we called her to come and eat. That morning when breakfast was ready, Al started down the hall, intending to lift Samantha off the bed and carry her into the kitchen because of her hurtie.

"No," I told him. "Stand where she can't see you and watch what happens next."

I called Samantha. We heard her jump off the bed and run down the hall. She was running like there was no tomorrow, and surprise, no hurtie—until she saw Al. She stopped on a dime and immediately began limping. We watched as she took a few steps. You could see the wheels turning in her beagle brain: Was it this leg or the other? Then she started limping on the other leg. Caught in the act!

Al and I laughed, both at Samantha and at each other, over what we called the Academy Award performance of the summer. In Hollywood, Samantha would have been given an award for "Best Actress in a Leading Role." Instead, we wrote, "The Best Beagle in the Northwest Territories Award" on a piece of paper and gave it to her. She seemed so proud of her performance and the award. Actually, we knew that she was the *only* beagle in the Northwest Territories, but we didn't tell her—we didn't want to spoil the magic.

Lynn Alcock

Pudgy

In 1975 my grandparents brought home a new pup and named him Pudgy. This came as no surprise since they always named their dogs Pudgy. In the course of their extremely long lifetimes, my grandparents must have had a dozen or more dogs named Pudgy.

At the time, Grandpa was ninety-two and Grandma was eighty-nine, and they had been married since she was thirteen. That seems shocking today, but it was quite ordinary in the small village on the Polish border where they were born, met and fell in love in the late 1800s. They emigrated to the United States and made a life together that lasted through the coming of the first automobiles, the Roaring Twenties, the Great Depression, four wars—and many Pudgys.

When anyone asked Grandpa why Pudgy was the only name he would ever give to his dog, he answered, "He's the same dog, come back."

Relatives told him that was crazy and that he should give new dogs new names, but he always stood firm. Rather than debate the issue, people simply accepted that "Pudgy" was Grandpa's dog.

Each Pudgy was about the size of a fox terrier and

white with black spots or patches. For the little kids in the family, like me, who lived in other states and traveled across the country to visit them in their big old brownstone in Chicago, using the same name for each dog did make it a lot easier to remember. And many of us believed it was the same dog, although I did wonder once why the Pudgy I saw when I visited them in 1949, 1950 and 1951 had shaggy, floppy ears and the Pudgy I played with over Easter vacation in 1952 had short, pointed ones. Since the Pudgy of 1952 was still black and white and about the same size, I simply assumed my grandfather was telling the truth when he told me that the dog had accidentally stuck his tail in a light socket and his ears had shot straight up and had never gone down again. It didn't explain where all the shaggy hair on his ears had gone, but at seven, I simply decided the electricity must have burned it off.

Looking at an old family album with photos from the various decades, one could see the dog change a little in height and definitely in bone structure. He went from having a long, slim nose to a short, puglike one and then back to something in between. In some photos he had curly hair; in others, smooth. One decade he had small black spots on the white coat; and the next, large, pinto-pony-type patches. One time he had no tail at all. It didn't matter: he was always Pudgy.

This last Pudgy was a short-legged, potbellied pup, a mixture of too many breeds to try to put a finger on any dominant one. He was the first "Pudgy" that really looked as if the name belonged.

About two weeks after the pup arrived at the house, Grandpa decided it was time to take him on his first walk. Grandpa was a great walker, and even in his nineties, he did a good two miles several times a week. His favorite destination was the park, a great place to let his dog run after a nice long walk down the busy city streets. He could sit and talk with his friends while their dogs romped together. That day, when Grandpa didn't come back at his usual time, Grandma simply thought he was spending more time at the park with his friends, showing off the new pup. Then she heard yapping at the front door. She opened it and there was the pup, leash dragging behind him. A panting boy ran up to the door. He'd been chasing the pup all the way to the house. Grandpa had been hit by a car!

The rescue unit that had come to his aid found no identification on him—only the pup, licking the unconscious man's face. They had taken Grandpa to the general hospital. But when they'd tried to grab the pup, he'd run away. The boy followed him over a mile and a half back to the house. How could this pup, who had only lived in the house only two weeks and had never been out walking in the city, have made a beeline right back to the front porch? It amazed everyone.

Grandpa had been admitted to the hospital as a John Doe and did not regain consciousness for several days. Thanks to Pudgy, Grandma was able to go immediately to see Grandpa and ensure that he received the best care possible instead of being relegated to languish in the charity ward until relatives could be found and notified.

Within two months Grandpa was back walking with Pudgy and sharing with his friends at the park the story of how his Pudgy brought help when it was needed the most. Of course, the story grew in heroic proportions every time it was told, but nobody seemed to mind. One thing was certain: nobody ever again contradicted Grandpa when he told them that Pudgy was, "The same dog, come back."

Joyce Laird

Felix, the Firehouse Dog

Firefighters everywhere love telling stories—and some of their favorites are about that select group of firefighters who are on duty twenty-four hours a day, seven days a week, 365 days a year: the firehouse dogs. One such dog, Felix, who lived in the first half of the twentieth century, remains a demigod among his firehouse brethren and stands alone as the dog that most influenced the Chicago Fire Department.

Felix was the Babe Ruth of Chicago firedogs. One of the earliest and most legendary firehouse dogs, he was a part of an elite group that went on every call, followed his crew into fires and rescued lives. This common street mongrel inspired memorials, remembrances and, eventually, television specials for more than a half century after his death. His firefighting colleagues truly considered Felix one of their own: a full-fledged Chicago fireman. The people in his neighborhood adored him as well. Loud cheers for Felix could be heard whenever Engine 25 rushed down a street.

Felix was born in 1910. How he arrived at Engine 25 will forever be in dispute. Some say Felix was among a litter of seven abandoned puppies donated to a local tavern that later gave one of the puppies to a firefighter. One woman distinctly remembers an injured dog wandering into her father's local coal office, which later donated the dog to Engine 25. Or perhaps Felix was simply another stray dog that found his way into one of Chicago's firehouses.

In any case, Felix grew to be a medium-sized mutt, mostly brown in color with some black-and-white patches. Although Felix served the majority of his career with horse-drawn fire engines, he later became a part of fire-fighting history due to a widely circulated picture taken of him in 1920 aboard one of Chicago's first motorized pumpers. Judging by his confident stance in the photo-graph, Felix adapted well to the new type of apparatus. The story goes that he made every run—except one. On that day, Felix wandered too far from the firehouse to hear the alarm, and when the firefighters returned, Felix was so ashamed that he couldn't bear to look at his com-rades. It never happened again.

Like most Chicago firedogs, Felix learned the different alarm bell sounds and would board the appropriate fire rig depending on the specific signal used. As a result, Felix was always on the rig, barking before the alarm finished sounding. Once at the fire, Felix served as guard to the rig, not allowing anyone near it. As time wore on, however, he wanted to get closer to the action, and his duties greatly expanded. He learned how to climb ladders, making his way behind the firemen into the belly of the fire. Once inside, Felix shadowed the men as they worked to extin-guish the flames. When the firefighters went down the ladder, Felix jumped on one of their backs, putting his front paws around the fireman's shoulders and his back legs tucked under his arms.

At one unusually intense fire, Felix followed the men into the flames as always, but the fire quickly overcame the two hose teams and outflanked the men. Because the path they had forged with their hoses was no longer available, they had to find another way out. Felix went to work. Through the smoke and flames, he left the firefighters to look for a back entrance. After a few minutes that seemed to the men like hours, he came back barking ferociously. As one man held onto Felix's tail, the dog led the entire team on their knees out of the building. At the end of the day, all the men owed their lives to Felix.

Felix also had an uncanny ability to know if anyone was still in a burning building, and he refused to leave the scene of an active fire if people were still inside. On one run, the men of Engine 25 extinguished a fire and believed they had evacuated the house when Felix went up to the porch door and began barking uncontrollably. After several minutes, the firefighters wondered why Felix was so focused on the house. Deciding to go back in for one more look, three firefighters followed Felix directly to one of the bedrooms. Moments later, a fireman emerged from the charred house with a screaming infant in his arms.

Stories of Felix's valor spread far and wide. One day P .T. Barnum from Barnum & Bailey Circus came to Engine 25 to see if Felix would join the circus. With his unusual intelligence and ability to climb ladders, there was no doubt he would have done very well in the show, but there was no way the firefighters were going to let him leave.

Felix enjoyed the simple pleasures of the everyday Chicago firedog. He thrived on the attention from the local children who looked forward to giving him treats on their way home from school. Like most firedogs, Felix loved to eat, especially the liver sausage brought to him by adoring neighbors.

In 1926, Felix was the victim of an accident common to Chicago firedogs; he was struck and killed by a car at the scene of a fire. Felix's long tour of service was recognized with the honors that the Chicago Fire Department reserves for those who die in the line of duty. Felix was given a wake in the firehouse, surrounded by an elaborate and expensive floral arrangement. A solid mahogany casket was donated by the owner of a local furniture company. As a sign of the great regard the workers at the company held for Felix, the casket was handcrafted with the highest workmanship: no nails were used in its production.

The entire neighborhood mourned the loss of their close friend. On the day of the funeral, all the schools in the neighborhood were closed so the children could attend the service. Six children, three boys and three girls, served as pallbearers. Tears streamed down their faces as they walked their friend to his final resting place. News media covered the event and took pictures for the newspapers. Televisions weren't yet popular, but a newsreel showed the story in the local theaters.

Eight automobiles and over twenty firefighters traveled from the firehouse to the Palos Forest Preserve where the chief of Engine 25 had obtained a permit from the county commissioner to bury Felix. To mark his final resting spot, the men placed a granite headstone that simply reads:

Felix
No. 25. C.F.D.

There is no mention that Felix was a dog.

To this day, people still bring flowers to his grave in gratitude for his service. Felix made such a profound impact on the community that the residents coined an expression in his memory. For years, whenever they won at playing cards or a stickball game, adults and kids alike would exclaim that they had "won one for Felix."

Today a statue of Felix stands outside the Palos Hills Library—a proud tribute to Felix and the Chicago Fire Department.

Trevor and Drew Orsinger
(Excerpted from The Firefighter's Best Friend*)*

Beau and the
Twelve-Headed Monster

The bicyclists are clad in black Lycra shorts and tight-fitting, bright-colored jerseys. They ride in a disciplined pace line. Sweat glistens on lean forearms and bulging quadriceps. They talk and joke and laugh as they ride. It is just past six on a warm Sunday morning in July.

A mile ahead at the top of a short steep rise is Beau's yard. Beau is a heavyset, sinister-looking black Labrador retriever who protects his yard and his family with unswerving diligence and a loud round of barking whenever strangers approach. If the threat is especially menacing, Beau supplements his barking with a swift hard charge that invariably sends the intruder packing. This morning Beau is stationed in his usual place under the porch. It is shady and cool there, and he can see all the territory he must defend.

The cyclists slow as they ascend the hill that leads to Beau's yard. As they labor against gravity, the only sound is the *whirr* of the freewheels and the *hooosh* of hard exhalations.

Beau sees the cyclists as they crest the hill. He has seen

cyclists before and takes pride in chasing them from his territory. But this is something new: a dozen cyclists moving as one. To Beau it is a twelve-headed monster with twenty-four arms and twenty-four legs. He has to protect his family. He has to be brave. He explodes from his hiding place under the porch and charges across the yard, hackles raised, fangs bared, barking his fiercest bark.

The cyclists are taken by surprise. It isn't the first time they've been attacked by an unrestrained dog. They usually avoid a confrontation by outrunning the beast. But this dog is unusually fast and is very nearly upon them. It is too late to run for it. The cyclists reach for the only anti-dog weapons they have: water bottles and tire pumps.

When Beau reaches the edge of his yard, he hesitates for a moment. He isn't supposed to go out of the yard, and the street is definitively off-limits. But this is a twelve-headed monster with forty-eight appendages. There is no telling what it will do to his family. He has no choice—he has to break the rules, and he clears the sidewalk and the curb with one great leap.

Among the cyclists is a man who has a Lab a lot like Beau. Instead of reaching for a water bottle or tire pump, he looks at Beau and says, "Hey, where's your ball? Where's your ball?"

A few minutes later one of the other cyclists says, "Man, I couldn't believe it. He just stopped and went looking for a ball. It was amazing. How did you know he had a ball?"

"He's a Lab. Labs are nuts about tennis balls. I had a friend once who swore he was going to name his next Lab 'Wilson' so all his tennis balls would have his name on them."

The cyclists laugh and then fall silent. The only sound is the *whirr* of the freewheels and the *hoosh* of hard exhalations.

Beau is back in his favorite spot under the porch. He

has a soggy green tennis ball in his mouth. If the twelve-headed monster with forty-eight appendages comes back, he's ready.

John Arrington

Sled Dogs without Snow

One summer day my dogs and I were hiking along, making our way through the Cleveland Metro parks, when we came to a picnic area. Off to our left I saw several Port-O-Lets—those portable toilets shaped like telephone booths—and noticed that one was being used in a very unusual fashion.

Parked next to this particular Port-O-Let was a cart. It looked like some sort of sled-training cart with wheels used when there is no snow, but that was pure speculation on my part. In any case, the cart was not the unusual part. What was truly unusual were the four Siberian husky/Alaskan malamute–type dogs in harnesses, all hooked to one gang line that went directly into the door of the Port-O-Let, making it appear that they were out on a Port-O-Let/sled-riding mission. I can only assume there was no way to anchor the cart and the dogs while taking care of business, so the cart driver got the brilliant idea to just take the gang line into the Port-O-Let and hold on to the dogs while using the facilities.

Perhaps you're thinking the same thing I was thinking when I saw this little setup. I began fishing in my pack for my digital camera to take a picture of the

"Port-O-Let-pulling team" when my dogs started yanking on their leashes, almost toppling me over. I looked around to see what in blazes had set them off.

It was a squirrel that had decided to stop in the middle of the wide-open field to my left, pick up a nut and chew on it. The problem was that my three dogs and the four Port-O-Let-anchored sled dogs were hanging out in the very same field. So far the potty chain gang hadn't seen the squirrel, but it was only a matter of time as my dogs were doing the if-we-weren't-on-this-leash-we-would-kick-that-squirrel's-butt dance with increasing intensity.

Sure enough, within seconds, the potty-pullers' heads all snapped in the direction of my dogs, then in the direction of the squirrel. They appeared to have the same idea as my pack, who were still straining vigorously at their leashes. At that point, my dogs saw the sled dogs spot the squirrel, and some sort of dog tribal-hunting, nonverbal communication thing happened: every one of the seven dogs on either end of the field realized that it was a race to see which of the two groups could get to the squirrel first. My dogs redoubled their pulling efforts, and the four-dog sled team reacted as one, barking furiously and lunging full steam for the squirrel.

The dogs' motion caused the Port-O-Let to spin about thirty degrees and rock like the dickens. Luckily it didn't tip over, just teetered back and forth a time or two, then righted itself. But nothing was going to stop the sled team in their pursuit of the squirrel. They gave another huge yank. The Port-O-Let spun yet again, and from inside the green tower of potty privacy came a human screech, finally piercing through the dogs' din. The screech had the immediate effect of slowing the port-o-pullers down, and they settled into a nervous stand.

Unfortunately, at this point, the squirrel realized that my dogs weren't going to get him, and the port-o-pullers *couldn't* get him, so he started doing some kind of nah-nah-nah-nah-nah-you-can't-get-me dance, once more infuriating the port-o-pullers and driving my dogs crazy.

If you've ever wondered why dogsleds are built long and low to the ground, as opposed to square and tall—like, say, the shape of a Port-O-Let—you needn't wonder any longer whether this is a design flaw. When the pulling and barking started up again, the Port-O-Let did its best to stay upright, rocking heavily back and forth. The dogs, sensing victory, forgot completely about the squirrel and started timing their pulls with the rocking. They gave one last enormous tug and yanked the Port-O-Let over. Toppling the tall green box seemed to give the dog team a sense of satisfaction; they immediately stopped pulling after the Port-O-Let crashed to the ground. The squirrel had finally gone, and with the dogs quiet, I could now hear a series of cusswords coming from the fallen Port-O-Let.

I figured I'd better head over that way and see if I could help. Sadly, the Port-O-Let had landed facedown, meaning the door was now the bottom—against the ground. I tied my dogs to a tree and ventured closer. I asked if the occupant of the tipped Port-O-Let was okay. A woman's voice said yes—actually, she used far more colorful language, but for the purpose of this story, we'll just say she said yes.

The Port-O-Let hadn't fared as well. You could tell it was badly hurt because there was a lot of blue fluid leaking from it. I told the woman that I would have to roll the Port-O-Let on its side so we could try opening the door, and that she should find something to hang on to. A couple of good shoves later, the Port-O-Let rolled 90 degrees, exposing the door. The door opened and out crawled Mama Smurf. The poor woman was covered in the blue "blood" of the dying Port-O-Let.

Her dogs came running over and decided she needed a bath, which did not make her at all happy. At this point, she suddenly realized she had skipped Step 10 in the bathroom process—pull your pants up—and with a yelp, she quickly disappeared back into the Port-O-Let to finish. When she reappeared, she was in absolutely no mood to talk about her ride on the wild side (I didn't blame her), so I told her the short version of what happened outside the Port-O-Let.

I helped her hook her dogs up to the cart, and off she went, glowing blue as she drove down the path and back into the Metro park woods. I had to laugh imagining the reactions of all the other people walking serenely through the park as they were passed by an irate Smurf and her merry band of blue-tongued dogs.

Dave Wiley

10

AMAZING CANINES!

She was such a beautiful and sweet creature . . . and so full of tricks.

Queen Victoria

Lucky Wows the Sheriff

Lucky was a dog of huge proportion—actually, *dispro-*portion. His neck was thick, his head was skinny, and his eyes were too close together, giving him a slightly stupid expression. I once had a friend who described his horse as a "cross between a freight train and a wire gate." When I found that big splotchy dog, stray and starving by the side of the road, I thought the description suited him, too. But in spite of his appearance, I brought him home to live with us.

Late one night I came home from work, driving up the long lane to our house in the country and—as usual—turned the car around in preparation for leaving the next morning. Lucky—also as usual—watched this routine, wagging mightily, and waited for me to open the car door. But this night, as I stepped out of the car, Lucky growled menacingly, barked and advanced toward me. I backed into the car seat and quickly closed the door against my big black-and-white, cow-spotted friend, who had now turned aggressive. In disbelief I contemplated the hundreds of cans of expensive dog food we had served him. *This is how he thanks me?* I sat there, safe in my metallic cocoon, puzzled. Then as my head cleared, I took heart and reasoned the dog was just playing a game and that it was silly to sit there in the dark. I pushed the door fully open. Lucky exploded, shooting up to display his full six-foot-plus "Bigfoot" imitation. Throwing his body weight across the door, he slammed it shut. Then standing guard, he never took his too-close-together eyes off the door again.

Our Tennessee fall had deepened. Though leaves would blow down from the woods for at least another month, frigid nights already frosted the leaves banked by our doorstep. Just as I was getting good and chilly, my husband drove into his parking spot beside my car. "What are you doing sitting out here in the cold?" he asked.

I cracked the window open an inch to explain that Lucky was now crazy and I could never get out of the car again.

"Well," my practical husband said, "Let's go see what's upsetting the big fellow."

Now that the mister was home, Lucky permitted me out of the car. As we approached the doorstep with a flashlight, the dog ran ahead and began a bizarre imper-sonation of a giraffe imitating a pointer. That's when we heard it—or more accurately, felt it—a buzzing sound from beneath a leaf pile. It could mean only one thing: a rattler. (When I encountered my first rattlesnake, what surprised me was that rattlers don't rattle; it's your teeth that rattle as the chills run up and down your spine.)

For some reason, the snake remained coiled in its cho-sen spot until the county sheriff arrived with his deputies and shotguns. As we raked the leaf cover aside, we saw that the timber rattler was so large that a man could not girdle it with the thumbs and middle fingers of both hands. We could also see why the snake had remained in place for so long. Picture a dozen little snakes squiggling around in all directions; with two large, uniformed deputies, armed with garden rakes and shovels, scrambling to collect the snake babies into a tall container; and a great black-and-white dog running back and forth, barking, dancing and "helping."

When the dancing was over and all the snakes caged, the exhausted sheriff said that he had worked the hills for many years, but had never seen "such a snake." Then he said, "Ma'am, it's a good thing you didn't step in that mess o' snakes in the dark. That dog saved your life tonight. I think you owe him a big Angus steak."

We all looked at Lucky who had returned to normal: a homely, friendly and slightly stupid-looking dog, wagging his tail at his teammates. He was an unlikely hero, but a hero all the same.

The sheriff then paid Lucky the highest compliment a country dog can receive, "Yes sir, that's a *fine* dog you've got there."

We had to agree.

Mariana Levine

A Dog's Day in Court

When I was growing up, we lived about a quarter mile from a train crossing. Our dog, Lenny, had a very annoying habit: he howled whenever a train whistled for the crossing. It probably stemmed from his very sensitive hearing. It did not matter if he was outside or in the house. He howled and howled until the train went by. On some days, when the wind was right, he would even howl for the crossings farther down the track. We learned to put up with the noisy ruckus, mainly because we loved our pet so much.

Early one morning while we were eating breakfast, we heard the squeal of a train's braking efforts followed by a terrible crash. My brother dashed out of the house, ran to the end of our lane and discovered a mangled mass jammed on the cowcatcher of the massive locomotive. Parts of a car were strewn everywhere. Unfortunately, the driver of the car had died instantly.

Back in the house, we guessed there had been a crash and called the local rescue squad. But we all immediately said to each other, "Lenny didn't howl. The whistle must not have blown!"

At the scene, my brother recognized what was left of the car as that of his buddy's father and knew immediately the sad, sad news that would now have to be conveyed to the family. When the chief of the rescue squad arrived, my brother told him, "The engineer could *not* have blown the whistle for the crossing, because our dog did not howl. And he always does!"

The story of Lenny's howling circulated rapidly around our small town as everyone shared in the grief of the wife and family. Speculation ran high as to whether the whistle had truly been blown as the engineer claimed. Some folks even came to witness the "howling dog" phenomenon and left convinced the whistle must not have sounded!

Left without the breadwinner, the family of nine was in dire straits. One of the county's best-known and most successful lawyers decided to pursue a claim against the, by now, infamous Soo Line on behalf of the widow and children. (On contingency, of course!) The lawyer hired an investigator and recording technician. For days, at all hours, the two men frequented our yard and our home listening for oncoming trains and faithfully recording Lenny's howl. Lenny never failed to echo with his characteristic, piercing howl the sharp wail of an approaching freight as it neared the crossing at which the tragedy had occurred. They even recorded his howling as a whistle was blown at the neighboring crossings in both directions when the wind was right. The lawyer was convinced.

The taped evidence, presented in court, along with the testimony of my family members, convinced the judge and jury. The settlement awarded to the family secured their home and future. County court records give evidence of the success of a "dog's day in court!"

Sr. Mary K. Himens, S.S.C.M.

The Bravest Dog

Lisa smiled, watching from the back door as her husband, Mike, disappeared into the woods surrounding their Tennessee home with Sadie, his two-year-old English setter, bounding at his side.

Mike had always wanted a dog of his own, and the year before, Lisa's father had rescued Sadie from a neglectful owner and brought her to them. At first she was pitifully timid and mistrustful. She'd cower and whimper at any sudden moves in her direction, yelp and run at the sound of loud noises.

But Lisa had combed the tangles out of the long hair of her white-and-black-spotted coat and Mike had spent hours gently coaxing and playing with her, winning her trust. With lots of attention and TLC, Sadie grew into a happy, adoring pet who shadowed Mike everywhere.

Lisa's dad had said it right from the beginning: "If you're good to this dog, she'll be good to you." And this morning Sadie would prove the power of that bond beyond all question. . . .

Sadie led the way along the familiar trail, the one she and Mike tramped every morning and evening. Sometimes she'd flush birds from the bushes, then sit watching, mesmerized, as they soared into the sky. This always amused Mike. Occasionally, she'd dive into the under-brush, lured by an interesting scent. But she'd always come when Mike called or blew his coach's whistle.

She's such a good dog, Mike thought, picturing her romp-ing with his three-year-old son, Kyle, and two-year-old daughter, Chelsea. She was always gentle, even patiently submitting to their inadvertent ear-tugging and tail-pulling.

They'd walked about a third of a mile, and Sadie was off exploring when Mike suddenly felt a sharp pain in his wrist. He'd experienced similar aches recently but shrugged them off when they quickly disappeared. Probably bursi-tis, he'd thought. This time, however, the burning pain began to shoot up his arm like wildfire, and a wave of nau-sea swept over him. *What's going on?* he wondered ner-vously, deciding: *I'd better turn back.*

But as he fumbled for the whistle around his neck to call Sadie, an excruciating pain slammed into his chest as though he'd been hit with an anvil. He dropped to his knees, gasping for breath. Desperate, he gave the whis-tle a short blow—all he could manage before collapsing facedown on the ground. With pain searing through his chest like a burning knife, and his left arm numb, he had a terrifying thought: *I'm having a heart attack—and I'm only thirty-six!*

Suddenly, he felt Sadie at his side, nudging him gently with a soft, wet nose. Sensing that Mike was in trouble, she whined softly and gazed at Mike with worried eyes that seemed to ask, *What's wrong?*

Mike realized Sadie was his only chance. He knew she'd never leave his side to go for help, even if he tried to send her. And Lisa wouldn't miss them for at least an hour—maybe more. *Maybe if I hang onto her, she can drag me close enough to call for help,* he thought. *But can she do it?*

Will she? he worried. With his last ounce of strength, he reached out and grabbed Sadie's collar with his good arm. "Home, girl!" he urged.

Sadie sensed it was up to her. Slowly the 45-pound dog started to drag the 180-pound man back down the rough trail. Groaning with pain, Mike struggled to hang on. He thought of Lisa waiting at home. Lisa, whom he'd met at work when he'd moved from California six years before. Beautiful and bright Lisa, who'd quickly captured his heart with her room-lighting smile and gentle soul. He recalled their wedding day, when he'd told her, "You've made me the proudest man in the world." And that feeling only intensified during their time together. *Not enough time!* Mike thought now. *We have our whole lives ahead of us.*

Sadie struggled and tugged, staggering beneath the burden of Mike's weight as it strained her muscles. As she dragged Mike over roots and rocks, his agony grew. The viselike pain constricted his chest as he thought *I'll never make it.*

Images of his children floated in his mind: little Chelsea toddling around the house clutching her precious Raggedy Ann doll. And Kyle, his constant shadow, helping Daddy work on his truck and playing catch in the yard.

I can't die, Mike told himself. *My family needs me!*

Suddenly, another picture popped into his mind. The card with the family photo they'd sent out last Christmas, with Chelsea on Lisa's lap and Kyle on his, and sitting pretty in front—Sadie, upon whose furry shoulders Mike's life now depended. But by that point he was starting to fade in and out of consciousness. Each time blackness descended and Sadie felt his fingers loosen their grip on her collar, she would stop and lick his face and whine urgently until his eyes flickered open again.

Somehow Mike managed to grasp her collar again and

hang on, in spite of the crushing pain in his chest as Sadie set out once more. Rocks and vines snagged and tore at his clothes as Sadie continued to pull him over the rough terrain, pausing only occasionally as she panted to catch her breath, marshaling her strength before plowing on.

Then she encountered an even greater test: a rolling hill. One which she easily bounded up and down most days—when she wasn't dragging a weight four times her size! Sadie paused for an instant, summoning her strength.

"You can do it, girl!" Mike urged.

With a lick of his face, Sadie set herself again and began the torturous climb, digging in her paws and straining with all her might, battling for every inch, growling with the effort.

"That's it, Sadie!" Mike encouraged as she slowly dragged him up the slope, foot by agonizing foot, until finally they reached the top—and then slipped down the other side.

Mike spotted his neighbor's house, but by now he was too weak and short of breath to call for help. *That's the last thing I'm ever going to see,* he thought, feeling unconsciousness slipping over him.

But somehow his fingers still clutched Sadie's collar. And she staggered stubbornly on and on, dragging Mike's unconscious dead weight, refusing to stop—until finally she tugged him through the opening in the fence, across the backyard and to the foot of the steps leading to the Millers' porch.

Once there, she barked and howled like never before.

Hearing the noise, Lisa wondered what was going on. She opened the back door and gasped, spotting her husband crumpled on the ground with Sadie hovering over him.

"Mike! What's wrong?" she screamed, racing to his side.

Mike's eyes blinked open. "My heart, I think," he moaned.

Dear God! she panicked, rushing to the phone to call 911, then dashing back to Mike.

While they waited for the ambulance, Mike croaked: "Sadie saved me. She dragged me home from the woods."

Lisa stared in disbelief at the panting dog who still refused to leave Mike's side. Then, still gripping Mike's hand, she threw her other arm around Sadie, pulled her close and choked, "Good girl, Sadie."

At the hospital, doctors discovered Mike had suffered a massive heart attack and performed emergency triple-bypass surgery. "You're going to be fine, but you're lucky to be alive," doctors told him afterward. Mike knew who to thank.

And he did. When he got home a week later, as Sadie bounced around him, overjoyed to see him, Mike produced a bag of bones from the butcher. "Treats for my hero," he said, hugging her.

Today Mike is fully recovered. He and his dog still walk together, and Mike spends many hours pitching sticks that Sadie happily retrieves. He can't do enough for her, knowing that if Sadie hadn't been with him, he wouldn't have made it home alive.

Lisa remains amazed that Sadie was able to drag Mike all the way back to the house by herself. She says, "I guess it just shows how strong the power of love really is."

Sherry Cremona-Van Der Elst
Previously appeared in Woman's World Magazine

OFF THE MARK, ©1997 Mark Parisi. Reprinted with permission of Mark Parisi.

A Pocketful of Love

If you think dogs can't count, try putting three dog biscuits in your pocket and then giving Fido only two of them.

Phil Pastoret

DebbieLynn never set out to be a fashion model, it just kind of happened. Although she had other interests she wanted to pursue, it was hard to walk away from the success she'd achieved modeling. The exciting lifestyle meant Deb traveled constantly, which left little time for other interests. She'd thought about taking the gamble, quitting and trying something new, but told herself she'd model just one more year. For more years than she could count, it had been, "Just one more year."

Everything changed the day Deb returned from an overseas modeling job and caught a taxi at the airport. Instead of delivering her home, the drunken cabbie stole her career and health in a horrible car accident that Deb barely survived. Suddenly, the "one more year" of modeling wasn't an option. Deb was left with a kaleidoscope of disabling health problems, some caused by side effects of the drugs meant to keep her alive. She had no choice— this time, Deb had to start over, from scratch.

Although she'd had dogs as a child and had wanted a dog for a long time, her travel schedule kept her from adopting a pet for many years. Finding the perfect canine companion was now the first thing on Deb's wish list. Not just any dog would do, though. The scleroderma racking her body left her skin so fragile, a tiny bump could tear it and cause bleeding. On top of that, secondary hemophilia kept cuts from coagulating, and Deb could die if the bleeding wasn't stopped in time. Doctors who feared a large dog could accidentally hurt her warned Deb that two and a half pounds was the top weight limit she could tolerate. With her lung capacity so severely diminished, shedding was also a problem.

Nevertheless, Deb was determined to have her dream dog. It took her eighteen months to find the perfect two-pound Yorkshire terrier, whom she named Cosette. Her puppy had special needs of her own—because of her tiny size, Cosette couldn't digest commercial dog foods and required a special vegetarian diet. Deb was happy to do whatever it took to keep her new companion healthy and happy.

They'd been together only a few weeks, and Cosette was only five months old when the pocket-size puppy began "acting weird." Cosette ran up to Deb, gently pawed her leg in an odd way, and squeaked a peculiar sound Deb had never heard before. The dog wouldn't stop—she repeated the behavior time and again. What was wrong? Deb worried the pup had gone nuts. Didn't Deb already have enough to deal with—what if the pup she'd fallen in love with had emotional problems? Deb knew she could manage the homemade diet, but could she handle something worse?

It never occurred to Deb that Cosette was trying to tell

her something, until the doctor saw them together. During a house call, Deb's doctor witnessed one of Cosette's strange episodes. Other patients of his had dogs who alerted them to health conditions, so he immediately recognized that the puppy somehow "knew" in advance Deb would suffer a health crisis. Sure enough, seven minutes later one of Deb's dangerous migraines began.

Deb was amazed! She had heard about this ability and knew dogs couldn't be trained to have it; they either "know" or they don't, and it's the bond between the pet and person that makes it happen. She'd never considered having a service animal, but Cosette had taken matters into her own paws. The pup's ability offered a freedom Deb never expected, and allowed her to take medicine and prevent the headaches that not only were painful, but also could cause bleeding and kill her.

The doctor told Deb that her puppy should get additional training and certification so Cosette could go with her everywhere. The Delta Society, a national group that certifies therapy dogs, recommended a trainer. It took only four months for the little dog, with her inborn service-dog instincts, to be certified.

Deb had also suffered hearing loss from the accident, making it difficult for her to hear buzzer-type sounds like the doorbell, the telephone, and the washer and dryer, so Cosette learned to alert her to any of these. She also was taught to tell Deb when something or someone approached from her peripheral blind spots.

But Cosette figured out ways to help Deb that not even the trainer anticipated. Cosette's acute sense of smell allows her to alert Deb to tiny cuts that Deb doesn't even know have happened. First, she pushes and pushes against Deb's ankles to make her get down to the dog's level. Then Cosette puts her tongue against the cut, finds a position that gives her good traction, then applies pressure. Deb says that the tiny dog can make herself feel like a lead weight. A treatment lasts for twenty to forty minutes—or until the bleeding stops, and somehow, Cosette knows when it has been long enough. Without Cosette's skillful attentions, Deb would need to spend all day at the emergency room.

Another serious health problem Deb faces are her heart irregularities. She's often not aware that her breathing has become shallower until she blacks out. Now when Deb's heart skips a beat, Cosette warns her so she can take medicine in time to ward off the problem. When Deb sleeps, sometimes her heart stops altogether, until Cosette leaps into action—literally, by jumping on Deb's chest. That almost always gets the heart going again, but if it doesn't start right away, Cosette even knows to dial 911!

Cosette was trained to dial 911 on any push-button telephone by tapping out the individual three numbers, so she can call for help anywhere, anytime, even from a cell phone when they're away from home. Deb leaves phones in their home always within paw-reach. Cosette has called 911 and saved Deb's life more than thirty times during their years together.

The little dog who saves her life also helps Deb make a living. Cosette inspired Deb to create three Web sites that cater to pet lovers. Cosette's Private Collection is a line of all-natural, botanical grooming products for dogs. Cosette's Choice includes organic biscuits, nutritional supplements for dogs with special nutritional needs (like Cosette herself), including a Biscuit-of-the-Month Club. The third, Cosette's Closet, leverages Deb's experience and taste from the world of fashion modeling to provide a specialty line of canine clothing, including doggy bridesmaid gowns, sundresses and tuxedos. Cosette, of course, has her own closetful of designer doggy togs.

Cosette wears her special outfits when she accompanies

Deb to restaurants. On her last birthday, Cosette enjoyed eating rice and beans at her favorite Mexican dining spot and greeting the restaurant manager, a member of her "fan club," who insisted on singing "Happy Birthday" to the special dog.

Her biggest fan, though, is DebbieLynn. The former model—now successful entrepreneur—never knew she could become so attached to a dog, yet her tiny companion and service dog has become everything to her. And Deb knows the feeling is mutual; she is amazed at the depth of Cosette's love for her. Today they live for each other.

Amy D. Shojai

Pedro the Fisherman

The most touching dog story I've ever heard was told to me thirty years ago by a neighbor on her return from a Mediterranean cruise.

The setting of the story is a little cove on the east side of the Spanish island of Mallorca. It was there that an Englishman, a professional diver, lived on his yacht with his dog, a springer spaniel. He had tied his yacht to a pier where diving conditions were ideal. Each time the Englishman made a dive, the dog sat anxiously on the pier, awaiting his return. One day the dog became so concerned when the Englishman disappeared into the water that he dove in after him.

Underwater, the dog saw a school of fish swim past. He grabbed a fish and carried it back to the pier. The Englishman, surprised and pleased, praised him. After that, the dog followed the man on his dives. In the course of the shared diving, the dog developed excellent fishing skills, to the man's considerable amusement. The Englishman told the island's residents of his dog's accomplishments, and they came to the pier to watch. Delighted, they began calling the dog Pedro, after Peter, the fisherman.

One day the Englishman became ill, and shortly there-after, he died. Townspeople tried to adopt Pedro, but the dog would never leave the beach for fear he would miss his master's return. He waited on the beach through hot sun and driving rain. People tried to feed him, but eventually they gave up. He wouldn't accept food from anyone other than his master. Finally, to feed himself, Pedro went back to fishing.

It happened that on this same island there were a number of stray cats. Ravenous, they would gather to watch Pedro dive into the schools of fish, select the fish he wanted and bring it back to eat on the shore. Then the cats would fight over what the dog had left uneaten. The dog must have observed this, for one morning when Pedro had eaten his fill, he dove into the water again and came back up with a large fish, which he placed on the sand before the group of cats. Then he backed off and watched. One black cat, with greater courage than the others, approached the fish, grabbed it and ran. After that, in addition to keeping vigil for his master, the dog also seemed to consider it his duty to feed those less fortunate. For every morning thereafter, Pedro the fisherman shared his catch with the hungry cats of Mallorca.

Bob Toren

Angel's Angel

When we first met Frisbee, she wasn't much to look at—a black-and-white lump of fur, being half-dragged and half-pushed by an impatient veterinary technician. Someone had left two six-week-old puppies in a box behind the hardware store outside of town. It was April in Texas, so the pups were lonely and hungry, but luckily not frozen. We agreed to foster them.

Over the next month, while the puppies grew, our family volunteered at the local shelter's Saturday adoption days and held the leashes of older dogs waiting for permanent homes. For three weeks in a row, my husband held an affectionate, gray and white one-year-old Weimaraner/cattle dog mix named Angel. A volunteer had found Angel lying at the side of the road. No one knew whether she had been hit by or thrown from a car, but in addition to her injuries, she also had heartworms and spent months at the veterinarian's office undergoing treatment.

Sometimes when a dog is adopted, the chemistry with the adoptive family isn't right, and the dog is returned to the shelter. We were surprised to learn that Angel had been returned three times for "erratic behavior," and was considered a "hard to place" dog. We held a family meeting and decided to bring Angel home. The next weekend, a family adopted one of our puppies, leaving just one: the girl we had named Frisbee. She and Angel got along well. In fact, we wondered about the other homes Angel had been in because she didn't act erratically with people or other dogs. Her only fault was that she tried to keep close to us, so we were constantly tripping over her. Her head appeared between the rungs of my chair. She leaned against my legs while I worked at the sink.

One evening, about a week after we adopted Angel, our family sat down to dinner. Angel and Frisbee lay under the table. Suddenly, there was a thump, followed by scraping as the empty chair next to me mysteriously pushed back. We heard more thrashing and saw Frisbee scramble out from under the table. I assumed the dogs were squabbling and bent down to scold them.

I had never seen a seizure before. Angel's eyes were dull and her head cartwheeled against the floor. Her legs twitched and thrashed as if she were racing from unseen demons. Our kids cleared the chairs, I cushioned Angel's head against the tile floor, and my husband dialed the vet. We hoped the episode would be a one-time event. Maybe she'd eaten something someone had thrown over the fence. Maybe she'd eaten a poisonous plant. (Sometimes she chewed on trees like a beaver!) But that evening's vet visit was the first of many.

Angel's seizures came more frequently. We tried a range of medications, read, contacted canine acupuncturists and visited specialists in Houston where Angel had a spinal tap. Angel was diagnosed with idiopathic epilepsy, a cruel diagnosis meaning that she suffered seizures for which there was no identifiable source. We could treat her symptoms, but not the cause. The veterinarians said that Angel's seizures were unusually severe, and she might live another year or two at most. At that point, we decided to adopt Frisbee. We reasoned that we would be able to bear Angel's loss better if we already had another dog.

Although medication eased Angel's seizures, several times a day she stiffened and stared into space in a petit mal seizure. Then she shook her head, as if to put her brains back in order, and continued as if nothing had happened. The grand mal seizures weren't as easy to watch. These episodes came unexpectedly, with brutal ferocity. If left alone, Angel sometimes hit her head on the floor until her jaw bled. We tried to rearrange our lives to be home more, but even so, we returned to disaster several times each week.

During the week of Thanksgiving, Angel had multiple grand mal seizures. I had to cut back her favorite activity and stay closer to home after a seizure midwalk left me struggling to carry her sixty-five-pound deadweight. Our family was heartbroken.

By then, our "puppy" Frisbee was a muscular seven-month-old, fifty-pound dog. She had grown up watching Angel's struggles, hearing "go sit" and "stay back" while I held Angel's head. One evening I heard Frisbee bark. It didn't sound like a "stranger at the door," or "squirrel in the yard" warning. I followed the bark and found Frisbee pinning Angel to the floor.

Some dogs have the innate ability to detect the onset of seizures. People use these dogs to detect their seizures so they can get to a safe location before a seizure starts. Other dogs, though not able to detect a seizure before it happens, stand over their charge during a seizure until the person regains consciousness. They hold their person steady and keep them safe. This is what Frisbee was doing for Angel, though she had never been trained to do so.

Frisbee has continued to assist Angel during her seizures. I don't know what Frisbee "tells" Angel when she holds her down. All I know is that if a seizure begins when my husband or I aren't in the room, Frisbee leaps into action. Apparently she watched us hold Angel and decided she could help. We used to worry every time we left the house, not knowing if a seizure was imminent. Now Frisbee fills in.

Frisbee is also Angel's "spare paws." Our dogs don't bark to go out or come back in. Instead they "tap" on the door. Angel loves her walk and does fine as long as all four paws are on the ground. However, her medications make her unsteady and she has trouble balancing on the back steps to tap on the door. If both dogs are outside, Frisbee taps on the door and then moves behind Angel, letting her go in first. If Frisbee is inside and sees Angel waiting outside, she taps as if she has to go out and then lies down when someone lets Angel in.

Frisbee isn't perfect. She hates to have her feet wiped. She growls at dogs she doesn't know. She pulls on her leash when we go for a walk. But that's okay. Thanks to Frisbee, five years after her grim diagnosis, Angel is still a tail-wagging, snack-snitching, treasured family member. What Frisbee can't do doesn't matter. For what she does, she's Angel's angel.

Wendy Greenley

Take Me Home!

As I gave Perrier, my black Labrador guide dog, the command, "Forward, inside," I could feel my heart thumping. Would he obey me and go up the three steps into the waiting train? Moments before, the commuter train had pulled into the station on its way from Philadelphia to Newark, New Jersey. As the brakes hissed and the train came to a halt near us, Perrier sat calmly beside me on the platform. But would he actually guide me on? Not to worry! Perrier conducted himself like a seasoned professional and smartly led me to the stairs and into the club car.

Four days earlier, we had returned home from the Seeing Eye in Morristown, New Jersey, after spending three and a half weeks learning to work as a team. At that time I was living with my wife, Phyllis, and daughter, Lori, in a suburb north of Philadelphia. Perrier quickly adapted to life in our apartment, and during the next few days we took frequent short walks around the neighborhood—a new experience without my long white cane. We visited some of the nearby stores and Perrier quickly learned to pause at an ice-cream parlor and see if this was one of those days when we would indulge my creamy passion. Now it was time to return to my job in New York, which would provide a true test of Perrier's skill.

My favorite conductor, Bobby, was on duty that morning and greeted the two of us with enthusiasm. Like a good old-time railroad conductor, he knew all the regular commuters by name. As I positioned Perrier under one of the tables in the club car, Jim, the waiter, came over to check on whether I wanted my usual coffee and muffin. This initial commute began a routine that lasted for five years, until I moved to New York to live. My commute normally lasted about an hour because it was a typical "local" with many stops along the way. On this first trip, however, several surprises were in store for me. When the train pulled into the first stop, Perrier got up and began pulling me to the exit. Since I knew we had more than an hour to go, I firmly resisted his attempt to disembark and resettled him under my seat. At each of the next few stops the scene was repeated. It finally dawned on me that during our training, all the teams got on a commuter train, went one stop, got off, crossed the platform, got on another train and went back one stop to Morristown. For Perrier, commuting to work meant going one stop and one stop only!

Another surprise was the attention lavished on us by my fellow commuters, many of whom I had been traveling with for several years without exchanging a word. Dog talk abounded, with questions about Perrier and reminiscences about the dogs in their own lives.

Once I reached the Newark station, I had two options: I could catch an Amtrak train from Newark into Manhattan, a fifteen-minute ride, or transfer to the Port Authority subway system. The advantage of the subway was I would be within easy walking distance of my office at Baruch College when I got off, but it took forty-five minutes. On this first day, as I left the commuter train in

Newark, an Amtrak train was just pulling into the station across the platform. I decided to take it. With my "Forward" command, Perrier swiftly crossed, made his way through the crowd waiting to board and guaranteed we would be the first ones to enter the waiting train. During this transfer I realized my new partner was a dog ideally suited for working in New York City.

On arrival in Manhattan, I opted to walk to work, a distance of slightly more than a mile. After walking several blocks south on Eighth Avenue, Perrier veered to the right, and the next thing I knew, he attempted to board a northbound bus! He was giving me a clear signal, which was repeated many times during our eight years of partnership: *I'd rather ride than walk!* Unfortunately for Perrier, the bus was going in the wrong direction.

Arriving at my office twenty minutes later, I was exhilarated. This thrilling sense of emerging independence was reinforced every time Perrier stopped at a curb, avoided rushing pedestrians and smartly crossed a traffic-filled street. What had been a chore for the last few years was now an exciting adventure!

During our years of intercity travel, Perrier and I shared many unique experiences. Stopping at stairs, avoiding open cellar doors, handling the hustle and bustle of city life, and weaving in and out of cars intruding into pedestrian walkways were all in a day's work for my magnificent canine partner. The one constant was that life was full of challenges.

One memorable occasion remains forever etched in my memory. On this particular day Perrier's intuitive guiding skill went well beyond his routine duties. I left the office just as a major blizzard hit the Northeast, and by the time I arrived at the station near my home, more than ten inches of snow had fallen. Stepping off the train, a strange new world encompassed me. Snow is to a blind person what fog is to a sighted person. Accustomed to being met by Phyllis, I listened for the sound of her voice or the car motor. As the train departed, I realized I was alone, since I had been the only passenger to disembark. The suddenness and severity of the storm not only kept Phyllis from picking me up at the station, but also kept all other cars off the usually crowded road. I knew Phyllis was probably stuck at home and frantic, but the road was impassable, even by emergency vehicles. The tiny station was closed, offering no protection from the snow.

With a sinking feeling, I realized that Perrier and I were on our own. Descending the steps of the station platform, it was eerie not to hear a single car moving. Snow, like dense fog, deadens the sounds I rely on for cues about the environment. That suppression of sound combined with the lack of traffic was totally disorienting for me. It was not only eerie, it was downright scary. I realized that I could easily become lost and wander around for hours looking for help. I knew I had to turn right after exiting the station, but had no idea where the sidewalks and curbs were. All I could do was give Perrier the "Forward" command and hope he knew where he was going. I said, "Take me home, Perrier!"

The snow continued falling as I followed my guide's slow but steady lead. As we walked along, the only sound I heard was the crunching of my shoes as we plodded on. I kept hoping a car would go by so I could determine if we were even on the sidewalk! No such luck. In the immense silence of the falling snow, it felt as if Perrier and I were the last two beings on Earth.

After walking for what seemed an interminable period, Perrier made a sharp right turn. At that point I said to him, "I sure hope you know where you are going." About ten minutes later he made another short right turn and I followed him up two steps where he unhesitatingly placed his nose on the doorknob of my apartment! Flinging open the door, I was enveloped by the safety and warmth of my home. The tension ebbed from my body and was immediately replaced by an incredible surge of gratitude for the skill and confidence of my canine partner. Dropping to my knees, I buried my face in Perrier's wet fur and whispered to him, "Thank you, buddy, for rescuing me!" His response was a warm tongue on my cheek.

Ed Eames, Ph.D.

More Chicken Soup?

Many of the stories and poems you have read in this book were submitted by readers like you who had read earlier *Chicken Soup for the Soul* books. We publish at least five or six *Chicken Soup for the Soul* books every year. We invite you to contribute a story to one of these future volumes.

Stories may be up to twelve hundred words and must uplift or inspire. You may submit an original piece, something you have read or your favorite quotation on your refrigerator door.

To obtain a copy of our submission guidelines and a listing of upcoming *Chicken Soup* books, please write, fax or check our Web site.

Please send your submissions to:

Chicken Soup for the Soul
Web site: *www.chickensoupforthesoul.com*
P.O. Box 30880, Santa Barbara, CA 93130
Fax: 805-563-2945

We will be sure that both you and the author are credited for your submission.

For information about speaking engagements, other books, audiotapes, workshops and training programs, please contact any of our authors directly.

Supporting Others

Join Us in Supporting
Pets to Stay in Their Homes "For Life"

The stories in this book celebrate the loving relationships between people and their animal companions. Yet in spite of all this love, an estimated 4 to 6 million animals are brought to shelters throughout the United States every year! Contrary to popular belief, most animals in shelters weren't abused, nor did they do anything "wrong" that caused them to lose their homes. Most animals are abandoned for "people reasons" like allergies, divorce and moving, or because of behaviors that pet owners don't understand and don't know how to address. If these reasons, which break the bond between pets and their families, could be eliminated, just imagine how many animals could remain in their homes.

That's the premise behind the Pets for Life program of the Humane Society of the United States (HSUS). Through Pets for Life, the HSUS provides information on the most common behavior problems and how to solve them, about dealing with allergies, tips on finding pet-friendly rental housing, and other issues affecting pets and their people. The HSUS also provides information on choosing the right pet, whether from a shelter or a reputable breeder. For information, go to *www.PetsForLife.org* or write to the address below.

Of course, pet overpopulation is still a factor that contributes to the large number of animals that end up in shelters. The HSUS continues to work to reduce pet overpopulation through education and programs like the Rural Area Veterinary Services (RAVS).

The Humane Society of the United States is the nation's largest animal protection organization with more than

8.5 million members and constituents. This nonprofit organization is a mainstream voice for animals, with active programs in companion animal and equine protection, disaster preparedness and response, wildlife and habitat protection, research and farm animal advocacy and the development of sustainable agriculture. The HSUS protects all animals through legislation, litigation, investigation, education, advocacy and fieldwork. The group is based in Washington, D.C., and has numerous field representatives across the country.

The HSUS depends on donations for its lifesaving work. To donate, go to *www.hsus.org*, or send your contribution to: The HSUS, 2100 L Street N.W., Washington, DC 20037. The HSUS can be reached at 202-452-1100.

Who Is Jack Canfield?

Jack Canfield is one of America's leading experts in the development of human potential and personal effectiveness. He is both a dynamic, entertaining speaker and a highly sought-after trainer. Jack has a wonderful ability to inform and inspire audiences toward increased levels of self-esteem and peak performance. Jack most recently released a book for success titled *The Success Principles: How to Get from Where You Are to Where You Want to Be.*

He is the author and narrator of several bestselling audio- and videocassette programs, including *Self-Esteem and Peak Performance, How to Build High Self-Esteem, Self-Esteem in the Classroom* and *Chicken Soup for the Soul—Live.* He is regularly seen on television shows such as *Good Morning America, 20/20* and *NBC Nightly News.* Jack has co-authored numerous books, including the *Chicken Soup for the Soul* series, *Dare to Win* and *The Aladdin Factor* (all with Mark Victor Hansen), *100 Ways to Build Self-Concept in the Classroom* (with Harold C. Wells), *Heart at Work* (with Jacqueline Miller) and *The Power of Focus* (with Les Hewitt and Mark Victor Hansen).

Jack is a regularly featured speaker for professional associations, school districts, government agencies, churches, hospitals, sales organizations and corporations. His clients have included the American Dental Association, the American Management Association, AT&T, Campbell's Soup, Clairol, Domino's Pizza, GE, Hartford Insurance, ITT, Johnson & Johnson, the Million Dollar Roundtable, NCR, New England Telephone, Re/Max, Scott Paper, TRW and Virgin Records. Jack has taught on the faculty of Income Builders International, a school for entrepreneurs.

Jack conducts an annual seven-day training called Breakthrough to Success. It attracts entrepreneurs, educators, counselors, parenting trainers, corporate trainers, professional speakers, ministers and others interested in improving their lives and lives of others.

For free gifts from Jack and information on all his material and availability go to:

www.jackcanfield.com
Self-Esteem Seminars
P.O. Box 30880
Santa Barbara, CA 93130
Phone: 805-563-2935 • Fax: 805-563-2945

Who Is Mark Victor Hansen?

In the area of human potential, no one is more respected than Mark Victor Hansen. For more than thirty years, Mark has focused solely on helping people from all walks of life reshape their personal vision of what's possible. His powerful messages of possibility, opportunity and action have created powerful change in thousands of organizations and millions of individuals worldwide.

He is a sought-after keynote speaker, bestselling author and marketing maven. Mark's credentials include a lifetime of entrepreneurial success and an extensive academic background. He is a prolific writer with many bestselling books, such as *The One Minute Millionaire, The Power of Focus, The Aladdin Factor* and *Dare to Win,* in addition to the *Chicken Soup for the Soul* series. Mark has made a profound influence through his library of audios, videos and articles in the areas of big thinking, sales achievement, wealth building, publishing success, and personal and professional development.

Mark is the founder of the MEGA Seminar Series. MEGA Book Marketing University and Building Your MEGA Speaking Empire are annual conferences where Mark coaches and teaches new and aspiring authors, speakers and experts on building lucrative publishing and speaking careers. Other MEGA events include MEGA Marketing Magic and My MEGA Life.

He has appeared on television (*Oprah, CNN* and *The Today Show*), in print (*Time, U.S. News & World Report, USA Today, New York Times* and *Entrepreneur*) and on countless radio interviews, assuring our planet's people that, "You can easily create the life you deserve."

As a philanthropist and humanitarian, Mark works tirelessly for organizations such as Habitat for Humanity, American Red Cross, March of Dimes, Childhelp USA and many others. He is the recipient of numerous awards that honor his entrepreneurial spirit, philanthropic heart and business acumen. He is a lifetime member of the Horatio Alger Association of Distinguished Americans, an organization that honored Mark with the prestigious Horatio Alger Award for his extraordinary life achievements.

Mark Victor Hansen is an enthusiastic crusader of what's possible and is driven to make the world a better place.

Mark Victor Hansen & Associates, Inc.
P.O. Box 7665
Newport Beach, CA 92658
Phone: 949-764-2640
Fax: 949-722-6912
Visit Mark online at: *www.markvictorhansen.com*

Who Is Marty Becker, D.V.M.?

What Jacques Cousteau did for the oceans, what Carl Sagan did for space, Dr. Marty Becker is doing for pets.

As a veterinarian, author, university educator, media personality and pet lover, Dr. Becker is one of the most widely recognized animal health authorities in the world. He is also passionate about his work, fostering the affection-connection between pets and people that we call, "The Bond."

Marty coauthored *Chicken Soup for the Pet Lover's Soul, Chicken Soup for the Cat & Dog Lover's Soul, Chicken Soup for the Horse Lover's Soul* and *The Healing Power of Pets*, which was awarded a prestigious silver award in the National Health Information Awards.

Dr. Becker has powerful media platforms, including seven years as the popular veterinary contributor to ABC-TV's *Good Morning America.* Dr. Becker authors two highly regarded newspaper columns that are internationally distributed by Knight Ridder Tribune (KRT) Services. And in association with the American Animal Hospital Association (AAHA), Dr. Becker hosts a nationally syndicated radio program, *Top Vet Talk Pets* on the Health Radio Network.

Dr. Becker has been featured on *ABC, NBC, CBS, CNN, PBS, Unsolved Mysteries* and in *USA Today, The New York Times, The Washington Post, Reader's Digest, Forbes, Better Homes & Gardens, The Christian Science Monitor, Woman's Day, National Geographic Traveler, Cosmopolitan, Glamour, Parents* and major Web sites such as *ABCNews.com, Amazon.com, Prevention.com, Forbes.com* and *iVillage.com.*

The recipient of many awards, Dr. Becker holds one especially dear. In 2002, the Delta Society and the American Veterinary Medical Association (AVMA) presented Dr. Becker with the prestigious Bustad Award, as the Companion Animal Veterinarian of the Year for the United States.

Marty and his family enjoy life in northern Idaho and share Almost Heaven Ranch with two dogs, five cats and five quarter horses.

Contact Marty Becker at:

P.O. Box 2775
Twin Falls, ID 83303
Phone: 208-734-8174
Web site: *www.drmartybecker.com*

Who Is Carol Kline?

Carol Kline is passionate about dogs! In addition to being a doting "pet parent," she is active in animal rescue work. Although she has recently relocated to California, she is still a member of the board of directors of the Noah's Ark Animal Foundation, *www.noahsark.org*, located in Fairfield, Iowa, a limited-access, "cageless," no-kill shelter that rescues lost, stray and abandoned dogs and cats. For the last eight years, Carol has spent many hours a week monitoring the fate of dogs and cats at Noah's Ark and working to find them good permanent homes. She also administered the Caring Community Spay/Neuter Assistance Program (CCSNAP), a fund especially designated for financially assisting pet owners to spay and neuter their pets. "The reward of helping these animals is more fulfilling than any paycheck I could ever receive. Volunteering time with the animals fills my heart and brings great joy to my life."

A freelance writer/editor for nineteen years, Carol, who has a B.A. in literature, has written for newspapers, newsletters and other publications. In addition to her own *Chicken Soup* books, she has also contributed stories and her editing talents to many other books in the *Chicken Soup for the Soul* series.

In addition to her writing and animal work, Carol is a motivational speaker and gives presentations to animal-welfare groups around the country on a variety of topics. She has also taught stress-management techniques to the general public since 1975.

Carol has the good fortune to be married to Larry and is a proud stepmother to Lorin, twenty-three, and McKenna, twenty. She has three dogs—all rescues—Beau, Beethoven and Jimmy.

To contact Carol, write to her at:

P.O. Box 521
Ojai, CA 93024
E-mail: *ckline@lisco.com*

Who Is Amy D. Shojai?

Amy D. Shojai is an animal behavior consultant, award-winning author, lecturer, and a nationally known authority on pet care and behavior. She is a passionate proponent of owner education in her books, articles, columns and media appearances, and has been recognized by her peers as "one of the most authoritative and thorough pet reporters."

The former veterinary technician has been a full-time pet journalist for more than two decades. She is a member of the International Association of Animal Behavior Consultants and consults with a wide range of animal care professionals, researchers and other experts, and specializes in translating "medicalese" into easily understood jargon-free language to make it accessible to all pet lovers. Amy answers pet questions in her weekly "Emotional Health" column at *www.catchow.com*, hosts "Your Pet's Well-Being with Amy Shojai" at *iVillage.com* and is section leader for the Holistic and Behavior/Care portions of the PetsForum. She is also the author of twenty-one nonfiction pet books, including *PETiquette: Solving Behavior Problems in Your Multipet Household* and *Complete Care for Your Aging Dog*, and a coauthor of *Chicken Soup for the Cat Lover's Soul*.

In addition to writing and pet care consulting, Amy's performance background (B.A. in music and theater) aids in her media work as a corporate spokesperson and pet product consultant. She has appeared on *Petsburgh USA*/Disney Channel Animal Planet series, *Good Day New York, Fox News: Pet News, NBC Today Show* and made hundreds of radio appearances including *Animal Planet Radio*. Amy has been featured in *USA Weekend, The New York Times, The Washington Post, Reader's Digest, Woman's Day, Family Circle, Woman's World*, as well as the "pet press." As a founder and president emeritus of the Cat Writers' Association, a member of the Dog Writers Association of America and the Association of Pet Dog Trainers, her work has been honored with over two dozen writing awards from these and many other organizations.

Amy and her husband, Mahmoud, live among 700-plus antique roses and assorted critters at Rosemont, their thirteen-acre "spread" in north Texas.

To contact Amy, write to her at:

P.O. Box 1904
Sherman, TX 75091
E-mail: *amy@shojai.com*
Web site: *www.shojai.com*

Contributors

Lynn M. Alcock is a registered professional counselor and advocate for self-care. Her first book—*The ABC's for Recovery from Depression*—will be published in 2005. She lives in rural Yukon outside of Whitehorse with her husband and a menagerie of pets. She enjoys gardening, mystery novels and needlecrafts.

After completing her B.S.Ed. with honors and master's degree from Arkansas State University, **Zardrelle Arnott** completed her Ed.S. at Southern Mississippi State University. Now retired, Zardrelle enjoys traveling, reading and writing. She has written several mystery stories and poems and is working on a novel. Contact her at: *zarnott@misn.com*.

John Arrington has been owned by Labs since he got his first one, a black female named Swamp, in 1969. John's Labs have been his companions, backpacking and camping partners, and best buddies. "Having a Lab at my side has become one of the few constant things in my life," he says. "Relationships come and go, but you can always count on a Lab to cheer you up when you're down or to keep you company when you're lonely. I just can't imagine living without a Lab to love."

Elizabeth A. Atwater resides in a quiet little village in North Carolina called Pfafftown. By day, disguised as a loyal technician for the Procter & Gamble Company, she blends in easily with the typical workforce. By night, she is a passionate, driven writer. She is currently trying to market her first novel.

David Ball is a person who has been dealing with a disablity for fifteen years. The introduction of a service dog into his life inspired him to write his first ever story. He is now going to school and plans to work in the corporate field.

Meghan Beeby is a full-time campaign coordinator for Farm Sanctuary, the nation's leading nonprofit farm animal protection organization: *www.farmsanctuary.org*. She lives in Ithaca, New York, with her husband, John, and twenty-seven companion animals. Meghan is also an active volunteer for human social service organizations. Her e-mail is: *meghanbeeby@hotmail.com*.

Marc Bekoff (*http://literati.net/Bekoff; www.ethologicalethics.org*) is a professor of biology at the University of Colorado, Boulder. Marc has published numerous books including *Minding Animals, The Ten Trusts* (with Jane Goodall), the *Encyclopedia of Animal Behavior* and *Animal Passions and Beastly Virtues*. He is also an optimistic activist with a dream for planetary unity and peace.

Millie Bobleter is an animal lover, mystery writer, cartoonist and sometimes-poet who lives in Southern California. She belongs to Sisters in Crime, Southern California Cartoonist Society, United Finnish Kaleva Brothers and Sisters Lodge #21, and the Independent Order of Totally Bewildered Innocent Bystanders.

Art Bouthillier resides in Washington State on Whidbey Island with his wife,

Jennifer, daughter, Sierra, and their Dobermans Kaos and Karma. Bouthillier freelances his artwork to magazines, calendars and tabloids. He just celebrated his twenty-first year in the business. He is also the editorial cartoonist for his local paper. You can contact Art at: *artb@whidbey.com.*

Susan Boyer resides with her husband and son in Pittsburgh, Pennsylvania. She enjoys caring for three dogs and a cat, reading, writing, collecting model horses, walking with her dogs and doing volunteer work with the elderly. Susan hopes to write a book about the various dogs in her life. Please e-mail her at: *offthetightrope@adelphia.net.*

Pat Byrnes is a frequent contributor to *The New Yorker* and *Reader's Digest.* The first anthology of his gag cartoons, *What Would Satan Do?* (Harry N. Abrams), hits bookstores in fall 2005, and his second, *Because I'm the Child Here, and I Said So* (Andrews & McMeel), in spring 2006.

JaLeen Bultman-Deardurff holds a B.A. in English/creative writing. She is married and has two grown children. She enjoys traveling with her husband, spending time with her dogs and cats, and collecting antiques. She is interested in pursuing a writing career focusing on the human interest genre.

Anne Carter, a native New Yorker and freelance writer, dedicates this story to all her amazing animals—Buster, Huckleberry, Princess, Penny, Sandra Dee, Tina and Peaches. She sends her love to Lucille McHugh—the animal kingdom's true champion. Anne's inspirational stories have appeared in major publications. Contact Anne at: *carteracdc@webtv.net.*

When **Carol Chapman** switched careers, she soon found herself on one of those roads less traveled. Arriving in Texas, she bought a ranch and created The Last Refuge, a sanctuary for unwanted dogs, cats and horses. She writes animal essays and inspirational life pieces. Please e-mail her at: *csylent@gmail.com.*

Meg Charendoff lives with her husband, four kids, two cats and her dog, D'Argo, in Elkins Park, Pennsylvania. An at-home mom and freelance writer, Meg is currently working on a novel and a collection of essays. Please e-mail her at: *MLCharendoff@comcast.net.*

Jennifer Coates graduated from the Virginia-Maryland Regional College of Veterinary Medicine as valedictorian in 1999 and has practiced small animal medicine ever since. She lives with her husband, dogs, cats and horses in western Wyoming and is currently writing a veterinary dictionary for animal owners. Please contact her at: *jencoates@silverstar.com.*

After a twenty-four-year career in newspapers, magazines, television and radio, **Sherry Cremona-Van Der Elst** received her Le Cordon Bleu Culinary Arts degree and is now a professional chef. She and her husband, Marcel, are planning to open a bed-and-breakfast in South Haven, Michigan. Please e-mail her at: *scremona@aol.com.*

Margaret P. Cunningham's short stories have placed in several national contests. Her stories have appeared in the anthologies, *Hello, Goodbye* and *Gardening at a Deeper Level.* She lives in Mobile, Alabama, with her husband, Tom. Margaret enjoys reading, writing and spending time at the beach with her children and granddaughters.

Atreyee Day is a double graduate in English (Honors) from Jadavpur University, Calcutta, and painting from M.S. University of Baroda, India. She stays in her rambling old family house in Calcutta. A poet and educator, she plans to travel extensively and write inspirational, travel and children's books. Her e-mail is *atreyee_d@vsnl.net.*

Pennie DeBoard is a registered nurse who works for the Red Cross. She lives with her husband in an old farmhouse on five acres in Oregon. Pennie enjoys spending time with her granddaughter, gardening organically, riding her Harley motorcycle and perfecting "fast Frisbee" with Josie. Reach her at: *wordbird@gmail.com.*

Gayle Delhagen is a certified equine sports massage therapist who lives with her family in northern Virginia. Gayle enjoys spending time with her family and her quarter horse, Handy. She plans on operating a farm for retired and rescued horses. Please e-mail her at: *gdelhagen1@yahoo.com.*

Tekla Dennison Miller (*www.teklamiller.com*), author of the novel *Life Sentences* and two memoirs, *The Warden Wore Pink* and *A Bowl of Cherries,* taught in riot-torn south central Los Angeles and worked with mentally-challenged enlisted men in Germany. She, her husband and three golden retrievers live in Colorado.

Lisa Duffy-Korpics is a freelance writer and global history teacher at Valley Central High School in Montgomery, New York. Her stories have also appeared in *Chicken Soup for the Cat & Dog Lover's Soul* and *Chicken Soup for the Mother's Soul 2.* Lisa lives in Dutchess County, New York, with her husband, Jason, son, Charles, and daughter, Emmaleigh.

Ed Eames, Ph.D. and his wife, Toni Eames, M.S., live with golden retriever guide dogs, Keebler and Latrell, and four cats. They are board members of the International Association of Assistance Dog Partners. As authors, lecturers and advocates, they claim their careers have gone to the dogs! Contact them at 559-224-0544; or via e-mail: *eeames@csufresno.edu.*

Blinded in a Nazi concentration camp, **Max Edelman** arrived in America with his wife in 1951. They worked and raised two sons and have five grandchildren. Now eighty-two years old, he writes and does public speaking on the subjects of the Holocaust and blindness. He is also a volunteer for the blind.

John Fenzel, Jr. is a Chrysler-Jeep-Dodge dealer in Hampshire, Illinois. He and his wife, Muriel, have four children. Their youngest boy, Michael, who sent Bashur to America, is currently a lieutenant colonel based in Afghanistan. The whole Fenzel family enjoys hiking, skiing and traveling.

Psychologist/Professor **Dr. Aubrey Fine** is an internationally known expert in the field of Animal Assisted Therapy. He is presently completing his new book titled *Afternoons with Puppy: A Therapist, His Animals and Life Lessons*. His life has been blessed with a wonderful family, which includes four dogs named Shrimp, Hart, PJ and Magic. Please e-mail him at: *ahfine@csupomona.edu*.

Susanne Fogle has written a weekly newspaper column about animals for the past six years. She has recently completed a book, tentatively titled *Animal Tails: A Guide to Loving, Respecting and Coping with the Animals in Our Lives*. You can e-mail her at: *Susannefogle@aol.com*.

Elisabeth Ann Freeman is an award-winning writer and speaker. She resides in Michigan with her husband, John, and four children. She attends Mount Hope Church in Ovid and serves in youth ministry. She has two books and over eighty articles/stories published. Please e-mail her at: *writeforlife@charter.net* or log on to her Web site: *http://writeforlife.com*.

Randy Glasbergen began his professional cartooning career at age fifteen and began freelancing full-time after a year of journalism studies in Utica, New York. Aside from one year spent as a staff humor writer at Hallmark Cards in Kansas City, he has been a full-time freelance cartoonist since 1976. Randy lives in a small town in northeastern USA with his family and several dogs and cats. He enjoys working at home in a cluttered studio that occupies the third story of his creaky old Victorian house.

Paula Gramlich has a master's degree in reading and special education. She writes a column about special education issues for StormWatch. Paula is now writing a children's book. You can e-mail her at: *pgramlich@sbcglobal.net*.

Wendy Greenley adopted her dogs from Twyla's Friends in Kingwood, Texas. Wendy graduated from the University of Delaware and Villanova University Law School. She is a member of the SCBWI and recently completed her first middle-grade novel. She lives outside Philadelphia with her husband, Dave, and two sons. Contact her at: *w.greenley@att.net*.

Jonny Hawkins's cartoons have been in over three hundred publications. His recent books are *Wild and Wacky Animal Cartoons for Kids, A Tackle Box of Fishing Funnies, Laughter from the Pearly Gates* and *Medical Cartoon-A-Day* and *Fishing Cartoon-A-Day* calendars that come out annually. He can be reached at *jonny hawkins2nz@yahoo.com*.

Christine Henderson lives in Minnesota with her husband, their three children and two Brittanys. She recently became a stay-at-home mom and works as a freelance writer in her spare time.

Margaret C. Hevel is a freelance author in magazines such as *Western Horseman, Bend of the River* and *Miniature Horse Voice*. She has also been featured in the books *Horse Tales for the Soul, Changing Course* and *Dog Tales for the Soul*. Her current nonfiction book, coauthored with a daughter, is *Parenting with Pets: The Magic of Raising Children with Animals*.

Mary K. Himens has been a Servant of the Holy Heart of Mary serving in various fields of education and ministry. In private practice as a psychotherapist, she has published poetry, *Images: Sights and Insights,* and is working on a collection tentatively titled *Listening with the Ear of the Heart.*

Jean Houston is a writer, scholar and researcher in human capacities and is the creator and leader of the twenty-year-old mythic studies workshop, Mystery School. Her books include *A Mythic Life* and *The Possible Human.* She lives in Ashland, Oregon.

Susan Huether battled breast cancer and survived. Getting another chance at life, Susan joined a small group named Wolfspirits Rescue who help give puppy mill survivors a new life. She lives modestly with her husband and eight dogs along with foster dogs and believes that each day is a gift from God.

Gary Ingraham is an award-winning documentary producer/director for Cornell University's Educational Television Center. He enjoys playing blues guitar, watching movies with wife, Patricia, and hanging out with their adopted dogs, Exley and Dobie Gillis. Gary is currently outlining a suspense novel. E-mail him at: *gri1@cornell.edu.*

Leigh Anne Jasheway-Bryant's writing is regularly carried in *Family Circle* and other national magazines. She won the 2003 Erma Bombeck Award for Humor Writing and has eleven published books including *Bedtime Stories for Dogs* and *If I Was a Dog, I'd Be a Better Person.* Her Web site is: *www.accidentalcomic.com.*

Pamela Jenkins lives in Henryetta, Oklahoma, with her husband and their four children. She is the office manager of her husband's veterinary practice and enjoys writing about the bond between people and their pets. E-mail her at: *calicoblessings@aol.com.*

Wendy Kaminsky is a software analyst at Dominion Virginia Power. Wendy enjoys traveling, running and working with animals. She and her husband, Dennis, volunteer at a local animal shelter. Through their rescue efforts they have adopted three dogs and two cats who are loved and spoiled beyond words.

Bill King has been an animal control officer for twelve years. Bill enjoys the outdoors, travel and his career. When you're looking for your new pet, consider your local animal shelter.

Roger Dean Kiser's stories have been published in seventeen books in five countries. Roger will never forget he was treated as though he was less than human while living in a Jacksonville, Florida, orphanage. Roger's story can be found at: *www.geocities.com/trampolineone/survive/noframe.htm.* Contact Roger at: *trampolineone@webtv.net.*

Mary Klitz resides in Michigan with an abundance of animals. She learned early of the dynamic relationship between people and pets. As the story in this book unfolded, she learned late in life the existence of another connection.

The sender of blessings will also be a receiver. Mary has secretly longed to be a writer. This is her first published story.

Edward H. Kostro's nonfiction animal book, *Curious Creatures—Wondrous Waifs: My Life with Animals,* available through *Amazon.com* and *Barnes & Noble.com,* depicts Ed's fifty-year love affair with all creatures—great and small. It was awarded a Certificate of Excellence in the 2004 International Cat Writers' Association Communications Contest.

Joyce Laird has been an industrial journalist since 1984. She has recently expanded her writing into the areas of fiction and creative nonfiction essays. Some of her work has been published in *Woman's World* magazine. Please e-mail her at: *jlcms@earthlink.net.*

Mariana Levine is a theatrical writer/director/choreographer and producer of Broadway-style musicals. She moved from Hollywood to Nashville where she founded Academy Center and Dance Academy of the South, emphasizing children's studies, and developed shows for Opryland USA and Ringling's Circus. An avid gardener, she paints and writes about country wildlife.

Elizabeth Lombard: wife, mother of five and fifth-generation south Boston resident. Animal lover actively committed to animal welfare. Stargazer, vegetarian, writer. Contributing author to the *South Boston Literary Gazette.*

Marjie Lyvers is a mother of four children, nine grandchildren and eight great-grandchildren. Her life story includes twenty-five years as a military wife, numerous adventures and travels, retiring in her hometown of Spokane, Washington. After the death of her husband, Marjie has filled her time with writing and crafts.

Laurie MacKillip currently lives in Florida and can be found on her motorcycle, at the beach, or spending time with family and friends when she can find time between work, training horses and writing.

Alexandra Mandis was born in Zimbabwe in 1958 and moved to the United States in 1983. Dogs are her passion and in particular her blue-eyed Dalmatian, Harry, and her two Great Danes, Elsa and Blue. She is working in New Zealand, with her work base in the United States, as an IT program manager. She also loves horses, books and the country life.

Shannon McCarty is a writer and humorist from Austin, Texas. She has three young children, a dog, three mice and numerous fish in her home. She enjoys playing soccer and writing about family life. Please e-mail her at: *smccarty@ austin.rr.com.*

Beth McCrea received her B.A. from Iowa State University in 2002. She teaches seventh-grade language arts in Littleton, Colorado. She enjoys traveling, hiking, reading and watching football.

Wilma Melville is the founder and executive director of the National Disaster Search Dog Foundation located in Ojai, California. Started in 1995, the foundation now has sixty-five active Canine Search Teams that are ready to be deployed to disasters around the world. For more information, visit *www.SearchDogFoundation.org* or call 888-4K9-HERO.

Rosemarie Miele is a graduate of Dominican College, Orangeburg, New York. She retired from KPMG where she was a senior human resources business consultant. She spends her free time traveling, doing volunteer work, enjoying her grandchildren and writing children's stories. Please e-mail her at: *rmiele109@aol.com.*

When not barricading his home against his ravenous dog, **Sam Minier** spends his free time in more lighthearted pursuits—writing horror stories and poetry! Brave souls can sample his work at: *www.samuelminier.com.*

Hester Mundis is an animal-loving comedy writer and the author of numerous books, including the autobiographical *No, He's Not a Monkey, He's an Ape and He's My Son.* She and her husband, Ron VanWarmer, currently share their upstate New York lives with a soft-coated wheaten terrier and a suave cockatiel.

Kelly Munjoy is currently working on her B.A. degree. She attends college classes part-time, as well as working a full-time job in customer service. Kelly enjoys spending time with her family and friends as well as reading and writing. She plans to write young adult fantasy novels and short stories. Please e-mail her at: *Kellymunjoy@charter.net.*

Eleanor Whitney Nelson, a geologist who has enjoyed a career in international mineral exploration, today concentrates on writing. Her stories have been published in *OASIS Journal* 2004 and *A Way with Murder: An Anthology of Arizona Mystery Writers.* She lives in Tucson with her dogs, horses, cat and husband.

Diane Nichols is the author of *A Prison of My Own,* the true story of her husband's incarceration for the murder of his mistress and their family's journey to forgiving and restoration (as seen on *The Montel Williams Show*). For more information, please visit her author's Web site at: *www.dianenichols.com.*

Lorena O'Connor is now a retired legal secretary. She has written and sold many stories to a variety of publications. She likes movies, music, sports and writing, not necessarily in that order. She plans to self-publish a children's book after recovering from a serious surgery. You can reach her at: *oldarmy4@aol.com.*

Born in Brooklyn, **Don Orehek** attended the High School of Industrial Arts and the School of Visual Arts. His cartoons have appeared in the *Saturday Evening Post, Good Housekeeping, Cosmopolitan* and *Playboy*—to name a few! Don has illustrated over thirty joke books, does caricatures and teaches cartooning to kids. He has won the National Cartoonists Society's Best Gag Cartoonist award four times.

Brothers **Trevor and Drew Orsinger** wrote *The Firefighter's Best Friend* for Lake Claremont Press (*www.lakeclaremont.com*), an independent publisher specializing in books on Chicago. A portion of the proceeds from this book are donated to the Illinois Fire Safety Alliance's summer camp for children who suffer from burn injuries.

Mark Parisi's "Off the Mark" comic panel has been syndicated since 1987 and is distributed by United Media. Mark's humor also graces greeting cards, T-shirts, calendars, magazines, newsletters and books, including his newest cartoon book *Chew This Book* with over 100 dog cartoons. Please vist his Web site at *www.offthemark.com*. Lynn is his wife/business partner, and their daughter, Jenny, contributes with inspiration.

After graduating from UCLA, **Eve Ann Porinchak** was a social worker, medical student and first-grade teacher. An active member of the Society of Children's Book Writers/Illustrators, she now writes children's books and paints. Eve enjoys tennis, traveling, snowboarding, hiking and running with her husband and beloved springer spaniels. Contact: *eporinchak@aol.com*.

Stacy Pratt received her bachelor's degree from Northeastern State University in Oklahoma and her master's degree from the University of Arkansas. A citizen of the Creek Nation of Oklahoma, she lives in Italy with her husband. She writes poetry and is currently researching the life of St. Valerie.

Robin Pressnall is a singer, a writer and cofounder of Small Paws Rescue, a worldwide nonprofit organization (*smallpawsrescue.org*) dedicated to saving the "unwanted" dogs of society and finding them "forever-homes." Robin lives in Tulsa with her husband, Dale, and their six dogs, ranging from a St. Bernard to a bichon frise.

Andrea Burke Redd, DVM, received her bachelor of science degree, cum laude, in zoology from North Carolina State University in 1993. She received her doctorate of veterinary medicine (DVM) from North Carolina State University College of Veterinary Medicine in 1997. She is currently practicing veterinary medicine at a mixed animal practice in Halifax, Virginia. She is married with two sons. She is active in her church and enjoys spending her free time with her family. She enjoys writing and has been published in *Veterinary Economics* magazine. E-mail her at: *abredd@gcronline.com*.

B. J. Reinhard writes to give readers hope and encourage them to live their dreams. Along with various magazine articles and stories, she is the author of an award-winning picture book, *Sanji's Seed,* and two nonfiction books, *Glow-in-the Dark Fish* and *Our Place in Space.* You can reach her through: *www. bjreinhard.com*.

Jennifer Renee Remeta has been an animal lover her entire life. Recently married, she and her husband, Nicklas, proudly own Diesel, the Great Dane, Abby, the wonderful Lab, and Pandora, the queen cat. They enjoy spending time with friends and family, and Jennifer hopes to continue her writing in the future.

Debbie Roppolo is a freelance writer and a student at St. Edward's University where she is pursuing a degree in anthropology. Debbie enjoys working with her horses, traveling and spending time with her family. She currently resides in San Marcos, Texas, with her husband and two boys.

Micki Ruiz lives in South Florida with her husband, Steve. A published author, she writes short stories and historical fiction, and is (still) hard at work on her novel, a fantasy adventure. This is her first nonfiction work. Please e-mail her at: *LadySunshine817@yahoo.com.*

Kathy Salzberg has been a professional pet groomer and owner of the Village Groomer in Walpole, Massachusetts, for thirty years. She is also an award-winning magazine writer who has written "How to Start a Home-Based Pet Care Business" and contributed several chapters to *The Dog Bible.* She is currently working on *The Everything Small Dogs Book* and can be reached online at: *kathog@aol.com.*

Linda Saraco is an animal massage therapist. At her Boston-area grooming shop, she offers holistic canine services and education. Linda also teaches the InTuneGroom method of energy work, which she developed. Linda loves spending time with her dogs and hopes to publish her series of children's books. E-mail her at: *linda@InTuneGroom.com.*

Valery Selzer Siegel received her B.A. in English from Binghamton University and her M.A. in Elementary Education from Adelphi University. She advocates on behalf of children in a variety of capacities, including writing inspirational picture books. Valery lives in New York with her husband and three children. Please e-mail her at: *vselzersiegel@yahoo.com.*

Stefany Lynne Smith is the founder and director of Southwest German Shepherd Rescue, a nonprofit, 501(c)3 organization, headquartered in Phoenix, Arizona. They are committed to the rescue, rehab and re-homing of German shepherd dogs in need, in addition to training and education.

Patricia Ann Smith is director of Operations/Programs at the Ronald McDonald House at Stanford, Palo Alto, California. She wrote the story "Can't Help Falling in Love" when on staff at the Humane Society Silicon Valley. Her book, *Introduction to Compassion Fatigue in the Helping Professions* will be published by Brunner-Routledge in 2005.

Laura Sobchik wrote her story, "Raising a Star," as her college entrance essay to the University of Notre Dame. She graduated from Notre Dame in 2002 and now teaches third grade in Fullerton, California. She and her family have raised eleven guide dog puppies for Guide Dogs for the Blind, Inc. in San Rafael, California. Five of their puppies graduated as guide dogs with a visually impaired partner and six were career-changed and now enjoy wonderful lives as pets. For more information about raising a guide dog puppy, please visit: *www.guidedogs.com.*

Jennifer Gay Summers is a contributing writer to *Whole Life Times* magazine and has also written for *Orange County Family Magazine.* She and her veterinarian have been married for twelve years, and their menagerie includes a dog, cat, fish and beloved daughter. Jennifer can be reached at: *jgsummers@verizon.net.*

Debra Szot has always loved animals. She volunteers for Boxer and Boston Terrier Rescue. She became involved in rescue because of a Scottish terrier named MacKenzie who saved her life and loved her unconditionally. She lives in Michigan with her husband, David, and daughter, Heather. Please e-mail her at: *dszot@net-port.com.*

Audrey Thomasson left a globe-trotting writing career to move to White Stone, Virginia, population: 360. Her choices were driven by Kody, a rescued dog whose therapy included daily swims in their river. When Kody passed, she found comfort in writing his memorial, and in the process realized this magnificent companion had taught her about living. His story inspired "Animal Tails," a public service newspaper column dedicated to pets and rescue volunteers. Audrey can be reached by e-mail at: *animaltails@verizon.com.* Information on her pet column is available at: *www.animaltails.org.*

Bob Toren is a pioneer in outdoor portraiture, photojournalist and a columnist for the *Georgetown Gazette,* Georgetown, California. He writes frequently of the cat family with whom he shares his Sierra hilltop. He is presently putting a collection of the columns together for book publication. Contact him at: *bobtoren@earthlink.net.*

Jackie Tortoriello currently resides in New Jersey, with her family, friends and two dogs. She's passionate about them, spirituality, music and writing, and is fervently pursuing a writing career. Until then, Jackie is honored to be instructing the mentally challenged at a life skills program. She may be reached at: *Jacmac@erols.com.*

Anne Watkins is the author of *The Conure Handbook* (Barron's Educational Series, Inc.). A full-time writer, her work has appeared in numerous magazines, newspapers, books and Web sites. She and husband, Allen, live in Vinemont, Alabama, where they love to spoil their grandchildren, Bailey, Chelsea and Tyler. See her Web site: *www.geocities.com/anne_c_watkins.*

Christine Watkins has been a flight attendant for over thirty years. In her spare time, she and her puppy, Maverick, volunteer with the Helen Woodward Animal Center in San Diego, California, where they visit children's centers. Currently, Christi is studying the craft of writing and editing.

Jean M. Wensink is an elementary teacher and freelance writer. She lives in rural Wisconsin with her husband and two daughters. She loves the outdoors, music, crafts and, of course, her dogs Rocky and Snickers.

Born in England, **Bill Westhead** received his bachelor of science degree in textile engineering from Leeds University. After working in the United Kingdom, he and his family emigrated to the United States in 1973. Retired, he enjoys writing (publishing three historical novels), community theater and several community service clubs. Contact him at: *westhead@accessatc.net.*

Dave Wiley is an information technology professional who enjoys just about anything. He likes taking on Tim-the-Toolman-like projects while achieving similar results, playing with his son, camping, hiking with the dogs, performing confirmation and obedience events with the dogs, and generally just doing stuff that helps him to avoid any type of housecleaning. He is hoping to become a writer someday when he grows up. He can be reached by e-mail at: *wiley@mayfran.com.*

Elizabeth Wrenn's first novel will be published by NAL/Penguin in 2006. When a wife and mother in a mid-life crisis volunteers to raise a puppy for K-9 Eyes for the Blind, an enthusiastic yellow Lab helps her to find what she didn't even realize was missing in her life—herself.

Permissions *(continued from page ii)*

Jethro's World. Reprinted by permission of Marc Bekoff. ©2004 Marc Bekoff.

The Great Dog Walk. Reprinted by permission of Anne Elizabeth Carter. ©2004 Anne Elizabeth Carter.

A Christmas for Toby. Reprinted by permission of Tekla Dennison Miller. ©1993 Tekla Dennison Miller.

Blu Parts the Veil of Sadness. Reprinted by permission of Margaret C. Hevel. ©2004 Margaret C. Hevel.

The Haunted Bowl. Reprinted by permission of John Ray Arrington. ©1997 John Ray Arrington.

You Have No Messages. Reprinted by permission of R. Zardrelle Arnott. ©2004 R. Zardrelle Arnott.

Bubba's Last Stand. Reprinted by permission of Lisa Duffy-Korpics. ©2004 Lisa Duffy-Korpics.

Some Snowballs Don't Melt. Reprinted by permission of Debbie A. Roppolo. ©2003 Debbie A. Roppolo.

Greta and Pearl: Two Seniors. Reprinted by permission of Stefany Lynne Smith. ©2004 Stefany Lynne Smith.

Bullet's Dog. Reprinted by permission of Elizabeth A. Atwater. ©2004 Elizabeth A. Atwater.

Daisy Love. Reprinted by permission of Kathleen R. Salzberg. ©1997 Kathleen R. Salzberg.

Devotion. Reprinted by permission of Marjie C. Livers. ©1994 Marjie C. Livers.

Dixie's Kitten. Reprinted by permission of Anne Culbreath Watkins. ©2001 Anne Culbreath Watkins.

Bashur, the Iraqi Dog. Reprinted by permission of John Fenzel, Jr. ©2004 John Fenzel, Jr.

After Dooley. Reprinted by permission of Gary Russell Ingraham. ©2004 Gary Russell Ingraham.

When Harry Met Kaatje. Reprinted by permission of David Michael Wiley. ©2003 David Michael Wiley.

Gremlin, Dog First Class. Reprinted by permission of JaLeen Alice Deardurff. ©2004 JaLeen Alice Deardurff.

My Blue-Eyed Boy. Reprinted by permission of Alexandra Mandis. ©2004 Alexandra Mandis.